James Mills, Dublin Holy Trinity priory

Account Roll of the Priory of the Holy Trinity

Dublin, 1337-1346 - with the middle English moral play "The Pride of Life"

James Mills, Dublin Holy Trinity priory

Account Roll of the Priory of the Holy Trinity
Dublin, 1337-1346 - with the middle English moral play "The Pride of Life"

ISBN/EAN: 9783337285715

Printed in Europe, USA, Canada, Australia, Japan

Cover: Foto ©Lupo / pixelio.de

More available books at **www.hansebooks.com**

PLAN OF THE CATHEDRAL OF THE HOLY TRINITY, DUBLIN.

A BAPTISTRY
B STRONGBOW'S TOMB
C CHAPEL OF ST. LAURENCE O'TOOLE
D CHAPEL OF ST. LAUD
E CHAPEL OF SANCTA MARIA ALBA
F CHAPEL OF ST. EDMUND
G CHAPEL OF THE B. V. MARY
   (Present Vestries & Grammar school)

NORTH

SOUTH

CHOIR

TRANSEPT   TRANSEPT

AMBULATORY   AMBULATORY

Site of
CLOISTERS

NAVE

Entrance

JOHN'S LANE

ST. MICHAEL'S HILL

Forster & Co Dublin.

Thomas Drew R.H.A.
Cathedral Architect
1886

ACCOUNT ROLL

OF THE

PRIORY OF THE HOLY TRINITY, DUBLIN

1337-1346

BEING

THE EXTRA VOLUME

OF THE

Royal Society of Antiquaries of Ireland

FOR

1890–1891

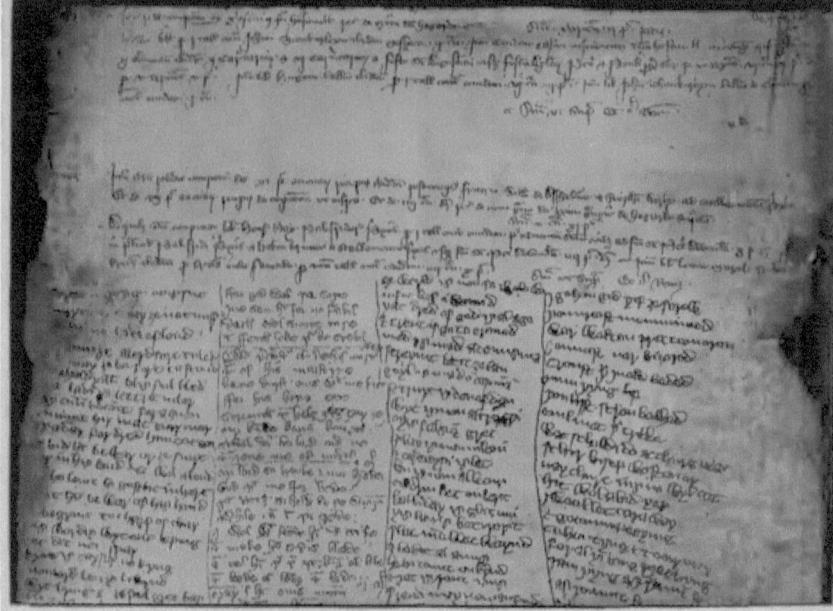

ACCOUNT ROLL

OF THE

PRIORY OF THE HOLY TRINITY, DUBLIN

1337-1346

WITH

THE MIDDLE ENGLISH MORAL PLAY

"The Pride of Life"

FROM THE ORIGINAL IN THE CHRIST CHURCH COLLECTION IN THE PUBLIC RECORD OFFICE, DUBLIN

EDITED WITH

Translation, Notes, and Introduction

BY

JAMES MILLS
M.R.I.A.

DUBLIN
PRINTED AT THE UNIVERSITY PRESS
FOR THE ROYAL SOCIETY OF ANTIQUARIES OF IRELAND

1891

PREFACE.

THIS Volume is issued by the Council, and presented to the Fellows of the Royal Society of Antiquaries of Ireland, in accordance with No. 27 of its General Rules.

In the same manner there have been published, in 1870, as the "Annuary" of this Society (under its former designation of the Royal Historical and Archæological Association of Ireland), for 1868 and 1869, "The Social State of the Southern and South-Eastern Counties of Ireland in the Sixteenth Century," edited by Herbert F. Hore, Esq., and Rev. James Graves; and as the "Annual Volumes" of the Association for 1870 to 1877, "Christian Inscriptions in the Irish Language," edited by Miss Margaret Stokes. Both these valuable works are long since out of print.

A proposed Annual Volume for 1878–80 was commenced by the late Mr. W. M. Hennessy, but it was not completed, and the circumstances of the Society for some subsequent years did not permit any new work to be produced.

The excellent monograph on Inismurray, by Mr. W. F. Wakeman, originally intended for an Annual Volume, was not so issued, but utilised in the Journal for October, 1885, becoming No. 64, vol. vii., New Series.

In 1889 Col. Wood-Martin's Papers on the "Rude Stone Monuments of Sligo," which had appeared in the Journal, were collected and issued as an extra volume for 1888–89.

Early in 1890 the Council of the Society desired to continue the printing of extra volumes, and appointed a Committee to choose a work worthy of being selected for the purpose. The Committee having reported in favour of the contents of the present volume, the Council, at its next meeting in June, authorized it to be printed as an extra volume for 1890. It was found impossible, however, to complete the work within that year, and it is now, therefore, presented as the volume for 1890–91. The Council contemplate the continuation of the Series with greater frequency, as the present financial position of the Society is such as to justify the additional outlay.

The frontispiece is a reproduction by photozinco-graphy of portion of the Roll; containing the concluding part of the Account of the Haggard of Gorman (pp. 52–4), and the beginning of the Poem. The four columns of the latter commence respectively with line 39 (p. 127), line 235 (p. 133), line 327 (p. 137), line 415 (p. 139).

CONTENTS.

INTRODUCTION.

AMONG the large number of early deeds and documents
preserved by the care of the canons of Christ Church,
Dublin, and saved from dispersion by the fact that that house
was not suppressed with the other religious houses in the 16th
century, is a group of early Accounts gathered together by some
old-time antiquarian canon. These Accounts have been stitched
together so as to form a roll of parchment 11 feet $8\frac{1}{2}$ inches in
length, and from $8\frac{1}{4}$ to $11\frac{1}{4}$ inches in breadth. They are now
placed as No. 235 in the Christ Church collection preserved in the
Public Record Office, Dublin. This Roll consists of four distinct
documents forming the Accounts II. to V. printed in this volume.
They must have been collected and sewn together for preservation
long, probably not less than 100 years, after they were made.
They stand on the Roll in this order, V., II., III., IV.

Accompanying this Roll is another membrane forming part of
the seneschal's account for parts of the years 1337–1339. This
membrane, though in excellent condition itself, is but a portion of
a much longer account, having been originally preceded and followed by other membranes, as is shown by marks of stitching, and
by a decayed fragment still attached to the top. In the course of
a careful examination of some detached and defaced parchments
accompanying the Christ Church collection, made after its removal
to the Record Office, a mutilated fragment was found which proved
to be an earlier part of this account, and was restored to its place
with it. This membrane and fragment form Account I. in this
volume.

L

The Roll attracted the attention of Dr. Lyon when examining the Christ Church records for the preparation of the *Novum Registrum*, towards the middle of the last century. But its length probably deterred him from having it copied into the Register like the other documents which he at the same time selected; and there are entered there only the headings of the four accounts, with his description of it as "an ancient roll of Accounts which contains things of no great moment, as it appears to me, reading it with some care" ("vetus Rotulus computorum qui continet res haud magni momenti, ut mihi videtur perlegenti eum non negligenter"). Archdall, in his *Monasticon*, makes only the following brief reference to it : " 1344.—An old parchment of the acts of the priory of this year informs us, that a pair of shoes was bought for the prior at the price of five pence."

The Roll remained therefore practically unknown until the rebuilding of the church in 1872 rendered it necessary to secure a place of safety for its muniments, and the original documents were transferred to the Record Office. There, after some years, they were carefully examined, and a calendar of the more ancient published. The portion of this calendar containing a notice of this Roll appeared as an appendix to the 20th Report of the Deputy Keeper of the Records in 1888 ; but enclosed in the cover of a Blue Book this notice failed to gain attention, until in 1890 the publication of the Roll in its entirety was proposed to the Council of the Society.

The Prior's Expenditure.

First in interest among the subjects dealt with in these accounts are the particulars of expenses incurred for the Prior and his chamber.[1] The term Prior's chamber meant the suite of apartments appropriated to the use of the Prior and his retinue.[2] It

---

[1] Pages 1–16, 99–101, 113–118.

[2] To illustrate the comprehensiveness of the term, I may point to Toulouse Abbey, in which according to an inventory made in 1246 the Camera Abbatis contained fittings for 18 beds, and among many other articles, three horses, a colt, and two mules.— *Mémoires, Soc. Arch. du Midi de la France*, tome xiv., p. 7.

must have included at least a hall for meals and reception of visitors, a sleeping room or cell, and accommodation for the Prior's retainers, including a chamberlain, esquires, and garciones or serving men. There is no indication of its position among the conventual buildings. Nor have we any inventory of its contents, but occasional purchases of articles required for it, give some idea of its furniture. The floors were bare, as there is no purchase of litter to cover them. A substantial table was bought for 6s. 1d. This was probably a regular table for the Prior's use, to replace the boards and trestles in general use, which may still have been retained here for the tables of the household. Chairs, seats, and stools of straw were used. These were not bought ready-made, but a man was employed to make them and paid 16d. for his work (p. 97). These may have resembled the chairs, foot-stools, and mats of straw work, made like the old beehives which were still in frequent use in Dublin until some years ago.

The table appointments were for the most part of pewter, or more properly tin (*peutreum*). On one occasion 12 dishes, 12 plates, 12 saucers or sauce vessels, and two large dishes or chargers of this metal were bought at a cost of 7s. (p. 89). They were considered sufficiently valuable to employ a goldsmith to mark them, who was paid 9d. for doing so. Mustard, which was much used, was brought to table in small earthenware pots, three of which were bought for 1d.

The lock and key for the chamber cost 3d.; ½d. was spent on earthenware vessels whose use is not specified. Fuel is occasionally bought; and candles cost 3d. for 2lb.

There is only an incidental notice of chamber or table linen, in the payment of the washerwoman, whose charge for half a-year ending Easter was 6d. (p. 99).

The Prior himself was warmly clad in tunic or coat of woollen cloth, over which he wore a surcoat, or the longer capa, each of which as well as his hood were plentifully furred (pp. 88-90). Shoes or boots, and gloves completed his street dress. Thus clad he must have appeared abroad in very much the ordinary dress of laymen of corresponding position. For religious dress he was furnished with rochets, over which a furred amice hung from his shoulders to his waist.[1] The amice worn by the prior and canons at a later time was of gray fur, lined with minever (p. 177). In addition he had special robes prepared for the great festivals, Christmas and Easter.[2]

The Prior rode abroad on his own palfrey, whose groom was a lay official called palfredarius. The seneschal also had a horse for his journeys, for which he paid 19s. 8d. The housings of the palfrey and of another horse cost 15d.; two pairs of spurs for the Prior and seneschal cost 8d, and the seneschal's saddle and bridle 4s. 6d.

The household retained by the Prior seems to have varied considerably. It consisted generally of one or two esquires, or clerks, who could be employed on responsible duties, such as over-seeing the harvest of the manors, commanding the levies of the priory tenants at hostings, and going on the more important missions for the Prior; a chamberlain or housekeeper; a palfreyman; a cook; and servingmen (garciones). Among his retinue were naturally often included relatives of the Prior.

At times when a need for retrenchment was pressing the household was much reduced. At one time it consisted apparently of one chaplain and a cook only (p. 99). At such times the seneschal undertook direct charge of the Prior's chamber.[3]

As at other religious houses the more prominent guests were entertained at the Prior's table. One account gives the names of

---

[1] Helyot, "Hist. des Ordres Monastiques," II., p. 23.

[2] Woollen cloth for 2 tunics cost 2s. 11d.; making 4 tunics 16d.; tailor for making 2 robes for Prior 16d.; making tunic and hood for esquire 7d.; gloves, 5d. a pair.

[3] A fuller illustration of household arrangements is supplied by the corrody granted by the Prior of Kilmainham (p. 170). This shows the Prior of that house sitting at the high table in his great hall, like a lay lord, while his retainers sat at different tables in other parts of the hall according to their rank. Honoured guests were entertained at the Prior's own table; clergy at the table of the brethren, which appears there to have been in the great hall instead of a separate refectory; and the retainers of the guest at the tables of the Prior's retainers of similar standing. When Walter de Istelep, to whom this grant was made, so wished he might mess in his own house within the priory close with his chaplain and 4 principal retainers, receiving then 10 gallons of the best ale, with meat as he desired from the kitchen, and certain quantities of bread.

the guests so entertained for a period covering about four months, in 1337–8. During these four months about 35 guests are named, besides on twelve occasions indefinite reference to "others" or "strangers." Among those named are the justices itinerant, who seem to have been formally entertained in their judicial capacity, the sheriff of the county and his followers, the archbishop's chancellor, the prior of S. Wolstan's in Co. Kildare, with his retinue of 2 canons and esquires, the prior of Holmpatrick in the north of Co. Dublin, the friars preachers and chaplains of Arklow. Of 25 others named 7 were prominent Dublin citizens, 2 local ecclesiastics, 2 government officials, 4 prominent men of the county, several holding land from the Priory; 3 were principal tenants of the manors belonging to the Priory, 2 were persons having business relations with the house, the remaining 5 only being not identified as neighbours or friends of the Priory. Casual strangers are comparatively rare, however, here, as the wealthier visitors to Dublin more commonly put up at Thomas-court, Mary's-abbey, and other houses outside the city walls.

In the Prior's chamber there were three meals daily : breakfast, dinner (apparently about noon[1]), and supper. The introduction of breakfast was an indulgence copied perhaps from the Prior's secular neighbours, the townsmen.[2]

The table though not supplied with the lavish variety to be found, somewhat earlier, in the Household Expense Books of Bishop Swinfield (Camden Soc.), was yet by no means ascetic. The English bishop's household observed two days a week for abstinence from flesh ; the Dublin Prior abstained on Friday only.

Breakfast was at least sometimes a substantial meal, including bread, capons, pasties, oysters or salmon, and wine or ale.

---

[1] Mr. Wright says that the dinner hour in England about this time was from 10 to 11 a.m.—*Hist. of Domestic Manners.*

[2] The writer of the description of England in Holinshed speaks of breakfast as a serious degeneracy of past times in England from which his country had in the sixteenth century recovered, in his own words, "Now these od repasts thanked be God are verie weil left, and eche one in maner (except here and there some young hungrie stomach that cannot fast till dinner time) contenteth himself with dinner and supper."

Dinner and supper were substantial, with abundance of meat, but without many different dishes. The principal articles of food were bread, beef and mutton, fowls, capons, geese (in autumn), and less frequently lamb (in season), pork, pigeons, goslings, rabbits, larks, plovers.[1]

As an example, the following is a bill of fare for a dinner and supper to the sheriff of the county and some of his followers:— Dinner, wine 9*d.*; 5 baked pasties of fowl 9½*d.* Supper, wine 6*d.*; roast fowls 4*d.*; half a lamb 2*d.*; roast beef 4*d.* (p. 8). This was only the 12th February, and lamb had already appeared at table on the preceding day—a quarter of lamb, 1*d.*

Very frequently the dishes were apparently bought ready cooked. The Priory stood some 100 yards from the Vicus Cocorum " the street of the cooks," still known as Cook-street, though the name has now quite lost its old significance. From the cook shops here came, no doubt, many of the dishes for the Prior's table, including the pies and pasties occasionally mentioned. On one occasion there is an entry of a present of 1*d.* from the Prior to two cooks in the Cook-street (p. 111).

In Lent, and on Fridays, there was a plentiful supply of fish. Salmon, oysters, stock-fish (salted cod, &c.), and herrings, were most common, but there were also eels, trout, turbot, tublynges, plaice, gurnard, salted eels; and other kinds may be included under the term " fish," used frequently; salmon pasties also occur. These days of abstinence were not marked by any other privation than that of the change of fish for flesh. Thus, one of the most elaborate dinners mentioned was upon an Ash-Wednesday, when the bill of fare included, herrings, 6*d.*, white fish, 12*d.*, salmon, 18*d.*, for cooking it, 2*d.*, almonds and rice,[2] 4*d.*, ginger and mustard, ½*d.*

Bread was in use at every meal. This was made in the Priory bake-house, but the frequency with which bread was bought for

---

[1] A carcase of beef cost 9*s.*, of mutton 1*s.* 1*d.* to 1*s.* 4*d.*, of pork 2*s.* 2*d.*, a quarter of lamb 1*d.*, a capon 2*d.*, fowl about 1*d.* each, a goose 3*d.*

[2] Almonds and rice are in these Accounts almost always mentioned together. Boorde, in his " Dyetary of Health " (E.E.T.S), says that " Ryce potage made with almon mylke, doth restore and doth comfort nature."

the Prior's table suggests that that made in the house was not very good. In the later accounts a finer kind of bread, Panis dominicus, lord's bread, the paindemaine of Chaucer and other contemporary writers, was frequently used by the Prior, especially for guests of more than usual importance.

Butter and cheese were in common use.

The only vegetable mentioned at table is the onion, and this but rarely. Beans and peas were largely grown, but were eaten only by the labourers and the horses.

Among groceries and foreign produce (which were in proportion much higher in price than the home-grown articles) are olive oil (6*d.* a quart), almonds, walnuts, rice (usually in conjunction with almonds), salt, white salt (the best qualities, the cheaper salts being very impure), pepper (20*d.* a lb.), verjuice, figs (2*d.* a lb.), mustard, saffron, spices. Fruit is very rare; pears appear once when the archbishop was entertained (p. 112).

The standing drink at every meal was ale (or beer). It was made in the Priory brew-house, under the direction of the cellarer. The home-brewed ale was probably not very good, as ale is frequently bought for the Prior's table. But the Prior and his guests were not limited to ale; wine is a continually recurring article, purchased sometimes two or three times in a day. It was but a step from the Priory gate to the street of wine shops, still called Winetavern-street, and so wine was bought as needed, by the quart or gallon. The price was 5*d.* or 6*d.* a gallon. White wine is sometimes distinguished, but is bought at the same price. Wine was usually bought retail, but was sometimes laid in in wood. It was then bought from a merchant named Stephen de Gascoyne, and if the wine came from the same quarter as the merchant's name, it was probably a claret.

Piment (a drink made with wine, honey, and various spices) rarely occurs, and then only as a present for the archbishop.

Such are the illustrations of life in the Prior's chamber. To complete its picture, there are a few entries relative to death there. In 1346 the Prior, Simon de Ludgate, died. There is no entry of the employment of a physician, none at least was paid, and there was

only one purchase of medicine, viz. rose-water and sugar, for 14*d.*
These not very active remedies were insufficient in the Prior's case,
as is shown by the fact that the next entries are preparations for
his burial. The body was, no doubt, arrayed in his canonicals,
but a pair of pinsons, or leather shoes, were bought for 3*d.* for
his feet. The boards and nails, and the making of the coffin, cost
4*s.* Only one entry occurs about him after the cost of the coffin.
This was the expenditure of 10½*d.* for paindemaine, wine, and ale,
for the dean of St. Patrick's, and others, at the Prior's wake.

The next item in the account (p. 113) is a breakfast given by
the Prior elect to his brethren, whose votes had advanced him to
be Prior and lord of Parliament. There were good reasons why
no delay should occur in the appointment of a successor. On the
last three occasions of vacancies, the escheator had endeavoured,
in the name of the Crown, to seize the possessions of the House
during the vacancy. It was, therefore, important that no time
should be lost in raising up a Prior legally entitled to hold
the lands. Prior de Ludgate's death is put down in the Obits at
Sept. 6. This was a Wednesday ; on the following Sunday the
required preliminaries had been gone through, and the Prior elect
entertained his brethren, although brother John Dolfyn, who
seems to have been Sub-Prior, was absent at Killenaule, in Co.
Tipperary. On Wednesday after the Exaltation of the Holy
Cross, a fortnight from the death of his predecessor, the new Prior
was installed, and gave his modest installation dinner, consisting
of two geese, 2*d.* worth of roast meat, and 4*d.* worth of wine and
ale (p. 115). The new Prior did not for some time, take up his
quarters in the Prior's chamber, and instead, entertained his guests
in the Sacristy.

The Priors who ruled the House at the times of these accounts
were :—

1320-25. Hugh de Sutton, called also le Joevene, or le Jeune,
became Prior about 1320, having been a canon of the House for
over 20 years. He resigned in 1325 (Cotton says in June), and
his resignation was made the occasion of putting forward the
claim of the Crown to the possessions of the vacant Priory, which

for more than 20 years was a source of annoyance and expense to
the House. On retirement, he was given a pension, and allotted
a separate chamber in the Monastery, where he could occasionally
entertain guests (p. 115).

1326-31. Robert of Gloucester succeeded. He was, perhaps,
not a canon of the House. In 1315 he appeared as proctor of the
abbey of Lanthony near Gloucester, in a suit against the Bishop
of Meath. While Prior, he became a baron of the Exchequer.
In 1330, he obtained a royal license to erect a battlemented bell
tower, but his death early in the following year must have prevented his carrying this work into execution.

1331-7. Roger Goioun succeeded, and ruled until 1337, on
the 6th July in which year he was deposed. Though frequent
references to the fact of his deposition occur, neither the registers
of the church, the Papal regesta, nor the public records, seem to
contain any explanation of the cause. No mention is made of him
afterwards, except in connexion with the claims of the escheator
on the possessions, or the debts left from his time of rule. That he
was not, however, lost sight of, or excluded from communion, may
be assumed from his obit being entered in the Mortilogium, where,
at Aug. 4, is " Ob. Rogerus Goyowne prior noster."

1337-43. Gilbert de Bolyniop was elected to succeed. He
was Prior during the period covered by account I., and resigned
about the middle of the year 1343, when account II. begins. On
resignation he was allowed a pension of two marks a-year. He
was living in 1346, when the accounts end.

1343-6. Simon de Ludegate followed. He was a canon of the
House. He is the Prior mentioned in accounts II., III., IV., and
the earlier entries of V. He died 6 Sept., 1346. Notices of his
death and burial occur on pp. 113-4.

1346-8. Robert de Hereford was at once elected to succeed.
Entries connected with his election and installation may be found
on pp. 113-5. In the following month (October, 1346), he
attended a Parliament at Kilkenny. He died, 1348, and was
succeeded by Stephen de Derby, a canon of the House, who continued to rule it for more than 30 years.

THE CONVENT.

Of the Convent itself the accounts give only incidental notices. It was a small body. There is no indication of its numbers at the time of these accounts, but a document of 1300, which appears to name all the members,[1] specifies only eleven brethren, and a visitation in 1468 states that it included only the Prior and seven canons. The officials mentioned, beside the Prior, were the sub-prior, the seneschal, cellarer, and kitchener (besides which were a sacrist and precentor). The seneschal managed the extern business of the House under the Prior, received rents, presided at the courts of the manors belonging to the House, directed the home farms, and sometimes looked after the housekeeping of the Prior's chamber. The cellarer saw to supplies of corn for the House, and controlled the brew-house and bake-house which supplied the ale and bread consumed. A specimen of a cellarer's account is printed in the Appendix (p. 202). The kitchener directed the supply of food (other than bread) for the refectory. In other monasteries he was subordinate to the cellarer, but in this Priory he was an important functionary, several of whose successors became Priors. The brethren included among their numbers two ex-Priors, Hugh de Sutton, or le Jeune, who had resigned the office of Prior in 1325, and Gilbert de Bolyniop, who resigned in 1337. The latter had a pension of two marks; the former somewhat more. These ex-Priors probably possessed special privileges, occupying separate chambers, where they sometimes entertained guests (p. 115).

We have no account of dietary in the refectory, similar to that of the Prior's chamber. This would have been supplied by the kitchener's accounts. But though the passing of such accounts is referred to, none survive. We are, therefore, left to cull incidental notices from the seneschal's accounts. These tend to suggest that if indulgence may have crept into the Prior's chamber it was not extended to the refectory. There were here, probably, only two meals a day, dinner and supper, though a breakfast for the

---

[1] Christ Church Deeds, No. 164.

brethren is mentioned on the special occasion of the election of a
new Prior. Bread was provided in considerable quantities ; when
purchased, the day's supply cost 16*d.* (p. 119). Debts of the
kitchener paid to fishermen show that fish was used. Ale was,
under ordinary circumstances, the drink exclusively used in the
refectory, a day's supply costing 16*d.* (p. 119), or somewhat less.
Wine appears to have been granted only on great festivals. A
list of the days upon which wine was provided for the refectory is
given in one of the accounts. It includes only twelve days in the
year—Christmas, Epiphany, Purification, Easter-day, Ascension—
on each of which 15*d.* worth of wine was allowed. Circumcision,
St. Patrick, Invention of the Holy Cross, 10*d.* each. Palm Sunday,
Vigil of Easter, Tuesday after Easter, Sunday after Easter, 5*d.*
each (pp. 101-2, see also pp. 6, 119). The refectory was, however,
on some occasions at least, provided with a varied *menu*—the Ash
Wednesday dinner, mentioned before, having been served there.

Other portions of the accounts give some idea of life outside the
Convent. The seneschal, the Prior, and others, found it necessary
to go abroad on business of various kinds. These journeyings
were made on horseback, the brother on his horse being attended
by a servant on foot, who took charge of the horse. The roads
were, no doubt, much too bad to give the horseman much advan-
tage in speed over his follower, who was, however, sometimes
mounted. Another fact which, perhaps, also illustrates the badness
of the roads, is the frequency with which it was necessary to have
the horses' shoes attended to, being almost a daily charge in the
travelling expenses.

One journey, made by the Prior (pp. 1-3), will serve to illustrate the manner of travelling: the Prior, accompanied by the
seneschal and a few followers on horseback, started from Dublin
on a Tuesday in November, for Balscadden, a manor near Balbriggan, belonging to the Priory. 10½*d.* worth of wine (about
two gallons) was sent from Dublin for their use. Food was provided from the larder of the manor house, the only article which
it was found necessary to purchase being candles. The party
remained at Balscadden on Wednesday and Thursday ; started

northward on Friday for another manor of the Priory at Drumshallon, Co. Louth, about six miles north of Drogheda. Passing
through the latter, they stopped and bought bread, wine, ale,
oysters, butter, cheese, and fish, on which, no doubt, they dined.
Before evening, they rode on the remaining six miles to Drumshallon, where it was necessary to buy 4*d.* worth of ale to accom-
pany the manor-farmhouse supper. The stock here seems to have
been so low, or so bad, that the next day ale, wine, oysters, fish, and
even oats for the horses, had to be bought. On Sunday the party
were back in Drogheda, where they again dined at their own
expense, notwithstanding the number of religious houses in the
town, which might be expected to show them hospitality. It is
not stated where this night was spent, but the following day finds
them on the road homeward, taking refreshment at Swords, and
on Tuesday the Prior is at home, receiving his guests. The
travelling represents an average journey of less than twenty miles
a-day. General messages were committed to foot servants, who
received an allowance for expenses of about 1*d.* a-day. These
were quite as expeditious as the mounted travellers, and seem
to cover more than twenty miles a-day. To such messengers
responsible duties, such as the collection of small sums of money,
were sometimes entrusted.

The most complete statement of the income of the House is to
be found in the valuation of its property at p. 200, in Appendix.
To the total of £226 there given (which includes property in
Dublin diocese only) must be added the value of Killenaule and
other possessions in Co. Tipperary ; Drumshallon, &c., Co. Louth ;
and the property in Lecale, Co. Down. These should bring
the total to at least £240. In addition still, the offerings in
church had been, in 1300, estimated at as much as £40 a-year.[1]
Taking them even at half this, the Convent must have been worth
say £260 a-year. It is a very difficult and in many respects mis-
leading thing to suggest any certain proportion between the value of
money in mediæval times and now ; but, accepting as an approxi-
mate average proportion, 1 to 15, which has been adopted by the

---

[1] Christ Church Deeds, No. 164.

editor of Bishop Swinfield's "Household Book," the income of Holy Trinity Priory would be equal to nearly £4000 of modern money.[1] Not a very great sum for the position which the Priory occupied in the country! It may be observed that this sum is much in excess of the income dealt with in the accounts. No. II. affords us the best means of estimating the revenue dealt with. The total receipts for a period of about half-a-year (omitting £5, which appears to be a balance in hand) were £72 19s. 8d. Of this, however, no less than £16 was money advanced as loans. Setting this apart, the remainder represents an annual income of about £112. This, however, is only that part of the revenues applicable to the general expenses managed by the treasurer of the House. Separate portions of the revenue were allocated to the expenses of the cellarer, kitchener, sacrist, and other convent officers. An account of a cellarer may be seen on p. 202. The small total of £11 10s. 9d. shown there does not at all represent the amount required for the cellar. It only indicates the sums of money which passed through the cellarer's hands. In addition, he seems to have received all the surplus produce of the manors of Clonken, Gorman, and Glasnevin.[2] The kitchener, too, must have had a considerable fund at his disposal, including probably the large property owned in the city of Dublin.

FARMYARDS AND WORKMEN.

Another very interesting portion of the accounts is that which relates to the management of the home farms. At Grangegorman (pp. 36-40), the farm buildings included a hall, off which were some private rooms. Round the yard stood a barn (kept dry by having its earthen floor raised above the general level of the ground), a malthouse, workshop, and haggard; the latter separated by a mud wall from the cowhouse and cattle yard. The great

---

[1] A lower relative value has been assigned to the money of the period by other authorities, but they have based their calculations on higher prices and wages than those current in these accounts.

[2] See Haggard Accounts, p. 78, &c.

gate was strengthened with 200 great nails, called spikings. The barn and workshop were also secured with strong doors, and the two locks for them cost 7*d.* Near the malt house was a well, from which the water was raised by a bucket attached to an iron chain. The bucket cost 5*d.*; the chain was made in the farm workshop.

On the manor farm of Clouken there was a similar group of buildings, as to the erection of which we have some details (pp. 60–1). They were probably not very substantial. We meet a mention of the fall of the cowhouse, which broke the head of one of the labourers (p. 79). Yet he was not so seriously wounded but that a gift of two pecks of corn, to enable him to lie up for a time, could cure him. The ruin of the cowhouse, however, seems to have been complete, and it had to be entirely rebuilt. Timber was bought and brought from Glenwhery at a cost of 3*s.* 6*d.* A carpenter took 10 days to make and put up the wooden frame of the house, which was apparently 16 yards long. The walls were erected by contract or piecework at 8*d.* a perch. They consisted apparently of mud, an instrument or vessel having been used to throw water on them in course of construction. Hurdles and wattle were used in the construction of another outhouse, but whether for walls or roof is not stated. All the farm buildings were thatched with straw, in applying which quantities of mud were used (pp. 37–8).

The clumsy farm-carts had to be bound together with iron bands and clamps, or tied round with ropes to keep them from shaking to pieces over the uneven roads. Their solid wooden wheels were bound with iron. In the country districts a vehicle called a "car" is distinguished from the carecta or cart. It seems to have been a kind of sledge without wheels, used for field work.

The ploughs were almost entirely of wood, with an iron share. Wooden spades seem to have been used, sometimes tipped with iron (p. 41).

In connexion with the frequent repairs of the farm buildings and utensils, are many examples of the rates of wages. Carpenters were hired generally at 2*d.* a-day with board ; sometimes without board at 2*d.* or 2½*d.*[1]

Smiths' wages 2*d.* a-day with board.

Labourers when engaged for short periods received with hardly an exception 1*d.* a-day.

Thatchers rarely 2*d.* a-day, generally the same as ordinary labourers. (Thatchers in England at this time had about 2½*d.* a-day).

Women employed as helpers to thatchers, &c., got only ½*d.* a-day.

The money wages of permanently employed servants was very small. Thus the bailiff, the responsible manager, or steward as he would now be called, of the farm and manor, took in money wages only 6*s.* 8*d.* a-year. Ploughmen and carters 5*s.* a-year. Drivers of the plough-teams 4*s.* a-year. Small additions of a few pence seem to have been made to the more deserving of these men (p. 34). But the chief part of the remuneration of these workmen consisted of allowances of corn for the food of them and their families. The bailiff of Clonken (p. 84) got 8 bushels of wheat, heaped measure, every 10 weeks. The ploughmen and other permanent farm workmen were allowed 6¼ bushels in the same time. Such allowances were governed, or rather perhaps, the custom relating to them was recognized, by the earliest extant statute of an Irish Parliament, 53 Hen. III., which enacted that servants who were accustomed to receive corn for their food should receive only a quarter of London measure for twelve weeks (Betham, *Constitution*, p. 254). The allowances made to the workmen at Clonken approximated closely to the quantities specified in this statute. The food allowance made to the bailiff was entirely in wheat. But those of the workmen, though estimated in wheat, were partly given in peas and beans, and in some mixed corn, the produce of the tolls taken in the manor mill. When these were substituted for the wheat, they were given in larger

---

[1] The average rate of wages of carpenters in England at the same time was over 3*d.* a-day. Thorold Rogers, "Hist. of Agriculture and Prices."

quantities, 8 pecks of peas, beans, or mixed corn, being given as
an equivalent to 7 pecks of wheat (pp. 84-5). The actual allowance for food made to one of these men during a year was 2
crannocs 5½ bushels of wheat, 1½ crannoc of peas and beans, and
more than ⅓ crannoc of the mixed corn from the mill, the
crannoc representing about a quarter. These allowances seem to
be a sufficient quantity for the food of an average family. They
may sometimes have left a small surplus to be exchanged for
clothes and other necessaries. There is no indication of any other
source of profit except the produce of the fowl, which must have
been kept universally by the cottagers, as is shown by the payment
of a hen at Christmas being a usual part of their service.

Except the small portion of grain from the mill the allowance
does not include any grain suitable for malting ; the money
payments could have afforded very little for the purchase of
meat ; so we may perhaps conclude that the farm labourer's
family must have lived mainly on wheat products and pulse, and
without other drink than water.

The farm servants lived in cottages near the manor, for which
they paid rents of about 1s. a-year, sometimes as much as 2s.—a
very considerable portion of their slender money earnings. The
village of Grangegorman consisted almost entirely of the farm
servants, most of whom had no surnames apart from the name of
their occupation. Of the 16 cottagers here, 3 were "holders" or
ploughmen, 1 a plough "driver," 2 carters, a lime burner, and a
thresher.

Poem.

The accounts contain incidental notices of a great number of
other matters bearing on the social and economic state of Dublin
and its neighbourhood in the fourteenth century. But it is notice-
able that among all the payments in these accounts there is not a
single penny spent on books. There are repeated entries of the
purchase of parchments for legal purposes, rentals, and letters,
but not one entry of the purchase of books or of parchment for
literary use in the Priory Scriptorium. But this neglect of the

Scriptorium was soon to be removed. Under Prior Stephen de Derby, whose government of the house commenced only two years after the end of these accounts, was written the beautiful Psalter of Christ Church, now preserved in the Bodleian Library, but known through the medium of Mr. Gilbert's National MSS. of Ireland (Vol. IV.—1, App.). This work must be acknowledged to be the most elaborate extant work of Anglo-Norman art in Ireland.

But we are reminded in a more direct way of the existence of literary interests in the convent, by the uses which have been made of some of the vacant portions of the parchment of the accounts. The pretty French verses printed on p. 125 were written there soon after the middle of the fourteenth century; and the English poem on pp. 126 to 142, was copied before the middle of the fifteenth century.

This English poem, which we have distinguished as the " Pride of Life," possesses many points of great interest. Written on the first parchment that could be found, by different hands relieving one another, sometimes at short intervals, we can realize the anxiety which existed in the Convent to secure without delay a literary treasure which may have been in the hands of some passing guest spending a night in the guest house of the monastery.

The "Pride of Life" is a Moral Play, or Morality, and consists of a Prologue containing 28 stanzas or 112 lines, and Play containing 97½ stanzas or 390 lines. The latter is now imperfect, a large part is wanting at the end, and two smaller gaps evidently occur, the position of which is explained in the note p. 185.

It is rendered of very special interest by being the only copy of the poem known to exist. The composition possesses a good deal of literary merit ; the style is vigorous ; and the part of the Queen is not without dramatic power. But perhaps the chief interest of the poem arises from its relation to other works of a kindred nature. "The Castle of Perseverance" has been held to be the earliest extant Morality, being usually attributed to the middle of the fifteenth century. The copy of the " Pride of Life " is perhaps slightly older than this, and its language is probably older still. But in the development of allegorical arrangement it

c

seems to occupy a distinctly earlier stage. In the "Castle of Perseverance" as still more in the Moralities of later date almost all the *dramatis personæ* are personifications of abstract qualities, gathered into a complicated allegory. In the "Pride of Life" the allegory is much simpler, and the personifications less numerous and less prominent. The principal character Rex Vivus, The King of Life, represents the man wholly engrossed by worldly success and heedless of the future, supported in his wantonness by Health and Strength (personified as his two knights), while he is further encouraged by Mirth, who as his herald (as in impious jest) challenges Death to combat. Death too is of course personified. But here the allegorical character of the piece seems to end. The other two persons are quite real. The Queen is a true woman, loving to her husband, earnest as to the future, faithful to the Church. The bishop too is no doubt a typical churchman of the time, though his interesting attack on the evils of the age has little reference to the object of his appeal, and justifies the King's advice that he should "learn bet to preach."

While this limitation of the allegory leaves more scope for dramatic interest, it also implies an earlier stage in the development of Moralities, in the later examples of which allegory and abstract personifications occupy almost the whole composition.

The Theology too is of a simpler type. Thus while in the "Castle of Perseverance" the state of the soul of Humanum Genus is the subject of argument, as in a court, between Justice, Mercy, and other characters, on which "Pater sedens in trono" gives his judgment. In "Pride of Life" the lost soul is rescued by the direct interposition of the Virgin alone.

On every ground the "Pride of Life" seems an earlier work than the "Castle of Perseverance"; and hence it may be claimed as absolutely the earliest composition of its kind yet discovered in the English language.

As to the source from which the poem was derived there is as yet no certain evidence. The dialect is mainly Southern, but with Midland influences; such as we might be prepared to find in the spoken tongue of Dublin, with its original Bristol connexion, but forced by position as a colonial capital to graft on its Southern dialect influences from other parts of England.

But that the work is an English not a Dublin composition seems certain from the three place-names which occur. Berwick-on-Tweed (line 285) is mentioned in a way which only one writing in England would be likely to refer to it. The earldom of Kent is conferred as a reward on the messenger, and it has been pointed out that this earldom was vacant from soon after the beginning of the fifteenth century. The third name is the Castle of Gailispire on the hill (line 301). Of this place I have not yet obtained any satisfactory identification ; but it is certainly an English, not an Irish name.

It may be added that like most other mediæval plays, though composed in popular language the representations were intended to be under the direction of the clergy. Accordingly all stage directions and the names of the speakers are written in Latin.

The literary treasure, hurriedly copied by two of the canons of the Priory four and a-half centuries ago, may have been acted in the church, or in the streets of Dublin, where it is almost certain that miracle-plays were at this time familiar. Then, having served its turn, it does not appear ever to have attracted attention again until the roll was examined in the Record Office. Dr. Lyon, when he inspected the roll, could not have read the poem ; at least he makes no mention of it. A brief reference was made to it in the 20th Report of the Deputy-Keeper of the Public Records ; but no public attention was secured to it until the editor of this volume pointed out its interest in a Paper read before the Royal Irish Academy in April, 1891. From the account thus given, Professor Morley, in the seventh volume of " English Writers " (published in the summer of 1891), gave a very interesting notice of the poem, before, however, the text had been fully transcribed.

THE APPENDIX.

A few contemporary documents have been added to the volume as an Appendix, to illustrate matters referred to in the accounts. Some of these have been noticed in passing.

The Rental (pp. 189–200) affords a species of information very rarely to be met with in Ireland. It supplies the names of all the cottagers in the villages of Glasnevin, Grangegorman, and Clonken or Kill-of-the-Grange, as well as of the farmers of those manors, and of Balscaddan in the extreme north of the county of Dublin ; with the amount of their rents, and a description of the customary services which they rendered. These services were now strictly defined and moderate in amount, and in most cases might be compounded for by a small money payment. The services of the larger holders are given in greater detail in the specimen lease printed at p. 207, and noticed on p. 172. The Rental is of importance as illustrating the position of the agricultural classes, and as giving some idea, by a comparison of names, as to the extent to which, about Dublin, the Anglo-Norman colonists had blended with the Irish in the lower classes.

The agreement for the celebration of Masses for John de Grauntsete (printed pp. 202–6, with a partial translation, pp. 148–51) gives some interesting details as to the conduct of the services in the Priory church.

Frequent references occur in the Accounts to the sojourn of members of the Convent on their possessions at Kilcullen and Killenaule. John Comyn, a canon of the House (who, in 1343-4, held the office of seneschal, and as such furnished the Accounts, Nos. II. and IV. in this volume), at one time seems to have been detailed for residence at Kilcullen. In the course of eight weeks there he incurred so much disfavour that a public inquiry into his conduct was held, the report of which is printed at p. 206.   The charges against the canon himself seem for the most part so trivial as to be only prompted by personal illwill, but they afford not the less an interesting illustration of the time.

In conclusion, I have to thank the Right Hon. the Master of the Rolls in Ireland for his permission to publish the Accounts and the other documents under his charge in the Record Office ; and Dr. La Touche, the Deputy-Keeper of the Records, for his help and encouragement in undertaking the work. The Very Rev. W. C. Greene, Dean of Christ Church, most kindly gave me every facility for examining the ancient books preserved in his Cathedral. The Rev. Denis Murphy, M.R.I.A., who read the proofs of the Accounts, has made many suggestions, whose value can only be surpassed by the very kind way in which they were given. I am very much indebted to Miss L. Toulmin Smith, J. A. H. Murray, D.C.L., J. K. Ingram, LL.D, and Mr. James Gairdner, who have been so good as to read the proofs of the Poem ; Miss Toulmin Smith especially, having most obligingly taken much trouble to solve some of its difficulties. Mr. Henry F. Berry, Mr. M. J. M'Enery, and Mr. A. J. Fetherstonhaugh, of the Record Office, Dublin, have each been ever ready with willing help in the progress of the work ; and lastly, I cannot omit to mention the patience and interest bestowed on its production by Mr. Weldrick of the Dublin University Press.

ACCOUNT ROLL

OF THE

PRIORY OF HOLY TRINITY, DUBLIN.

————·⚊·————

I.

[ACCOUNT OF THOMAS DE BEULEY, SENESCHAL, TO
25TH APRIL, 1339.]

. . . .

. . . . In vino empto in refectorio . . . . . adventu Mauricii
Howel, Johannis Aket & aliorum superventorum. Item
eodem die in vino empto in cameram Prioris, pro priore
de Holmpatrik, iii d.

Die [Martis] in octaba Sancti Martini. In oystreis emptis pro
camera Prioris, i d., in . . . i d. ob.; in vino empto ibidem
post prandium, pro adventu Johannis de Novo Castro &
Roberti de Houton, i d. ob. Item eodem die, in vino
empto & misso apud Balyscadan pro Priore ibidem, Senescallo, W. Dasscheburne & aliis, x d. ob. Et in candelis
emptis i d. ob.

————————— ———————

TRANSLATION.

. . . .

[Monday, 17th November, 1337.] In wine bought for the refectory
. . . . . for the coming of Maurice Howel, John Aket, and other
strangers. Also on the same day, in wine bought for the Prior's
chamber, for the prior of Holmpatrick, 3d.

Tuesday, the octave of S. Martin. In oysters bought for the Prior's
chamber, 1d., in . . . . 1½d., in wine bought after dinner there
for the coming of John de New Castle and Robert de Houton, 1½d.
Also on same day, in wine bought and sent to Balscaddan for the
Prior there, the seneschal, W. de Assheburne, and others, 10½d.
And in candles bought, 1½d.

B

Diebus Mercurii & Jovis, nil nisi stauro.

Die Veneris proxima post festum Sancti Edmundi Regis & Martiris. Apud Droghda, in pane pro Priore, iii d., in vino, xii d.; in cervisia, v d.; in oystreis, i d.; in botir & caseo, i d.; in pisse, iii d.; in . . . i d.; in pane pro vii equis ibidem, ii d. ob.; in feno, i d. ob. Item in stablagio, i d.; in ferura equorum ibidem, v d. Item eodem die apud Dromsalan, in cervisia, iiii d.; in . . . pro equis ibidem ii d.

Die Sabbati proxima sequente ibidem. In pane pro Priore, Senescallo, W. de Assheburne & aliis, iii d.; in cervisia, xiii d.; in vino vii d.; in oystreis & pisce viii d.; in avena pro prebenda equorum ibidem, ix d.

         Summa vii s. vii d. Probata.

Die Dominica proxima sequente. Ad prandium apud Droghda; in pane pro predictis, iii d.; in vino, iii d.; in cervisia, vi d.; in carne b[ovina] iiii d.; in gallinis furniendis missis de Dromsolan apud Droghda, ii d. Item ad cenam eodem die pro W. de Assheburne & Johanne Passeleu, ii d. ob. In feno pro equis ibidem, i d.; in pane pro eisdem [equis] . . .; in ferura equorum ibidem, iiii d.

Wednesday and Thursday. Nothing except from the stock.

Friday next after the feast of S. Edmund, king and martyr. At Drogheda, in bread for the Prior, 3*d.* ; in wine, 12*d.* ; ale, 5*d.* ; oysters, 1*d.* ; butter and cheese, 1*d.* ; fish, 3*d.* ; . . . . 1*d.* ; in bread for 7 horses there, 2½*d.* ; hay, 1½*d.* Also stabling, 1*d.* ; shoeing horses there, 5*d.* Also same day at Drumshallon, in ale, 4*d.* ; in . . . . for horses there, 2*d.*

Saturday next following, at same place. In bread for the Prior, seneschal, W. de Assheburne, and others, 3*d.* ; ale, 13*d.* ; wine, 7*d.* ; oysters and fish, 8*d.* ; oats for provender of horses there, 9*d.*

         Total 7*s.* 7*d.* Checked.

Sunday next following. At dinner at Drogheda, in bread for those above named, 3*d.* ; in wine, 3*d.* ; ale, 6*d.* ; beef, 4*d.* ; fowl cooked, sent from Dromshallon to Drogheda, 2*d.* Also at supper, same day, for W. de Assheburne and John Passeleu, 2½*d.* In hay for the horses there, 1*d.* ; in bread for the same [horses] . . . . .; in shoeing of horses there, 4*d.*

Die Lune proxima sequente. In . . . empt. pro eisdem apud Sword, iii d.

Die Martis proxima sequente . . . . empt. ad cameram Prioris pro adventu . . . . aliorum extraneorum, iiii d. ob.

Die Mercurii. Omnia de stauro.

Die Jovis proxima sequente. In vino pro camera Prioris ad prandium [et] cenam, x d. ob., pro adventu magistri Hugonis de Saltu, marescalli archiepiscopi & aliorum. Item in cervisia pro eisdem, x d. In cer[visia in refect]orio pro Conventu, iiii d.

Die Veneris proxima sequente. In camera Prioris, pro adventu diversorum canonicorum & armigerorum, in vino . . . . In cervisia empta pro Conventu in refectorio & firmaria, xii d. Item in penettes emptis & liberatis magistro R . . . . . vi d.

[Die Sabbati in vig]ilia Sancti Andree apostoli. In cervisia empta, ad cameram Prioris ad nonam & sero, vi d. ob. Item . . . . . .

   Summa viii s. viii d. Probata.

[Die Dominica in]festo Sancti Andree apostoli. In cervisia empta ad cameram Prioris ad nonam & sero, & pro Con-

---

Monday next following. In . . . . bought for the same at Swords, 3d.

Tuesday . . . . bought for the Prior's chamber for the coming of . . . . and other strangers, 4½d.

Wednesday. All from stock.

Thursday. In wine for the Prior's chamber at dinner and supper, 10½d., for the coming of master Hugh de Saltu, the marshal of the archbishop, and others. Also in ale for them, 10d. In ale in the refectory for the convent, 4d.

Friday. In the Prior's chamber, for the coming of sundry canons and esquires, in wine . . . . In ale bought for the convent in the refectory and infirmary, 12d. Also in penettes bought and delivered to master R . . . . 6d.

Saturday, the vigil of S. Andrew the apostle. In ale bought for the Prior's chamber at noon (or none) and evening, 6½d. Also . . . .

   Total 8s. 8d. Checked.

Sunday, the feast of S. Andrew the apostle. In ale bought for the Prior's chamber at noon and evening, and for the convent in the refectory

ventu in refectorio & [firmaria] .... empta eodem die pro
eisdem ob defectum celarii, xix d. Item pro Priore alias
eodem die, ii d.

Die Lune ..... [ad camer]am Prioris, pro adventu magistri
Thome de Kylmor, iii d. Item sero pro adventu Ricardi
Eliot & armigeri Prioris ; in ......

[Die Martis proxima se]quente. In cervisia empta ad cameram
Prioris, ob defectum Celarii, ii d.

Die Mercurii proxima sequente. In cervisia empta ....
....

Die Veneris in vigilia Sancti Nicholai. In cervisia empta ad
cameram Prioris, iii d. ; in vino empto, iii d. ....
.... empt. pro Priore, quia jejunavit ad aquam i d.
Summa iii s. .... Probata.

.   .   .   .

Die dominica proxima sequente. Omnia de stauro precomputato.

Die Lune proxima sequente. In camera Prioris ad cenam ; in
vino iii d.

----

and infirmary .... bought on same day for the same owing to
default of the cellarer, 19*d.* Also for the Prior at another time
on same day, 2*d.*

Monday. [Wine] for the Prior's chamber, for the coming of master
Thomas de Kylmor, 3*d.* Also at evening for the coming of Richard
Eliot, and the esquire of the Prior, in ....

Tuesday. In ale bought for the Prior's chamber, owing to default of the
cellarer, 2*d.*

Wednesday. In ale bought ....
....

Friday, the vigil of S. Nicholas. In ale bought for the Prior's chamber,
3*d.*; wine, 3*d.* ......

[Saturday, 6th December, 1337.] .... bought for the Prior, because
he fasted on water, 1*d.*
Total 3*s.* .... Checked.

.   .   .   .

Sunday next following [18th January, 1338]. All from the stock previously accounted for.

Monday. In the Prior's chamber at supper, in wine, 3*d.*

Die Martis proxima sequente. In Sacrista, pro Priore, & priore
de Holmpatrik, Johanne Passelewe, et aliis, ad prandium;
in vino iii d. Item in ii paribus cirotecarum ad donandum
p[recep]to Prioris iii d.

Die Mercurii, in festo Sancte Agnetis virginis. In vino empto ad
jantaculum Prioris & magistri Simonis cancellarii Archiepiscopi iii d. Et eodem die; in vino pro adventu Johannis
Welsshe, Walteri Brayhenogh, procuratorum, ad prandium
ibidem iii d.; in ii caponis furnitis & carne assata viii d.
Eodem die ad cenam ibidem; in cervisia ii d., in carne
assata ii d. ob.

Die Jovis proxima sequente. In camera Prioris pro adventu
Johannis de Granc' [et] capellani sui ad jantaculum; in
pane i d., in vino iii d., in i capono furnito iii d. In cervisia
sero i d.

Die Veneris sequente. In vino empto pro camera Prioris, pro
adventu dominorum Thome Wogan eschaetoris Hibernie,
Elie de Assheburne, justiciariorum itinerariorum, et aliorum
superventorum, ad prandium, ii s.; in oystreis iiii d., in ii
libris de ffyges emptis iiii d. Item sero eodem die in
camera Prioris, in cervisia i d.

Tuesday. In the sacristy, for the Prior, the prior of Holmpatrick, John
Passalewe, and others, at dinner, in wine, 3*d.* Also in 2 pairs of
gloves for gifts by command of the Prior, 3*d.*

Wednesday, the feast of S. Agnes the virgin. In wine bought for breakfast of the Prior and master Simon, chancellor of the Archbishop,
3*d.* And the same day, in wine for the coming of John Welsshe
(and) Walter Brayhenogh, proctors, to dinner there, 3*d.*; in 2
cooked capons and roast meat, 8*d.* Same day at supper there, in
ale 2*d.*; roast meat, 2½*d.*

Thursday. In the Prior's chamber for the coming of John de Grancet
and his chaplain to breakfast, in bread, 1*d.*; wine, 3*d.*; a cooked
capon, 3*d.* In ale at evening, 1*d.*

Friday. In wine bought for the Prior's chamber, for the coming of sir
Thomas Wogan, escheator of Ireland, and sir Elias de Assheburne
justices itinerant, and other strangers, to dinner, 2*s.*; in oysters,
4*d.*; 2 pounds of figs bought, 4*d.* Also at evening same day, in
the Prior's chamber, in ale, 1*d.*

Die Sabbati sequente. In oystreis emptis pro Priore, senescallo, et celerario, in celario, ad prandium i d., iu vino iii d.
Summa v s. x d. ob. Probata.

Die Dominica, in festo conversionis Sancti Pauli. In anguillis salsatis emptis pro Priore viii d., et in ii pluvers emptis ii d.

Die Lune. In vino empto in camera Prioris iii d., in cervisia ii d., in cinape i d., in volatilibus i d.

Die Martis sequente. In vino empto, in camera Prioris iii d.

Die Mercurii. Omnia de stauro.

Die Jovis sequente. In cervisia empta pro Priore apud Glasnevin iii d.

Die Veneris sequente. In camera Prioris ad prandium, in pane i d.

Die Sabbati sequente. In pane empto, in camera Prioris, i d.
Summa ii s. i d. Probata.

Die Dominica, in festo Sancte Brigide virginis. Omnia de stauro.

Die Lune in festo Purificationis Beate Marie virginis. In vino empto in refectorio pro Conventu, ix d. Et eodem die in vino empto sero pro camera Prioris, iii d.

Saturday. In oysters for the Prior, seneschal, and cellarer, in the cellar, at diuner, 1d. ; in wine, 3d.
Total 5s. 10½d. Checked.

Sunday, the feast of the conversion of S. Paul. In salted eels bought for the Prior, 8d. ; in 2 plovers bought, 2d.

Monday. In wine bought for the Prior's chamber, 3d.; ale, 2d.; mustard, 1d. ; fowl, 1d.

Tuesday. In wine bought for the Prior's chamber, 3d.

Wednesday. All from stock.

Thursday. In ale bought for the Prior at Glasnevin, 3d.

Friday. In the Prior's chamber, at dinner, in bread, 1d.

Saturday. In bread bought for the Prior's chamber, 1d.
Total 2s. 1d. Checked.

Sunday, the feast of S. Brigid the virgin. All from stock.

Monday, the feast of the Purification of the Blessed Virgin Mary. In wine bought in the refectory for the convent, 9d. And same day in wine bought at evening for the Prior's chamber, 3d.

Diebus Martis, Mercurii, Jovis, et Veneris.   Omnia de stauro.

Die Sabbati proxima sequente.   In vino empto pro Priore, Johanne Haket, Gilberto de Moenes, in ffirmaria, iiii d. ob. Summa xvi d. ob.

Die Dominica et die Lune proxima sequente.   Omnia de stauro.

Die Martis.   Apud Dublin, in camera Prioris, pro adventu Johannis de Balygodman, ad prandium, in i gallina furnita & ii pyes furnitis, iii d.   Item in vino iii d.   Et sero ibidem pro eisdem, in vino, iii d.; et in gallinis & carne assatis, iiii d.

Die Mercurii sequente.   Ad jantaculum in camera Prioris, pro Priore, senescallo, coquinario, & aliis; in vino, iii d.; in i pastello i d.   Et eodem die sero ad cenam, pro adventu Johannis de Balygodman, Johannis Haket, & aliorum superventorum in firmaria; in vino, iii d.; in i gallina & volatilibus assatis, ii d. ob.   Item in i quarterio agni assati, i d.; in candelis, i. d.

Die Jovis proxima post festum sancto Scolastice virginis.   In

---

Tuesday, Wednesday, Thursday, and Friday.   All from stock.

Saturday.   In wine bought for the Prior, John Haket, Gilbert de Moenes, in the infirmary, 4½d.

Total, 16½d.

Sunday and Monday following.   All from stock.

Tuesday.   At Dublin, in the Prior's chamber, for the coming of John de Balygodman at dinner, in one fowl and 2 pies cooked, 3d.; also in wine, 3d.; and at evening there for the same, in wine, 3d., and in fowl and meat roast, 4d.

Wednesday.   At breakfast in the Prior's chamber, for the Prior, seneschal, kitchener, and others, in wine, 3d.; 1 pasty, 1d.   And on same day at evening at supper, for the coming of John de Balygodman, John Haket, and other strangers, in the infirmary, in wine, 3d.; in one hen and fowl roasted, 2½d.   Also in a quarter of roast lamb, 1d.; candles, 1d.

Thursday next after the feast of S. Scolastica the virgin.   In the Prior's camera Prioris, pro adventu W. Comyn vicecomitis, Ricardi fratris sui, Johannis Haket, Willelmi Haket, Hugonis Lumbard, Nicholai clerici vicecomitis & aliorum ; in vino, ix d. ; in v pastellis gallinarum furnitis, ix d. ob.   Et eodem die sero ad cenam pro eisdem ; in vino, vi d. ; in ii gallinis assatis & volatilibus emptis, iiii d. ; in dimidio agno, ii d. ; in carne bovium assata, iiii d. ; in candelis, iii d.

Die Veneris.   Omnia de stauro.

Die Sabbati, in festo Sancti Valentini.   In oystreis emptis ad cameram Prioris, i d. ; in vino, iiii d. ob. ; in volatilibus, ii d., pro die crastina ; in ii li. candelarum, iii d.

Summa vi s. ob.   Probata.

Diebus Dominica, Lune, Martis, & Mercurii, in festo Sancti Fintani.   Omnia de stauro.

Die Jovis proxima sequente.   In i gallina empta pro Priore apud Glasnevin, i d.   Item in i gallina furnita, i d. ob.

Die Veneris sequente.   In cervisia empta pro Conventu in refectorio ad prandium, pro defectu celarii, & ad cenam, v d.

---

chamber, for the coming of W. Comyn, sheriff, Richard his brother, John Haket, William Hacket, Hugh Lumbard, Nicholas clerk of the sheriff and others, in wine ; 9*d*. ; 5 pasties of fowl baked, 9½*d*. And on same day, at evening at supper for the same, in wine, 6*d*. ; 2 hens roast and fowl bought, 4*d*. ; half a lamb, 2*d*. ; roast beef, 4*d*. ; candles, 3*d*.

Friday.   All from stock.

Saturday, the feast of S. Valentine.   In oysters bought for the Prior's chamber, 1*d*. ; wine, 4½*d*. ; fowl, 2*d*. for the day following ; 2 lb. of candles, 3*d*.

Total, 6*s*. ½*d*.   Checked.

Sunday, Monday, Tuesday, and Wednesday, the feast of S. Fintan.   All from stock.

Thursday next following.   In one fowl bought for the Prior at Glasnevin, 1*d*.   Also in a cooked fowl, 1½*d*.

Friday.   In ale bought for the convent in the refectory at dinner, through default of the cellarer, and at supper, 5*d*.

Die Sabbati proxima sequente. In camera Prioris ad prandium
pro Priore, senescallo, W. de Assheburne, quorum unus
ivit versus Kylcolyn et alius versus Mackyngan ad
wardam; in vino, iii d.

Summa x d. ob.

Diebus Dominica & Lune proximis sequentibus. Omnia de
stauro.

Die Martis in festo Carniprivii. Pro Johanne de sancto Wlstano,
in camera Prioris, in carne assata, i d.; in vino, sero, iii d.,
in ii gallinis, iii d.

Die Mercurii in festo Cinerum. Pro conventu in refectorio, &
pro adventu magistri Johannis de Pylattenhale ad prandium; in allece, vi d.; in pisso albo, xii d.; in salmone,
xviii d.; in dicto salmone furniendo, ii d.; in amigdalis
& rys emptis, iiii d.; in gingibero & cinape, ob. Item in
focali, iii d.

Die Jovis in crastino Cinerum. In vino empto pro Priore apud
Glasnevin, iii d.; in oystreis emptis ad prandium, i d.

Die Sabbati proxima sequente. In camera Prioris pro adventu

Saturday. In the Prior's chamber at dinner for the Prior, seneschal,
and W. de Assheburne, of whom one went towards Kilcullen, and
the other towards Mackyngan [Newcastle, co. Wicklow], to ward,
in wine, 3*d*.

Total, 10½*d*.

Sunday and Monday next. All from stock.

Tuesday in the feast of Carnival. For John de S. Wulstan, in the
Prior's chamber, in roast meat, 1*d*.; in wine at evening, 3*d*.;
2 hens, 3*d*.

Ash Wednesday. For the convent in the refectory, and for the coming of
master John de Pylattenhale at dinner, in herrings, 6*d*.; white
fish, 12*d*.; salmon, 18*d*.; baking the salmon, 2*d*.; almonds and
rice, 4*d*.; ginger and mustard, ½*d*.; also in fuel, 3*d*.

Thursday on the morrow of Ash Wednesday. In wine bought for the
Prior at Glasnevin, 3*d*.; oysters for dinner, 1*d*.

Saturday. In the Prior's chamber for the coming of Thomas Blakeburne,

Thome Blakeburne; in oystreis, ii d.; in iiii pastellis salmonum emptis, iiii d.; in cervisia, iii d.; in candelis, iiii d.

Summa v s. ix d. ob.   Probata.

Dominica prima Quadragesime.   In camera Prioris pro jantaculo suo, in oystreis, i d.; in salmone empto, ii d.

Die Lune proxima sequente.   In camera [Prioris] pro adventu fratrum Predicatorum & capellanorum de Arclo; in oystreis, ii d.; in salmone, ii d..

Die Martis sequente.   In camera Prioris pro adventu Gilberti Moenes, Thome de Stokton & aliorum superventorum; in oystreis, ii d.; in stokfych, ii d.; in salmone, ii d.

Die Mercurii.   De stauro.

Die Jovis.   In camera Prioris, ad prandium; in oystreis, i d.; in i quarta de oleo olivo, vi d.; in cervisia, i d. ob.; in cepis, ob.; in iii parvis ollis luteis pro cinape inponendo, i d.

Die Veneris.   Apud Glasnevin pro Priore; in cervisia, iiii d.; in oystreis, i d.   Item sero apud Dublin in camera Prioris; in cervisia, ii d.

---

in oysters, 2*d.*; in 4 salmon pasties bought, 4*d.*; ale, 3*d.*; candles, 4*d.*

Total, 5*s.* 9½*d.*   Checked.

First Sunday of Lent.   In the Prior's chamber for his breakfast, in oysters, 1*d.*; in salmon bought, 2*d.*

Monday.   In the Prior's chamber for the coming of the friars Preachers and chaplains of Arklow, in oysters, 2*d.*; salmon, 2*d.*

Tuesday.   In the Prior's chamber for the coming of Gilbert Moenes, Thomas de Stockton, and other strangers; in oysters, 2*d.*; stockfish, 2*d.*; salmon, 2*d.*

Wednesday.   From the stock.

Thursday.   In the Prior's chamber at dinner, in oysters, 1*d.*; one quart of olive oil, 6*d.*; ale, 1½*d.*; onions, ½*d.*; 3 little earthenware pots for putting mustard in, 1*d.*

Friday.   At Glasnevin, for the Prior, in ale, 4*d.*; oysters, 1*d.*   Also at evening, at Dublin, in the Prior's chamber, in ale, 2*d.*

Die Sabbati. In camera Prioris ibidem; in oystreis, i d.; in vino, iii d.; in cervisia empta, i d.

      Summa ii s. xi d. Probata.

Die Dominica secunda Quadragesime. Omnia de stauro.

Die Lune. De stauro.

Die Martis. In camera Prioris, pro priore Sancti Wlstani, ii canonicorum & armigeris. In oystreis, i d.; in vino empto, iii d.; in stokfich, i d.; in walnotes, ii d. Item post prandium pro magistro Thoma de Kylmor, in vino, iii d.

Die Mercurii. De stauro.

Die Jovis. De stauro.

Die Veneris. De stauro.

Die Sabbati. In camera Prioris, in amigdalis, ii d.

      Summa xii d. Probata.

Dominica iiiᵃ Quadragesime. Pro priore apud Clonken; in vino, vi d.; in amigdalis, iii d. Et eodem die pro adventu Johannis de Moenes, Thome de Stokton, & aliorum; in vino, iii d.; in candelis, i d. ob.

Saturday. In the Prior's chamber there, in oysters, 1d.; wine, 3d.; ale bought, 1d.

      Total, 2s. 11d. Checked.

Second Sunday of Lent. All from stock.

Monday. From stock.

Tuesday. In the Prior's chamber, for the prior of St. Wulstan's, 2 of the canons, and esquires, in oysters, 1d.; wine bought, 3d.; stockfish, 1d.; walnuts, 2d. Also after dinner, for master Thomas de Kylmor, in wine, 3d.

Wednesday. From stock.

Thursday. From stock.

Friday. From stock.

Saturday. In the Prior's chamber, in almonds, 2d.

      Total, 12d. Checked.

Third Sunday of Lent. For the Prior at Clonken [Kill of the Grange, Co. Dublin], in wine, 6d.; almonds, 3d. And on same day, for the coming of John de Moenes, Thomas de Stokton, and others, in wine, 3d.; in candles, 1½d.

Die Lune sequente. In pisse empto pro eodem ibidem, vi d.

Die Martis. In camera Prioris pro adventu Roberti de Clifford, ad prandium; in oystreis, i d.; in salmone, ii d.

Die Mercurii. Pro adventu dicti Thome de Stokton & aliorum; in salmone furnito, i d.; in stokfich, i d. Et post prandium pro adventu Roberti Tanner; in vino, iiii d. ob.

Die Jovis sequente. In camera Prioris, pro adventu magistrorum Hugonis de Saltu, Thome de Kylmor, & aliorum; in pane, i d.; in vino, xii d.; in cervisia, iii d.; in allecibus, iii d.; in tublynges, ii d. ob.; in plays, iii d.; in troytes, i d,; in amigdalis & rys, iiii d.

Die Veneris proxime sequente. Apud Glasnevin, pro Priore; in pane, ob.; in vino, iii d.; in amigdalis & rys, ii d.

Die Sabbati. In camera Prioris, ad prandium; in oystreis, i d.; in vino, i d. ob.

Summa v s. ii d. ob.   Probata.

Dominica iiii^a Quadragesime, qua cantatur Letare Jerusalem. Pro Priore apud Clonken, pro le mustrysoun; in allecibus, iii d.; in amigdalis pro eodem ibidem, i d. ob.

Monday. In fish bought for the same there, 6*d.*

Tuesday. In the Prior's chamber, for the coming of Robert de Clifford to dinner, in oysters, 1*d.*; salmon, 2*d.*

Wednesday. For the coming of said Thomas de Stokton and others, in cooked salmon, 1*d.*; stockfish, 1*d.* And after dinner, for the coming of Robert Tanner, in wine, 4½*d.*

Thursday. In the Prior's chamber, for the coming of masters Hugh de Saltu, Thomas de Kylmor, and others, in bread, 1*d.*; wine, 12*d.*; ale, 3*d.*; herrings, 3*d.*; tublynges, 2½*d.*; plaice, 3*d.*; trout, 1*d.*, almonds and rice, 4*d.*

Friday. At Glasnevin, for the Prior, in bread, ½*d.*; wine, 3*d.*; almonds and rice, 2*d.*

Saturday. In the Prior's chamber, at dinner, in oysters, 1*d.*; wine, 1½*d.*

Total, 5s. 2½*d.*   Checked.

Fourth Sunday of Lent, on which is sung *Lætare Jerusalem.* For the Prior at Clonken, for the muster, in herrings, 3*d.*; in almonds for him there, 1½*d.*

Die Lune. Omnia de stauro.

Die Martis. Apud Glasnevin. In pane, i d.

Die Mercurii in festo Annunciationis Dominice. Apud Clonken; in pissibus, iii d.

Die Jovis ibidem. Pro senescallo, W. Dasseburne, & aliis, ad le mustrison; in allecibus, ii d.; in pissibus, iii d.

Die Veneris. In camera Prioris; in pane, i d.; in vino, ii d.; in oleo de olivo, iii d.; in walnotes, ob. quad.

Die Sabbati. In camera Prioris, ad prandium; in oystreis, i d.; in vino, ii d. ob.

     Summa ii s. quad. Probata.

Dominica vᵃ Quadragesime. Pro Priore apud Glasnevin; in vino, ii d. ob.

Die Lune. Apud Clonken, pro T. B. senescallo, W. Dasscheburne, & aliis hominibus euntibus ibidem, cum equis armatis, pro mustrisoun faciendo & ad wardam comorandam; in pissibus & allecibus, v d.

Die Martis. Ibidem, pro eisdem, Gregorio Taunton, Johanne Baly-godman, & aliis; in pisse, vii d. ob.; in vino, ii d. ob.

Monday. All from stock.

Tuesday. At Glasnevin, in bread, 1*d.*

Wednesday, the feast of Annunciation of Our Lady. At Clonken, in fish, 3*d.*

Thursday. In the same place, for the seneschal, W. de Assheburne, and others at the muster, in herrings, 2*d.*; fish, 3*d.*

Friday. In the Prior's chamber, in bread, 1*d.*; in wine, 2*d.*; olive oil, 3*d.*; walnuts, ¾*d.*

Saturday. In the Prior's chamber, at dinner, in oysters, 1*d.*; wine, 2½*d.*

    Total, 2s. ¼*d.* Checked.

Fifth Sunday of Lent. For the Prior at Glasnevin, in wine, 2½*d.*

Monday. At Clonken, for T[homas de] B[euley], seneschal, W. de Assheburne, and other men going there with horses armed for making the muster and to keep ward, in fish and herrings, 5*d.*

Tuesday. In the same place, for the same persons, Gregory Taunton, John Balygodman, and others, in fish, 7½*d.*; wine, 2½*d.* Also on

Item eodem die in camera Prioris apud Dublin, pro adventu Johannis Grancest, Johannis Callan & aliorum ; in oystreis, ii d. ; in pane, ii d. ; in vino, xii d. ob. ; in turbut, v d. ; in gurnard, i d. ; in amigdalis & rys, iiii d. ; in anquillis, iii d. ; in salmone, v d. ; in cepis, i d. ob.   Et eodem die, in Sacrista, sero ; in vino, ii d. ob.

Die Mercurii.   In camera Prioris, ad prandium, pro adventu Gilberti Moenes, Gregorii Taunton, Petri Howel & aliorum ; in pane, i d. ; in oystreis, i d. ; in vino, iiii d.

Die Jovis & Die Veneris.   Omnia de stauro.

Die Sabbati.   In camera Prioris ad prandium ; in amigdalis, ii d. ; in cervisia, i d.

Summa v s. v d.   Probata.

Die Dominica in Ramis Palmarum.   Omnia de stauro.

Die Lune proxima sequente.   Ad prandium, pro senescallo, Waltero fratre Prioris, qui comederunt ante nonam eo quod iverunt apud Kylcolyn pro diversis negotiis domus ; in pisse, ii d. ob. ; & eodem die apud le Nas post nonam versus Kilcolyn, in cervisia, i d. ; in pane pro equis . . . .

---

same day, in the Prior's chamber at Dublin, for the coming of John Grancest, John Callan, and others, in oysters, 2*d.* ; bread, 2*d.* ; wine, 12½*d.* ; turbot, 5*d.* ; gurnard, 1*d.* ; almonds and rice, 4*d.* ; eels, 3*d.* ; salmon, 5*d.* ; onions, 1½*d.*   And on same day, in the sacristy at evening, in wine, 2½*d.*

Wednesday.   In the Prior's chamber, at dinner, for the coming of Gilbert Moenes, Gregory Taunton, Peter Howel and others, in bread, 1*d.* ; oysters, 1*d.* ; wine, 4*d.*

Thursday and Friday.   All from stock.

Saturday.   In the Prior's chamber, at dinner, in almonds, 2*d.* ; ale, 1*d.*

Total, 5*s.* 5*d.*   Checked.

Palm Sunday.   All from stock.

Monday next following.   At dinner for the seneschal, Walter, brother of the Prior, who eat together before noon because they went to Kilcullen for diverse business of the house, in fish, 2½*d.* ; and on same day, at the Naas after noon, on the way to Kilcullen, in ale, 1*d.* ; in bread for horses . . .

Die Martis & Die Mercurii. Omnia de stauro precomputato.

Die Jovis in Parasceve. Pro eisdem apud Kyldar ad recipiendum oleum sacrum, ad prandium ; in pane, i d. ; in cervisia, ii d. Panis pro equis, i d.

Die Veneris & Die Sabbati. Omnia de stauro.

Summa x d. ob. Probata.

Die Pasche. In Refectorio ; in vino pro Priore & conventu, viii d.

Die Lune. Pro Priore, apud Glasnevin, in vino empto, ii d.

Die Martis. Ibidem pro eodem ; in vino, ii d.

Die Mercurii. In camera Prioris, ad prandium ; in vino, i d. ; in candelis, i d.

Die Jovis. Apud Clonken, pro Priore, & adventu Johannis Haket, Gregorii Taunton, Willelmi Haket, Petri Howel, & aliorum ; in pane, i d. ; in vino, x d. ; in cervisia, iii d. ; in carne bovina & porcina, ix d. ; in gingibero & croco, i d.

Die Veneris. Apud Dublin, in camera Prioris ; in fructu, i d.

Die Sabbati. In refectorio pro adventu Roberti Hony & aliorum ; in vino, ii d.

Summa iii s. ii d. Probata.

Tuesday and Wednesday. All from stock previously accounted for.

Thursday in the Preparation. For the same at Kildare to receive the holy oil, at dinner, in bread, 1d. ; ale, 2d. ; bread for horses, 1d.

Friday and Saturday. All from stock.

Total 10½d. Checked.

Easter day. In the refectory, in wine for the Prior and convent, 8d.

Monday. For the Prior at Glasnevin, in wine bought, 2d.

Tuesday. In the same place for him, in wine, 2d.

Wednesday. In the Prior's chamber at dinner, in wine, 1d. ; candles, 1d.

Thursday. At Clonken for the Prior, and for the coming of John Haket, Gregory Taunton, William Haket, Peter Howel, and others, in bread, 1d. ; wine, 10d. ; ale, 3d. ; beef and pork, 9d. ; ginger and saffron, 1d.

Friday. At Dublin, in the Prior's chamber, in fruit, 1d.

Saturday. In the refectory for the coming of Robert Hony, and others, in wine, 2d.

Total 3s. 2d. Checked.

Die Dominica in festo clausi Pasche, & Die Lune. Omnia de
    stauro.

Die Martis sequente. In cervisia empta pro Priore, apud Glas-
    nevin, iiii d.

Die Mercurii sequente. Pro Priore ibidem ; in vino, ii d.

Die Jovis. Die Veneris. Omnia de stauro.

Die Sabbati. In camera Prioris apud Dublin ; in vino empto,
    & pro adventu Willelmi Mareschall & aliorum . . . . iiii d.
                Summa x d.   Probata.

. . . .

[Johan.] de Castro eunt. apud Trim ad Eschaetorem Hibernie,
    vi d.

Item in expensis W. Dassheburne, Thome . . . . apud Rat . . .
    hill ; in cervisia, i d. ; in pane pro equis, i d. ; videlicet die
    Martis proxima post festum Inventionis Sancte Crucis.

Item eodem die apud Kyl . . . In carne, i d. ob. Die . . . apud
    Poynteston in redeundo versus Dublin, iii d. in cervisia.
    In cervisia empta sero pro eisdem apud Gorman . . . .

Magistro Johanni de P[il]atehal pro subsidio spiritualium con-
    cessos, x s.
    _____

Sunday, the feast of the close of Easter, and Monday. All from stock.

Tuesday. In ale bought for the Prior at Glasnevin, 4*d.*

Wednesday. For the Prior in the same place, in wine, 2*d.*

Thursday, Friday. All from stock.

Saturday. In the Prior's chamber at Dublin, in wine bought, and for
    the coming of William Mareschall and others [strangers], 4*d.*
                Total 10*d.*   Checked.

. . . .

. . . . John de Castro going to Trim to the escheator of Ireland, 6*d.*

Also in expenses of W. de Assheburne, Thomas . . . at Rat . . . hill, in
    ale, 1*d.* ; bread for horses, 1*d.*, viz. on Tuesday next after feast of
    the Finding of the Holy Cross.

Also on the same day at Kyl. . . . In meat 1½*d.* ; . . . day at Poyntes-
    ton in returning towards Dublin, 3*d.* in ale. In ale bought at
    evening for them at Gorman . . .

To master John de Pilatehal granted in aid of the spiritualities, 10*s.*

Item W. Dassheburne pro spiritualibus de Kilcolyn, iiii s.

Item in . . . . emptis & missis Thesaurario Hibernie de exbennio per consensum Prioris & couventus, v marc' di'.

Item cuidam nuncio eunti apud Kilcolyn ad . . . pro utilitate domus, ii d.

Item liberatum hominibus hobellariis euntibus cum Thesaurario super les Obrennes, vi d. Et in i equo empto de Milone Passelew ad . . . . xv s., qui perditus erat in eodem voyagio.

Item cuidam nuncio eunti ad magistrum Johannem Desewell cum litera apud Morrath, vi d.

Johanni de Evesham apud Dublin de subsidio domino Regi concesso versus partes Scocie, xxvi s. viii d.

Item cuidam nuncio eunti apud Kylcolyn . . . . N. de Barton directis, ii d.

Item liberatum domino Roberto capitali & supervisori brevium cancellarie per ordinacionem Prioris & conventus pro i brevi Thesaurario Hibernie & alio brevi Eschaetori Hibernie pro dictis brevibus sigillandis, v s. iiii d.

———————

Also to W. de Assheburne for the spiritualities of Kilcullen, 4s.

Also in . . . bought and sent to the treasurer of Ireland as a present by consent of the Prior and convent, 5½ marks.

Also to a certain messenger going to Kilcullen to . . . for service of the house, 2d.

Also given to the light horsemen going with the treasurer against the O'Byrnes, 6d. And in one horse bought of Milo Passelew to . . . . . . 15s., which was lost in that expedition.

Also to a certain messenger going to master John Desewell with a letter to Morrath, 6d.

To John de Evesham at Dublin, of the subsidy granted to the lord the king towards the parts of Scotland, 26s. 8d.

Also to a certain messenger going to Kilcullen . . . . directed to N. de Barton, 2d.

Also given to sir Robert, chief and supervisor of writs of Chancery by ordinance of the Prior and convent, for one writ to the treasurer of Ireland, and another writ to the Escheator of Ireland, for sealing the said writs, 5s. 4d.

Item carpent' Joh' Grancest, in cimiterio Predicatorum, iii d.

Item Hen . . . . mercatorum & mensurarum, domini Regis in Hibernia pro feodo suo de mensuris Gorman & alibi non attemptis, xv s. iiii d.

Item liberatum domino Roberto C . . . Cancellarii Hibernie pro vino de dono Prioris & conventus eidem Cancellario, v marc'.

Item datum filiis & filiabus Johannis Passelewe, vi . . . . recipere vult pro expensis Senescalli ibidem quando curias te[nui]t.

Item liberatum pro i capella ferrea pro warda, xi d.

Item cuidam garcioni moranti . . . . pro warda, iiii d.

Item in grayves emptis & factis ad opus Wal. fratris Prioris apud Clonken, viii d.

Et pro zonis & bokeles ad eosdem, ii d.

. . . . . . Rolegh subeschaetori comitatus Kyldarie ad inquisitionem capiendum & parcendum Priori & conventui de injuria facienda, xx s.

Also for the wooden structure of John Grancest in the cemetery of the [Friars] Preachers, 3*d*.

Also to Henry [clerk of] markets and measures of the lord the king in Ireland for his fee for the measures at Gorman and elsewhere which were not tested, 15*s*. 4*d*.

Also given to sir Robert . . . . of the chancellor of Ireland for wine, of the gift of the Prior and convent to the same chancellor, 5 marks.

Also given to the sons and daughters of John Passelewe 6 . . . . [which] he desires to receive for the expenses of the seneschal there when he held courts.

Also paid for an iron head-piece for the ward, 11*d*.

Also to a certain boy remaining . . . . for the ward, 4*d*.

Also in greaves bought and made for the use of Walter, brother of the Prior, at Clonken, 8*d*.

Also for belts and buckles for the same, 2*d*.

. . . . to . . . Rolegh the subescheator of county Kildare to take an inquisition and spare the Prior and convent from injury, 20*s*.

Item Henr. Whyte de dono Prioris . . . .
. . . . de Kylcolyn, vi s.
Et eidem Nicholao de dono Prioris, xii d.
Et in reparacione unius paris de . . . .
. . . . Clonken & Novum Castrum
in servicio Prioris & conventus, ix d.
Item in cena Senescalli apud Cl. . . . .
. . . . qui venit
de Curia Romana, iiii s.
Item cuidam nuncio venienti de Kyldenh[al] . .
. . . & redeunti, precepto Prioris, viii d.
Item Tubaccionibus Justiciariorum qui fuerunt in Refect
. . . .
Item Johanni Faytour Waffrer, ex dono eiusdem, iii d.
Item cuidam parvo Cittheratori ex dono domini, iii d.
Item . . . . clerico ex dono domini, vi d.
Item Johanni Janitori Johanni Wheler euntibus ad inquirendum
post Johannem Grancest' per . .

Also to Henry Whyte of the gift of the Prior . . . .
of Kilcullen, 6s.
And to the same Nicholas of the gift of the Prior, 12d.
And in repair of one pair of . . . . Clonken, and New Castle
in the service of the Prior and convent. 9d.
Also in supper of the seneschal at Cl[onken] . . . .
. . . . who came from the Roman Court, 4s.
Also to a certain messenger coming from Killenaule . . . . and
returning, by command of the Prior, 8d.
Also to the trumpeters of the justices who were in the refectory . . . . .
. . . .
Also to John Faytour waferer, of the gift of the same, 3d.
Also to a certain little harper of the gift of the lord (Prior), 3d.
Also . . . . clerk, of the gift of the lord, 6d.
Also to John the doorkeeper and John Wheler going to inquire after
John Grancest by . . . .

[Item] Johanni de Castro eunti ad curiam domini Regis in Anglia pro negociis domus expediendis, cvi s. viii d.

Item . . . . .

Item Fynnok Otozill precepto Prioris, ii s.

. . . .

Item Mariote Dawenoy pro debito cervisie de tempore Roberti ballivi de Glasnevin, ii s.

Item Roberto de Moenes in partem solucionis xl s., per literam aquitancie, xx s.

Item liberatum Priori quando senescallus ivit versus partes Momonie, xxxvi s.

Item liberatum archiepiscopo Cassellensi pro synodalibus & amerciamentis per diversas vicarias per i literam quam Prior habet penes, xx s. Et apud Dublin, xx s. Et pro procuratione apud Kildenhale, archiepiscopo, . . . et apud . . . . . officiali, v s. Decano & aliis clericis adjuvantibus, iii s. iiii d.

Item liberatum Willelmo ballivo pro . . . . debito, de debitis Nicholai de Esenden coquinarii, x s.

———

Also to John de Castro going to the court of the lord the king in England to transact business of the house, 106s. 8d.

Also . . . .

Also to Fynnok Otooll by command of the Prior, 2s.

. . . .

Also to Mariota Dawenoy for a debt of ale from the time of Robert the bailiff of Glasnevin, 2s.

Also to Robert de Moenes in part payment of 40s., by letter of acquittance, 20s.

Also given to the Prior when the seneschal went towards the parts of Munster, 36s.

Also paid to the archbishop of Cashel for synodals and penalties for diverse vicarages, by one letter which the Prior holds, 20s., and at Dublin, 20s. And for proxies at Killenaule to the archbishop . . . . and to the official, 5s. To the dean and other clergy assisting, 3s. 4d.

Also paid to William the bailiff for . . . debt, of the debts of Nicholas de Esenden, kitchener, 10s.

Item Rogero de Kyldar pro feodo suo, xx d.

Item cuidam Kenewrek de debito dicti R. Goioun pro panno ab eo empto, in partem solutionis xx s. per literam obligatoriam, x s.

Item Roberto de Moenes, xiii s. iiii d. tam de debitis R. Goioun quam Prioris qui nunc est.

Item liberatum Pencoyt pro panno capto de Hugone Lonestok tempore R. Goioun, ix s., unde idem Pencoyt Priorem inplitavit.

Item Willelmo de Assheburne pro autumpno apud Clonken, xl s.

Item Johanni Haket pro lorica & alia armatura ei inpignoratis per R. Goioun, xiii s. iiii d.

Item Edwardo piscatori pro antiquo debito Roberti de Sancto Neoto nuper coquinario, xix d.

Item liberatum Willelmo Sterre coquinario pro seldis quas magister Johannes Desewell tenuit pre Priore, x s.

Item liberatum Stephano cissori de Oxmanton pro brasio ab eo empto, xxxviii s. iiii d. die mercurii proxima ante festum Sancti Thome apostoli.

Also to Roger de Kildare for his fee, 20*d*.

Also to a certain Kenewrek of a debt of said R. Goioun for cloth bought from him, in part payment of 20*s*. by letter obligatory, 10*s*.

Also to Robert de Moenes, 13*s*. 4*d*, as well of the debts of R. Goioun as of the Prior who now is.

Also paid to Pencoyt for cloth taken from Hugh Lonestok in the time of R. Goioun, 9*s*., for which the same Pencoyt sued the Prior.

Also to William de Assheburne for the harvest at Clonken, 40*s*.

Also to John Haket for a corselet and other armour pledged to him by R. Goioun, 13*s*. 4*d*.

Also to Edward the fisherman, for an old debt of Robert de Saint Neot, late kitchener, 19*d*.

Also paid to William Sterre, kitchener, for shops which master John Desewell held by reason of the Prior, 10*s*.

Also paid to Stephen the tailor of Oxmanton, for malt bought from him, 38*s*. 5*d*., on Wednesday next before feast of S. Thomas the apostle.

Expense facte circa Hosbonderiam de Gorman per tempus compoti.

In primis idem computat, in carucis emptis, emendacione earundem, virgis pro hartis, fabricacione & emendacione ferri carucalis, rotis, carectis, stradels, basses, trays, stipendiis famulorum, ferura equorum ad carectas, per tempus compoti, & cirotecis contra autumpnum, ut patet per parcellam, iiii li. xiiii s. iii d.

Et in domibus de novo ibidem construendis, antiquis domibus emend', & muris faciendis et emend' cum hostii serura & huiusmodi, & stacione cisterne facienda apud Gorman, per dictum terminum, xxxvii s. viii d.

Item in i bove empto de Galfrido de Fyncham pro caruca apud Gorman, v s.

Et in i equo empto Andrea ballivo pro eodem, viii s. vi d.

Item in i equo empto Johanni Callan pro eodem, x s.

Gorman xxi li. vi s. iiii d. ob.   Et in iii bobus emptis de Willelmo ballivo pro eodem, xxiiii s. viii d.

Et in i affro empto de Petro Howell pro eodem, vi s. viii d.

Expenses incurred about the husbandry of Gorman for the time of the account.

Gorman. £21 6s. 4½d.   In the first place he accounts, in ploughs bought, mending of them, rods for handles, making and mending of plough iron, wheels, carts, straddles, basses, trays (traces?), wages of servants, shoeing of cart horses, for the time of the account, and gloves for harvest as appears by schedule, £4 14s. 3d.

And in houses built anew there, old houses repaired, and walls made and repaired, with a lock for the gate and the like, and preparing the site of the cistern at Gorman during said term, 37s. 8d.

Also in one ox for the plough at Gorman, bought of Geoffrey de Fyncham, 5s.

And in one horse bought of Andrew the bailiff, for same, 8s. 6d.

Also in one horse bought of John Callan for same, 10s.

And in 3 oxen bought of William the bailiff, for same, 24s. 8d.

And in one farm horse bought of Peter Howell for same, 6s. 8d.

Item in i nigro equo empto ad Milon. Passelewe pro eodem, vii s. vi d.

In i bove empto apud Clonken pro eodem, vi s. viii d.

In iii bobus & i tauro emptis ad Joh. Passelewe pro eodem, xxii s. vi d.

Item in sarclacione bladorum de Grangia Gorman hoc anno per tempus dicti Thome, ii s. i d. ob.

Item in messione omnium bladorum hoc anno manerio de Gorman crescentium, ut patet per pacellam, viii li. v s. iii d. quad.

Item in expensis senescalli et aliorum apud Gorman commorancium per autumpnum pro blado ibidem intrando ad mensam, per totum autumpnum, ut patet per parcellas, xxxv s. vii d.

Item idem computat in custibus carucarum, carectarum, emen- Glasnevin, dacione domorum & portarum, cum muris, sarclacione, fal- ix li. iii s. cacione, et messione bladorum apud Glasnevin, factis per iii d. ob. tempus compoti, ut patet per parcellam, absque stauro empto, viii li. viii s. x d. ob.

Et in ii equis emptis pro carucis et carectis ibidem, xv s. vi d.

Item idem computat in omni husbonderia, facta apud Clonken ; ut Clonken x s. ii d.

Also in one black horse bought at Milo Passelewe's for same, 7s. 6d.

In one ox bought at Clonken for same, 6s. 8d.

In 3 oxen and one bull bought at John Passelewe's for same, 22s. 6d.

Also in hoeing the corn of Grange Gorman this year for the time of said Thomas (de Beuley being in charge), 2s. 1½d.

Also in the harvesting of all corn growing this year in the manor of Gorman, as appears by a schedule, £8 5s. 3¼d.

Also in expenses of the seneschal and others remaining at Gorman through the harvest time for the corn coming in there, at board, through the whole harvest time, as appears by schedules, 35s. 7d.

Also he accounts in cost of ploughs, carts, repair of houses and gates, Glasnevin, with walls, weeding, mowing, and harvest of corn at Glasnevin, £9 4s. 4½d. done during the time of the account as appears by schedule, ex- cluding stock bought, £8 8s. 10½d.

And in 2 horses bought for ploughs and carts there, 15s. 6d.

Also he accounts in all husbandry done at Clonken, as in carts, repair of Clonken. 10s. 2d.

in carectis, emendacione domorum, ut patet per parcellam per tempus compoti, x s. ii d.

Item in bordis clavis meremio & calce emptis pro domibus infra clausum Sancte Trinitatis, ut patet per parcellam, xviii s. iii d. ob.

Item in v bendis ferri & iii vomeribus emptis pro omnibus grangiis sustinendis, set ignoratur quot pro quanto, xx s. ii d.

Item idem computat liberatum Willelmo de Burthon pro debitis Domus Sancte Trinitatis prout patet per literam obligatoriam, xl marc. de redditu de Balyscadan.

Summa xl marc.   Patet.

Summa Summarum omnium Expensarum, clx li. xviii s. ii d. ob. Et sic debet iiii li. v s. iii d. ob. quad.

Postea idem Thomas oneratur de ix s. receptis de perquisitionibus curie de Balyscadan per idem tempus. Unde non oneratur superius quia non habuit rotulos nec extractas curie de dicto tempore. Item de iii s. iiii d. receptis de quodam fine facto apud Balyscadan de quodam Hybernico de villa de

---

houses, as appears by schedule during the time of the account, 10s. 2d.

Also in boards, nails, timber, and lime, bought for houses within the close of Holy Trinity, as appears by schedule, 18s. 3½d.

Also in 5 bends of iron and 3 ploughshares bought for supplying all the granges, but he knows not how much for each, 20s. 2d.

Also he accounts as paid to William de Burthon for debts of the house of the Holy Trinity, as appears by letter obligatory, 40 marks of the rent of Balscaddan.

Total, 40 marks, is manifest.

The sum of the totals of all the expenses, £160 18s. 2½d. And so he owes £4 5s. 3¾d.

Afterwards the same Thomas is charged with 9s. received of the profits of the court of Balscaddan during the same time. He was not charged with this above, because he had not the rolls or estreats of the court for the said time. Also with 3s. 4d. received of a certain fine made at Balscaddan by a certain Irishman of the

Dermodeston pro ingressu habendo in xl acris terre. Summa debiti cum superoneracioue adhibita iiii li. xvii s. vii d. ob. quad. Quos debet de claro.

Et memorandum quod in isto pede suprascripto, omnes compoti Thome de Beuley de toto tempore quo erat senescallus terrarum & tenementorum Prioris & Conventus Ecclesie Cathedralis Sancte Trinitatis Dublin usque festum sancti Marci Evangeliste anno regni regis xiii⁰ finaliter percladuntur, ita quod dictis arreragiis suprascriptis plenarie solutis usque in festum Sancti Marci Evangeliste supradictum, ab omni actione compoti quietus permaneat.

---

town of Dermotstown for having entry in 40 acres of land. Total of the debt, with the additional charge added, £4 17s. 7¾d., which he owes clear.

And be it remembered that in above written foot of this account, all the accounts of Thomas de Beuley for the whole time in which he was seneschal of the lands and tenements of the Prior and Convent of the Cathedral Church of the Holy Trinity, Dublin, to the feast of Saint Mark the Evangelist in the thirteenth year of the king's reign are finally closed, so that the said arrears above written being fully paid up to the feast of Saint Mark the Evangelist aforesaid, let him remain free from all action of account.

II.

COMPOTUS FRATRIS JOHANNIS COMYN, SENESCALLI DOMUS SANCTE
    TRINITATIS, DUBLIN, a die Lune in crastino Apostolo
    rum Petri et Pauli Anno Domini Millesimo ccc^{mo}
    xliii⁰ usque vigiliam Epiphanie Domini proximam
    sequentem ; videlicet, de Officio Senescalli.

In primis idem reddit compotum de lxviii s. iii d. ob. receptis de
    redditu de Gorman de termino Omnium Sanctorum, ut patet
    per rentale.

Et de vii li. xviii s. vi d. receptis de redditu de Glasnevyn de eodem
    termino ut patet per rentale.

Et de lxvi s. viii d. receptis de Roberto Poer pro redditu de Kyn
    turk de eodem termino.

Et de xxxiii s. iiij d. receptis de redditu de Mablyeston de eodem
    termino.

Et de l s. receptis de capitali redditu de Kynsaly de eodem termino.

Et de v s. receptis de redditu de Killestre per annum integrum.

Et de xviii d. receptis de Jacobo Laweles pro redditu de Coulok de
    eodem termino.

ACCOUNT OF BROTHER JOHN COMYN, Seneschal of the house of the Holy
    Trinity, Dublin, from Monday (30th June), the morrow of the
    feast of the Apostles Peter and Paul, A. D. 1343, to the vigil
    (5th January) of the Epiphany of our Lord next following :
    of his Seneschalship.

In the first place he renders account of 68s. 3½d., received from the rent
    of Gorman, of the term of All Saints, as appears by the rental.

And of £7 18s. 6d. received from the rent of Glasnevin, of same term, as
    appears by the rental.

And of 66s. 8d. received from Robert Poer, for rent of Kynturk, of same
    term.

And of 33s. 4d. received from rent of Mabestown, of same term.

And of 50s. received from chief rent of Kinsaley, of same term.

And of 5s. received from rent of Killester for a whole year.

And of 18d. received from James Laweles for rent of Coolock, of same
    term.

Et de xvi d. ob. receptis de redditu ii acrarum iii stanguorum terre in Nehoyhery, quam Walterus Baysham tenet, de eodem termino.

Et de xiiii li. xiiii[1] s. ix d. ob. receptis de redditu de Clonken de eodem termino, ut patet per rentale.

Et de c s. receptis de domino archiepiscopo Dublin de prestito pro avena inde emenda.

Et de c s. receptis de fratre Thoma de Beuley, per unam talliam contra eundem.

Et de xv li. receptis de redditu de Balyscadan, de termino Nativitatis Beati Johannis Baptiste, ut patet per rentale.

(Et de iiij s. receptis de Hugone de Belynges per unam talliam contra eundem.)[2]

Et de iiij li. xiii s. iiij d. receptis de Johanne Cordel in plenam solucionem viii marcarum pro decimis de Kyldenhale per unum annum, et non ultra se onerat quia frater Gilbertus de Bolyniop inde recepit i marcam tempore quo stetit Prior.

Et de liii s. iiij d. receptis de decimis de Glasnevyn hoc anno venditis.

And of 16½d. received from rent of 2 acres 3 stangs of land in Nehoyhery, which Walter Baysham holds, of same term.

And of £14 14s. 9½d. received from rent of Clouken of same term, as appears by the rental.

And of 100s. received from the lord archbishop of Dublin, as an advance to buy oats.

And of 100s. received from brother Thomas de Beuley, by one tally against him.

And of £15 received from rent of Balscaddan, of the term of the Nativity of S. John the Baptist, as appears by the rental.

(And of 4s. received from Hugh de Belynges, by one tally against him.)

And of £4 13s. 4d. received from John Cordel, in full payment of 8 marks for the tithes of Killenaule for one year. And he does not charge himself further, because brother Gilbert de Bolyniop received of them one mark during the time that he remained Prior.

And of 53s. 4d. received from the tithes of Glasnevin, sold this year.

---

[1] Altered from iii to xiiii s.   [2] This entry is struck out in original.

Et de xx s. receptis de Ada Louestok de prestito.

Et de vi li. xiij s. iiij d. receptis de Roberto de Moenes de prestito.

Et de lx s. receptis de magistro Johanne Petyt de prestito.

Et de ii s. iii d. receptis de i herieta de Clonken vendita.

Et de viii s. receptis de viii suibus debilibus venditis.

Et de xxii d. receptis de stipula hoc anno vendita.

. . . . receptis de herbagio iii vaccarum apud Gorman de termino Omnium Sanctorum.

Et de vj s. viii d. receptis de Roberto de Hoghton de prestito.

    SUMMA TOTIUS RECEPTUS, lxxvii li. xix[1] s. viii d. ob. Probata.

In primis idem computat in conduccione unius carpentarii facientis unam carucam novam, de meremio de stauro, & corrigentis alias carucas ut inponendo eisdem chip[pes], & facientis juga boum & alia pertinentia ad quartam carucam levandam, & corrigentis magnam portam, hostium granarii, presepia & maniours pro equis & affris, per viii dies ad tascham, xx d. : per diem ii d. ob.

And of 20*s.* received from Adam Louestok as a loan.

And of £6 13*s.* 4*d.* received from Robert de Moenes as a loan.

And of 60*s.* received from master John Petyt as a loan.

And of 2*s.* 3*d.* received for one heriot of Clonken sold.

And of 8*s.* received for 8 old sows sold.

And of 22*d.* received for straw (or stubble) sold this year.

[And of 18*d.*] received for pasture of 3 cows at Gorman, for the term of All Saints.

And of 6*s.* 8*d.* received from Robert de Hoghton as a loan.

    Total of all receipts, £77 19*s.* 8½*d.* Checked.

In the first place he accounts in hire of a carpenter making a new plough of timber from stock, and repairing other ploughs (as in fitting chippes to them), and making ox yokes and other requisites to fit up a fourth plough, and mending the great gate, the door of the barn, stalls and mangers for horses and affers, for 8 days at full wages, 20*d.* : 2½*d.* a day.

---

[1] viii changed to xix in original.

Item in meremio empto pro chippes & plohubemes inde faciendis, vi d.

Item in conduccione unius carpentarii facientis ii carucas estivales & v [caru]cas iemales, per vii dies ad tascham, xiiii d. : per diem ii d.

Item alia vice in vi plohubemes, iiij⁰ʳ axibus, & meremio pro chippes carucarum emptis, xv d. ob.

Item in conduccione unius [car]pentarii aptantis meremium & inde facientis carucas & emendantis, per iiij⁰ʳ dies & dimidiam, ad tascham, ix d. : per diem ii d.

In butiro empto pro collis boum ungendis & affris de . . . sanandis & salvandis, xxi d.

Item in sulphure empto pro eisdem, iii d. ob.

Item cuidam medico boves & affros predictos sananti xv d.

Item in i benda ferri pro ferro caruca[li] sustinendo, iiii s.

Item in ii bendis ferri emptis pro eodem, ix s. : precium bende, iiii s. vi d.

Item in i benda ferri empta pro eodem, iiii s. i d.

Item in v peciis ferri emptis pro eodem, x d.

Also in timber bought for making chippes and plough beams, 6*d*.

Also in hire of a carpenter, making 2 summer ploughs and 5 winter ploughs, for 7 days at full wages, 14*d*. : 2*d*. a day.

Also another time for 6 plough beams, 4 axle-trees, and timber for chippes of ploughs bought, 15½*d*.

Also in hire of a carpenter, preparing timber and making and mending ploughs with it, for 4½ days, at full wages, 9*d*. : 2*d*. a day.

In butter bought for anointing the necks of the oxen, and healing and curing farm horses, 21*d*.

Also in sulphur bought for the same, 3½*d*.

Also to a certain medical man healing the same oxen and farm horses, 15*d*.

Also in one bend of iron to supply the plough iron, 1*s*.

Also in 2 bends of iron bought for same, 9*s*. : price of a bend, 4*s*. 6*d*.

Also in one bend of iron bought for same, 4*s*. 1*d*.

Also in 5 pieces of iron bought for same, 10*d*.

In calibe empto pro eodem, i d.

Item in quatuor vomeribus emptis, ii s.

Item in vi lezerlegges emptis pro carucis, xii d.

Item liberatum pro stipendio fabri, pro ferro carucali faciendo &
    emendando, de duobus beudis xv peciis ferri, quatuor novis
    vomeribus emptis ut supra levandis, & quatuor vomeribus
    antiquis in emendacione ferri carucalis fabricandis viii s. xi
    d. ob. : pro pecia videlicet i d. [ob.], pro vomere levando
    i d., pro vomere antiquo i d. ob. quad. pro pecia.

Et memorandum quod idem frater Johannes liberavit Hugoni
    Belynggs per i talliam contra eundem xliiii pecias ferri pro
    ferro carucali quarum idem Hugo respondebit.

Summa xxxviii s. vii d. ob.   Probata.

Item idem computat in omnimodis expensis pro xiii carucis ad
    quas fuerunt xxvi viri ad warectandum, quasi per ii dies
    cito post installacionem Prioris iiii s. iiii d. : cuilibet per
    diem i d.

Item in omnimodis expensis pro xii carucis ad rebinandam terram

---

In steel bought for same, 1*d.*

Also in 4 ploughshares bought, 2*s.*

Also in 6 lezerlegges bought for ploughs, 12*d.*

Also paid for wages of a smith for making and mending plough iron
    with two beuds and 15 pieces of iron, mounting 4 new plough-
    shares bought as above, and working up 4 old ploughshares in
    repair of plough iron, 8*s.* 11½*d.* : viz. for a piece, 1½*d.*, for mounting
    a ploughshare, 1*d.*, for an old ploughshare, 1½*d.* a-piece.

And be it remembered that the same brother John delivered to Hugh
    Belynges, by one tally against him, 44 pieces of iron for plough
    iron, for which the said Hugh will answer.

Total, 38*s.* 7½*d.*   Checked.

Also he accounts in all expenses for 13 ploughs, to which were 26 men
    to plough the fallow land for 2 days shortly after the installation
    of the Prior, 4*s.* 4*d.* : for each, 1*d.* a day.

Also in all expenses for 12 ploughs for the late ploughing of the demesne dominicorum videlicet in autumpno ex regatu, quasi per unum diem, ad quas fuerunt xxiiii viri, ii s. : cuilibet per unum diem i d.

Summa vi s. iiii d.

Item in conduccione duorum carpentariorum facientium unum par rotarum cum corpore ad ligandum cum ferro, per iii dies ad mensam, xii d. : cuilibet eorum per diem ii d.

Item in strakenail emptis pro . . . rotis ferratis emendandis iii d.

Item in i stapul de ferro empto pro le wayn & uno circulo ferreo empto pro eodem iii d.

Item in quadam ligatura ferrea pro antiqua carecta . . . ii d. ob.

Item in una benda ferri empta pro uno novo pare rotarum ligando, iiii s.

Item in xii lezerleggis emptis pro eisdem ligandis, ii s.

Item in v peciis ferri emptis pro d[icta] ligatura, x d.

Item in stipendio fabri pro strakes & strakenail gropis & integra ligatura pro dicto pare rotarum ligando, de dictis xxx peciis ferri & xii lezerlegges ex certa conven[cione] v s. ii d. ob., videlicet pro qualibet pecia i d. ob. quad. & pro xii lezer- legges x d.

---

lands, videlicet, in autumn, by custom, for one day, to which were 24 men, 2s. : for each, 1d. a day.

Total, 6s. 4d.

Also in hire of two carpenters, making one pair of wheels with a body to bind with iron, for 3 days at board, 12d. : to each, 2d. a day.

Also in nails for tires bought for mending . . . iron-shod wheels, 3d.

Also in one staple of iron bought for the wain, and an iron hoop bought for same, 3d.

Also in an iron band for an old cart, 2¼d.

Also in one bend of iron bought for binding a new pair of wheels, 4s.

Also in 12 lezerlegges bought for binding the same, 2s.

Also in 5 pieces of iron bought for said band, 10d.

Also in wages of a smith, for tires and nails for the tires, hooks, and a complete band for binding said pair of wheels, with said 30 pieces of iron, and 12 lezerlegges, by fixed agreement, 5s. 2¼d., viz. for each piece, 1¾d., and for 12 lezerlegges, 10d.

Item in ii karris emptis, v d.

Item in ii stradell emptis und' ii d.

Item in xii clutis emptis pro carectis, viii d.

Item in iiii^{or} paribus tractuum de canebo emptis, viii d.

Item in xii clutis pro les waynes emptis, xvi d.

Item in cc de clavis emptis per tempus compoti pro dictis clutis firmandis, viii d.

Item in uno pare rotarum lanearum empto, ii s. viii d. quad.

Item in cepo empto & unguento pro carectis & waynes per tempus compoti ungendis, xii d.

Item in i corda de canabo empta pro . . . ligandis v d.

Item in conduccione unius carpentarii aptantis ii paria rotarum in autumpno usarum, pro ligatura ferrea portanda per iiii^{or} dies & dimidiam diem ad tascham ix d. : per diem ii d.

Item in iii capistris de canabo emptis, ii d.

Item in xii clutis emptis pro carectis & missis apud Kylcolyn, ad fratrem Johannem de Castro precepto Prioris, vi d.

Item in ii cordis de canabo emptis & missis ibidem, x d.

Also in 2 cars bought, 5*d.*

Also in 2 straddles bought for them, 2*d.*

Also in 12 clouts bought for carts, 8*d.*

Also in four pairs of hemp traces bought, 8*d.*

Also in 12 clouts bought for the wains, 16*d.*

Also in 200 nails bought during the time of account for securing the said clouts, 8*d.*

Also in one pair of woollen wheels bought, 2*s.* 8¼*d.*

Also in tallow and grease bought for greasing the carts and wains during the time of the account, 12*d.*

Also in one cord of hemp bought for binding . . . 5*d.*

Also in hire of a carpenter fitting two pairs of wheels, used in harvest for carrying an iron band, for four and a-half days, at full wages, 9*d.* : 2*d.* a day.

Also in 3 halters of hemp bought, 2*d.*

Also in 12 clouts bought for carts, and sent to Kilcullen to brother John de Castro by command of the Prior, 6*d.*

Also in 2 cords of hemp bought and sent there, 10*d.*

Item in xii ferris equinis emptis & missis ibidem, vi d.

Item in ii capistris de canabo emptis & missis ibidem, i d.

Item in i freno empto & liberato dicto fratri Johanni ibidem, viii d.

Summa xxv s. iii d. quad.

Item idem computat liberatum magistro Johanni Mareschall pro ferura palefridi & aliorum equorum de debito de tempore fratris Gilberti de Bolyniop nuper prioris, ut patet per talliam inter dictum magistrum Johannem & Johannem le Wode palefridarium & Henricum le Carter de celario, viii s. vii d. ob.

Item in ferura affrorum per tempus autumpnale & pro equis de carecta celarii & pro aliis equis ad carectas de grangia per ii tallias contra magistrum Johannem, v s. iiii d. ob.

Item in ferura palefridi & aliorum equorum deserviencium armigeris & familie domini Prioris per tempus compoti per i talliam contra Henricum Hay palefridarium Prioris, iii s. xi d.

Item in ii houces emptis pro palefrido & alio equo & liberatis eidem Henrico palefridario, xv d.

Also in 12 horse shoes bought and sent there, 6d.

Also in 2 halters of hemp bought and sent there, 1d.

Also in one bridle bought and delivered to said brother John there, 8d.

Total, 25s. 3½d.

Also he accounts, as delivered to master John Mareschall for shoeing the palfrey and other horses, a debt from the time of brother Gilbert de Bolyniop, late prior, as appears by a tally between said master John, and John le Wode palfrey keeper, and Henry, the carter of the cellar, 8s. 7½d.

Also in shoeing of the farm horses for the harvest time, and for the horses of the cart of the cellar, and for other horses for the carts of the grange, by 2 tallies against master John, 5s. 4½d.

Also in shoeing of the palfrey and other horses for use of the esquires and household of the lord Prior, during the time of the account, by one tally against Henry Hay, palfrey keeper of the Prior, 3s. 11d.

Also in 2 housings bought for the palfrey and another horse, and given to the same Henry, the palfrey keeper, 15d.

D

Item in iii supercingulis emptis & liberatis eidem Henrico, vi d.

Item in emendacione unius celle antique iiii d.

Item in una cella cum freno empto pro senescallo & liberata eidem
Henrico, iiii s. vi d.

Item in ii paribus calcarium emptis pro Priore & senescallo, viii d.

Summa xxv s. ii d.

Item idem computat in stipendio unius messoris vocati Ricardi
Watte de servicio suo de tempore Spennyngges anno xvi^{mo}
usque festum Omnium Sanctorum proximum sequens, ii s.
vi d.

Item liberatum Johanni Watte tentori caruce in plenam solucionem
servicii sui de termino Omnium Sanctorum anno xvi° usque
Spennynges proximum sequens, xiii d.

Item Petro Hanan tentori caruce in plenam solucionem servicii sui
de eodem termino, ii d.

Item Roberto Jurdan tentori caruce in persolucionem servicii sui
de eodem termino, ix d.

Item Roberto Dryvere in persolucionem servicii sui de eodem termino, iiii d.

Also in 3 surcingles bought and given to the same Henry, 6d.

Also in repair of one old saddle, 4d.

Also in one saddle with a bridle, bought for the seneschal, and given to
the same Henry, 4s. 6d.

Also in 2 pairs of spurs, bought for the Prior and Seneschal, 8d.

Total, 25s. 2d.

Also he accounts in wages of one reaper called Richard Watte, for his
service from the time of Spennyngs, in the 16th year, to the
feast of All Saints next following, 2s. 6d.

Also paid to John Watte, ploughman, in full payment of his service from
the term of All Saints, in the 16th year, to Spennyngs next following, 13d.

Also to Peter Hanan, ploughman, in full payment of his service for the
same term, 2d.

Also to Robert Jurdan, ploughman, in full payment of his service for the
same term, 9d.

Also to Robert Dryvere, in full payment of his service for same term, 4d.

Item liberatum carectario de celario, uni carectario de manerio, Willelmo le Rous messori, Johanni Chamburleyn messori & ballivo, & quatuor tenentibus carucarum a festo Spennynges anno xvii° usque festum Omnium Sanctorum proximum sequens, xx s. : cuilibet, ii s. vi d.

Item iiii°ʳ fugantibus carucas per dictum terminum, viii s. : cuilibet ii s.

Item cuidam mulieri siccanti brasium de termino Omnium Sanctorum anno xvi° usque Spennyges ii. s. vi d.

Item Johanni Coco pro servicio suo de tempore fratris Gilberti Bolyniop nuper prioris, v s.

Item Ricardo garcioni senescalli pro stipendio suo, per unum annum, xvi d. de tempore fratris Gilberti prioris.

Item Henrico Hay, pro salario suo, ex certa convencione per annum, vi s. viii d.

Item Johanni Gibbe garcioni senescalli pro indumento suo & calciamento, per annum, vi s.

Summa liiii s. iiii d.   Probata.

Item idem computat in uno bove empto pro carucis, vii s.

Also paid to the carter of the cellar, to one carter of the manor, William le Rous, reaper, John Chamburleyn, reaper and bailiff, and four ploughmen, from the feast of Spennyngs in the 17th year to the feast of All Saints next following, 20s. ; to each, 2s. 6d.

Also to 4 plough drivers for the said term, 8s. ; to each, 2s.

Also to a certain woman drying malt, from the term of All Saints in the 16th year to Spennyngs, 2s. 6d.

Also to John the cook, for his service from the time of brother Gilbert Bolyniop, late prior, 5s.

Also to Richard, the seneschal's serving man, for his wages for one year, 16d., from the time of brother Gilbert, prior.

Also to Henry Hay, for his salary by a fixed agreement for a year, 6s. 8d.

Also to John Gibbe, the seneschal's serving man, for his clothing and shoes for a year, 6s.

Total, 54s. 4d.   Checked.

Also he accounts in one ox bought for the ploughs, 7s.

Item in ii bobus emptis pro carucis, xiii s.

Item in i bove empto, v s. vi d.

          Summa xxv s. vi d.

Item idem computat in ix copulis de quercu emptis pro granario & domo proxima edificanda, xx d.

Item in ii seruris emptis pro granario & domo operis, vii d.

Item in bordis emptis pro hostio granarii, iii d.

Item in c tabulis de Wykinglowe bordis emptis pro dicto granario, xiiii d.

Item in ccc clavis emptis pro eisdem firmandis pro dicto granario, vi d.

Item in cc de spykynges emptis pro magna porta emendanda, v d.

Item in c de Doublebordnaill emptis pro eadem porta & hostio granarii, iii d.

Item in conduccione quatuor garcionum fodientium le Boly & implentium carectas de fimis & purgantium hagardam & facientium murum inter bostar & grangiam & circa hostium bostaris & portantium terram ad exaltandam aream de granario & pro le Beemfullyngges per vi dies ad tascham, iiii s. : cuilibet per diem, ii d.

Also in 2 oxen bought for ploughs, 13s.

Also in 1 ox bought, 5s. 6d.

          Total, 25s. 6d.

Also he accounts in 9 couples of oak bought for building the barn and house adjoining, 20d.

Also in 2 locks bought for the barn and workshop, 7d.

Also in boards bought for the door of the barn, 3d.

Also in 100 planks of Wicklow boards bought for said barn, 14d.

Also in 300 nails bought for securing the same for the said barn, 6d.

Also in 200 large nails bought for mending the great gate, 5d.

Also in 100 double-board-nails bought for same gate and for the door of the barn, 3d.

Also in hire of four serving men digging the cattle yard and filling carts with dung, and cleaning the haggard, and making a wall between the ox house and the grange and about the door of the ox house, and carrying earth to raise the floor of the barn and for the beamfilling, for 6 days at full wages, 4s.; to each by the day, 2d.

Item in conduccione cujusdam cooperientis granarium & domum proximam usque ad aulam per vi dies ad mensam, vi d.

Item uni mulieri tractanti stramen & eidem servienti per dictos vi dies, iii d.

Item in conduccione unius coopertorii scarpilantis & aptantis copulas pro domo operis & facientis granarium & alia necessaria pro quadam camera privata de novo reparanda per vi dies ad mensam, xii d.

Item in conduccione ii garcionum fodientium lutum & facientium le Bemfullynges circa dictam domum per i diem, ii d.

Item in conduccione unius hominis fodientis lutum & servientis[1] cuidam coopertorio per sex dies ad tascham, vi d.

Item uni garcioni eunti ad quartam carucam per sex dies quia fugator infirmabatur & facienti alia opera necessaria per diversa loca, vi d.

Item in carne empta pro diversis operariis supradictis ad mensam qui erant per sex dies, viii d.

Also in hire of a man thatching the barn and adjoining house as far as the hall for 6 days, at board, 6*d*.

Also to a woman drawing straw and supplying it to the thatcher for said 6 days, 3*d*.

Also in hire of a roofer planing and fitting roof couples for the workshop, and making the barn, and other things necessary for repairing anew a private chamber, for 6 days at board, 12*d*.

Also in hire of 2 servants digging mud and making the beamfilling about the said house for one day, 2*d*.

Also in hire of one man digging mud and serving a roofer for 6 days at full wages, 6*d*.

Also to a serving man going to the fourth plough for six days, because the driver was invalided, and doing other necessary work in different places, 6*d*.

Also in meat bought for divers workmen above mentioned who were at board for 6 days, 8*d*.

---

[1] Servienti in original.

Item in conduccione unius coopertorii cooperientis stabulum & alias
domos usque ad magnam portam, per sex dies ad mensam,
vi d.

Item in conduccione unius garcionis levantis lutum & stramen, per
vi dies, vi d.

Item in allocatione ii mulierum tractancium stramen & portancium
aquam per sex dies vi d. : cuilibet per diem, ob.

Item iu conduccione duorum garcionum prosternencium watlaturam
pro granario per ii dies, iiii d. : cuilibet per i diem, i d.

Item in conduccione cujusdam Thome Dassheburne aptantis dictam
watlaturam super dictum granarium & alias domos proximas per quatuor dies ad mensam, iiii d.

Item cuidam garcioni allocato ad caruem per vi dies quia fugator
erat infirmus & pro aliis necessariis faciendis post prandium,
vi d.

Item in carne & pisce emptis pro supradictis ad mensam per vi dies,
vii d.

Item in conduccione iii garcionum aptantium lutum & Beemful-
lingges cameram juxta aulam, per i diem ad mensam, iii d.

Also in hire of a thatcher roofing the stable and other houses as far as the
great gate, for six days at board, 6*d.*

Also in hire of a serving man carrying up mud and straw for six
days, 6*d.*

Also in payment of two women drawing straw and carrying water for six
days, 6*d.* ; to each by the day, ½*d.*

Also in hire of two serving men cutting down wattle for the barn for
2 days, 4*d.* ; to each by the day, 1*d.*

Also in hire of a certain Thomas de Assheburne fitting the said wattle
upon the said barn and other adjoining houses, for four days at
board, 4*d.*

Also to a certain serving man employed at the plough for 6 days because
the driver was sick, and to perform other necessary duties after
dinner, 6*d.*

Also in meat and fish bought for the aforesaid men at board for 6
days, 7*d.*

Also in hire of 3 serving men applying mud and beamfilling to the
chamber next the hall for one day at board, 3*d.*

Item uni carpentario facienti fenestras dicte camere, ad mensam per i diem, ii d.

Item in carne empta pro dictis servientibus ad mensam, v d.

Item in conduccione dicti Thome Dassheburne cooperientis iii tassos avene i longum tassum pisarum, rastrantis & aptantis quatuor tassos magnos frumenti, ne pluvia ingressum haberet per vii dies ad mensam, vii d.

Item ii mulieribus tractentibus stramen & coopertorio portantibus ad tascham per dictos vii dies, vii d : per diem, ob.

Item in carne & pisce emptis pro supradictis ad mensam, v d. ob.

Item in conduccione unius coopertorii facientis speres inter granarium & alias domos propinquiores, per ii dies ad tascham, v d.

Item in conduccione ii garcionum temperancium lutum & servientium pro dictis speres per unum diem ad tascham, ii d.

Item in conduccione unius carpentarii facientis dependenciam fontis juxta torale & alia pertinentia pro eodem, fenestras & duo hostia pro cameris intrinsecis juxta aulam, per quatuor dies ad tascham, x d. : per diem ii d. ob.

Also to a carpenter making the windows of the said chamber, at board for one day, 2*d.*

Also in meat bought for said servants at board, 5*d.*

Also in hire of said Thomas de Assheburne thatching 3 stacks of oats, 1 long stack of peas, raking and preparing four great stacks of wheat lest the rain should get in, for 7 days at board, 7*d.*

Also to 2 women drawing straw and carrying it to the thatcher, at full wages for said 7 days, 7*d.*; by the day, ½*d.*

Also in meat and fish bought for the abovesaid at board, 5½*d.*

Also in hire of a roofer making beams between the barn and other houses next it, for 2 days at full wages, 5*d.*

Also in hire of 2 serving men tempering mud and assisting about the said beams, for one day at full wages, 2*d.*

Also in hire of a carpenter making the hanging gear of the well next the kiln and other belongings for the same, windows and two doors for the inner chambers next the hall, for four days at full wages, 10*d.*; by the day, 2½*d.*

Item in vi spyres de quercu emptis pro necessariis ad fontem & pro aliis necessariis infra manerium, ut iu presepibus & hujusmodi, ix d.

Item iu bordis emptis pro hostiis camerarum intrinsecarum faciendis, iiii d.

Item in iiii^c de clavis emptis viii d.

Item in i p^c de calce empta pro emendacione vasorum infra domum toralis, i d.

In bithumine empto pro eodem, i d.

Item in bordis emptis pro hostio domus toralis emendando, iii d.

Item in i clave empta pro hostio janitoris, i d.

　　　　　Summa xxi s. ix d. ob.　Probata.

Item idem computat in vii p^c avene emptis pro prebenda equorum, xiiii d.

　　　　　Summa xiiii d. Patet.

Item idem computat in i boketto empto ad deserviendum fonti pro torali v d.

Item in xi peciis ferri emptis pro eodem ligando convenienter & pendendo & pro cathena ferrea pro eodem facienda, xxii d.

Also in 6 beams of oak bought for requisites for the well, and for other necessaries within the manor, as in stalls and the like, 9*d.*

Also in boards bought for making doors of the inner chambers, 4*d.*

Also in 400 nails bought, 8*d.*

Also in one peck of lime bought for repair of the vessels in the kiln house, 1*d.*

In tar bought for same, 1*d.*

Also in boards bought for repairing the door of the kiln house, 3*d.*

Also in one key bought for the gate-keeper's door, 1*d.*

　　　　　Total, 21*s.* 9½*d.*　Checked.

Also he accounts in 7 pecks of oats bought for provender of horses, 14*d.*

　　　　　Total, 14*d.*, is manifest.

Also he accounts in one bucket bought for use of the well for the kiln, 5*d.*

Also in 11 pieces of iron bought for binding the same suitably and hanging it, and for making an iron chain for it, 22*d.*

Item fabro pro eodem faciendo de dictis peciis & aptando, xxii d.

Item in i secure empta vii d.

Item in ii vangis cum ferura emptis, vi d. ob.

In quatuor vangis nudis emptis, iii d. quad.

In percameno empto per tempus compoti pro curia tenenda, pro diversis scribendis, vii d.

In discis & platellis emptis pro autumpno, iiii d.

In iii quartis de ligno emptis, iiii d.

In pykforkes emptis, pro garbis levandis, v d.

In pykstelus emptis, ii d.

In ollis luteis emptis, ii d. quad.

Item pro fovea antiqua implenda, iii d. ob.

Item in v caseis emptis & missis diversimode ex precepto domini per Petrum Camerarium, ii s. vii d.

Item in percameno empto & liberato dicto Petro pro necessariis scribendis, iiii d.

Summa x s. vii d. ob.

Also to a smith for making the same of the said pieces, and for fitting it up, 22*d.*

Also in one axe bought, 7*d.*

Also in 2 spades with iron tips bought, 6½*d.*

In four spades not tipped bought, 3¼*d.*

In parchment bought during the time of the account, for divers documents to be written for holding the court, 7*d.*

In dishes and plates bought for harvest time, 4*d.*

In 3 quarts of wood bought, 4*d.*

In pitchforks bought for lifting sheaves, 5*d.*

In handles for forks bought, 2*d.*

In earthenware pots bought, 2¼*d.*

Also for filling in an old dike, 3½*d.*

Also in 5 cheeses bought and sent in divers directions by command of the lord (Prior) by Peter the chamberlain, 2*s.* 7*d.*

Also in parchment bought and delivered to said Peter for documents required to be written, 4*d.*

Total, 10*s.* 7½*d.*

Item in vadiis diversorum garcionum euntium pro fratre Johanne
de Castro apud Kylcolyn per vii vices pro negociis domus,
xiiii d.

Item in cervisia empta pro Henrico Taloun & domino Philippo
capellano de Balycor per ii noctes, iii d.

Item cuidam garcioni eunti apud Kylgon & Castrum Martyn pro
procuracionibus Archidiaconi Glyndlagh ii d.

Item cuidam Hugley clerico Willelmi de Boseuorth pro cirotecis
precepto Prioris, i d.

Item liberatum marescallo de Banco pro brevibus magistri Walteri
de Istelep cassandis seu cassatis, ii s. vi d.

Item Johanni Rous clerico apud le Naas circa negocia domus
videlicet post Johannem de Kynton narratorem, vi d.

Item liberatum eidem pro parcameno emendo, ii d.

Item uni garcioni eunti apud Dynelek precepto domini, i d.

Item fratri Willelmo Dasscheburne semel eunti versus Urgal[liam]
& fratri Johanni Dolphyn semel eunti ibidem, iiii s. vi d.
Summa ix s. v d.   Probata.

Also in wages of different serving men going for brother John de Castro
to Kilcullen on 7 occasions on business of the house, 14*d.*

Also in ale bought for Henry Taloun and sir Philip, chaplain of Ballycor,
for 2 nights, 3*d.*

Also to a certain serving man going to Kilgowan and Castlemartin for
proxies of the archdeacon of Glendalough, 2*d.*

Also to a certain Hugley, clerk of William de Bosworth, for gloves by
command of the Prior, 1*d.*

Also delivered to the marshal of the Bench for writs of master Walter de
Istelep quashed or to be quashed, 2*s.* 6*d.*

Also to John Rous, clerk, going to Naas about the business of the
house, viz. after John de Kynton, pleader, 6*d.*

Also delivered to the same to buy parchment, 2*d.*

Also to a serving man going to Duleck by command of the lord
(Prior), 1*d.*

Also to brother William de Assheburne going once towards Uriel, and
brother John Dolphyn going once there, 4*s.* 6*d.*
Total, 9*s.* 5*d.*   Checked.

Item computat in sarclacione omnium bladorum hoc anno manerio crescencium, iiii s. iii d. ob.

Summa iiii s. iii d. ob.

Item idem computat in omnimodis bladis hoc anno manerio crescentibus metendis ligandis colligendis & in campo tassandis ut patet per dietas in i cedula cum victualiis cirotecis socularibus & aliis ad ingressum bladorum pertinentibus prout patet in dicta cedula, cxv s. vii d. quad.

Item cuidam colligenti decimas & custodienti apud Gorman in autupno, xii d. & facienti alia necessaria que sibi fuerunt precepta erant per totum autumpnum, xii d.

Summa cxvi s. vii d. quad.

Item idem computat liberatum magistro Ade de Kyngeston pro negociis de Dromsalan versus Drohgda expediendis, iii s. iiii d.

Item liberatum Petro Camerario pro necessariis ad cameram pertinentibus per i talliam contra eundem xxviii s. ob.

Item liberatum domino archiepiscopo pro debito, ut patet per literam, x li.

Also he accounts in hocing of all the corn this year growing on the manor, 4s. 3½d.

Total, 4s. 3½d.

Also he accounts in reaping, binding, collecting, and stacking in the field all kinds of corn this year growing on the manor, as appears by daily particulars in a schedule, with food, gloves, shoes, and other expenses connected with the bringing in of the corn, as appears in said schedule, 115s. 7½d.

Also to a certain man collecting tithes and guarding them at Gorman in the harvest time, and doing other necessary things which were commanded him, for the whole time of harvest, 12d.

Total, 116s. 7½d.

Also he accounts as delivered to master Adam de Kyngeston (going) towards Drogheda to execute business touching Drumshallon, 3s. 4d.

Also delivered to Peter the chamberlain for necessaries connected with the (Prior's) chamber, as by one tally against him, 28s. 0½d.

Also delivered to the lord archbishop, for a debt as appears by a letter, £10.

Item Petro clerico, ut patet per unam literam, in partem solucionis de quatuor marcis, xxx s.

Item liberatum domino Elie Dasscheb[urne] militi, pro feodo suo, de terminis Omnium Sanctorum anno r. r. xvi° & Omnium Sanctorum anno r. r. xvii^{mo} ut patet per ii literas aquietancie, xxvi s. viii d.

Item liberatum Nicholao Lumbard clerico tastatore mensurarum, pro feodo suo, de fine, xiiii s. iiii d.

Item magistro Hervico Bagot, pro procurationibus de Kylcolyn & capellis, x s.

Item Johanni Haket pro feodo suo, per literam aquietancie, xx s.

Item Willelmo Pistori pro pane ab eodem empto in autumpno, xxxiii s. iiii d.

Item clericis de Cancellaria pro ii brevibus de supersedeas de temporalibus viii s.

Item liberatum privato clerico domini Justiciarii pro i billa, clericis Cancellarie directa, de supersedeas, ii s.

Item magistro Thome de Kylmor clerico pro debito fratris Gilberti de Bolyniop, v s.

Also to Peter the clerk, as appears by a letter, in part payment of four marks, 30s.

Also delivered to sir Elias de Assheburne, knight, for his fee of the terms of All Saints in the 16th year of the king's reign and of All Saints in the 17th year, as appears by two letters of acquittance, 26s. 8d.

Also delivered to Nicholas Lumbard, clerk, examiner of measures, for his fee, by composition, 14s. 4d.

Also to master Hervey Bagot for proxies of Kilcullen and its chapels, 10s.

Also to John Haket for his fee, by letter of acquittance, 20s.

Also to William the baker, for bread bought from him in the time of harvest, 33s. 4d.

Also to the clerks of the Chancery, for two writs of " Supersedeas " of the temporalities, 8s.

Also delivered to the private clerk of the lord Justiciary for a bill directed to the clerks of the Chancery concerning the " Supersedeas," 2s.

Also to master Thomas de Kylmor, clerk, for a debt of brother Gilbert de Bolyniop, 5s.

Item liberatum Stephano de Gascoyne, in persolucionem vi li., pro
vinis ab eo emptis, vi li.

Item liberatum eidem Stephano, pro duobus doleis vini, xxxv s.

Item liberatum Willelmo Petyt narratori, ex dono domini, xiii s.
iiii d.

Item liberatum Thome Whyte, de tempore vacacionis, xii d.

Item Laurentio Raggley versus ordines, xii d.

Item fratri Hugoni de Suttone, xxiii s. iiii d.

Item fratri Gilberto de Bolyniop, precepto domini Prioris, videlicet de redditu de Mablieston, xiii s. iiii d.

Item Nicholao Chamburleyn ballivo de Glasnevyn, pro husbonderia
ibidem ordinanda, per i talliam contra eundem, l s. ob.

Item Johanni Chamburleyn ballivo de Clouken, per i talliam
contra eundem, xxix s. ix d.

Item liberatum domino Priori per manus Petri Camerarii, de
quatuor marcis receptis de decimis de Glasnevin venditis,
iii s.

Item liberatum Johanni Gernoun narratori, pro feodo suo de termino

---

Also delivered to Stephen de Gascoyne, in full payment of £6 for wines
bought from him, £6.

Also delivered to same Stephen for two tuns of wine, 35s.

Also delivered to William Petyt, pleader, of the gift of the lord
(prior), 13s. 4d.

Also delivered to Thomas Whyte, for the time of the vacancy, 12d.

Also to Laurence Raggley, towards orders, 12d.

Also to brother Hugh de Suttone, 23s. 4d.

Also to brother Gilbert de Bolyniop, by command of the lord Prior; viz.
of the rent of Mabestown, 13s. 4d.

Also to Nicholas Chamburleyn, bailiff of Glasnevin, for managing the
husbandry there, as by one tally against him, 50s. 0½d.

Also to John Chamburleyn, bailiff of Clonken, by one tally against him,
29s. 9d.

Also delivered to the lord Prior, by the hands of Peter the chamberlain,
of the four marks received for the tithes of Glasnevin sold, 3s.

Also delivered to John Gernoun, pleader, for his fee for the term of All

Omnium Sanctorum anno r. r. xvii°, per i aquietanciam, xiii s. iiii d.

Item Willelmo de Burton, ut patet per i aquietanciam, xv li.

(Item liberatum Hugoni de Belynges ballivo de Gorman, per i talliam contra eundem, pro avena emenda, iiii li)[1].

Item Hugoni Broun narratori, pro feodo suo de termino Omnium Sanctorum, ut patet per i aquietanciam, x s.

Item liberatum Henrico Abbot mercatori pro panno ab eodem, ut patet per literam obligatoriam, xxx s. pro panno ab eodem empto.

Item liberatum Petro Camerario, de i herietta de Clonken, ii s. iii d.

Item fratri Johanni de Castro versus Kylcolyn, vi s. viii d.

Item Roberto Decer, pro debito coquine de tempore Willelmi Sterre, lxvi s. viii d.

Summa liiii li. xix s. v d. Probata.

Item idem petit allocanciam de x s. viii d. de redditu Johaunis de

———

Saints, in the 17th year of the king's reign, by one acquittance, 13s. 4d.

Also to William de Burton, as appears by one acquittance, £15.

(Also delivered to Hugh de Belynges, bailiff of Gorman, by one tally against him, for buying oats, £4.)

Also to Hugh Brown, pleader, for his fee for the term of All Saints, as appears by one acquittance, 10s.

Also delivered to Henry Abbot, merchant, for cloth from him, as appears by letter obligatory, 30s., for cloth bought from him.

Also delivered to Peter the chamberlain, from one heriot of Clonken, 2s. 3d.

Also to brother John de Castro, (going) towards Kilcullen, 6s. 8d.

Also to Robert Decer, for a debt of the kitchen, of the time of William Sterre, 66s. 8d.

Total, £54 19s. 5d. Checked.

Also he claims allowance of 10s. 8d. of the rent of John de Morton, at

———

[1] This entry struck out in original.

Morton, apud Gorman, de i termino unde superius oneratur, quia dicit quod solvit pre manibus diversis celerariis unde respondebunt.

Item in decasu ii cotagiorum, videlicet Henrici Cerney & Rogeri Janel, de dicto termino, xii d., unde superius oneratur & nihil inde recepit, quia jacent vasta.

Item in decasu redditus unius cotagii quondam Willelmi Vestham, de eodem termino, xv d., quia vastum, & inde superius oneratur, & nihil inde recepit, videlicet apud Glasnevin.

Item petit allocanciam de viii s. iii d. de redditu Thome Balle ibi-[dem], de eodem termino, quia nihil inde recepit, nisi xvi s., & superius oneratur de xxiiii s., quia non solvet plenum redditum usque ad terminum spennynges prox. futurum, & quia dimidia acra ab eo capta est & liberata Thome Wauter, ut patet per indenturam.

Item petit allocanciam de x s., de redditu Johannis Whyt de Balytiperd, quos frater Thomas de Beuley recepit, pro custibus autumpni & inde superius oneratur.

———————

Gorman, for one term, whereof he is above charged, because he says that he paid it beforehand to divers cellarers who will answer for it.

Also in loss (of rent) of two cottages, viz. of Henry Cerney and Roger Janel for said term, 12*d*., whereof he was above charged, and he received nothing thereout because they lie waste.

Also in loss of rent of one cottage, formerly of William Vestham, for same term, 15*d*., because it is waste, and he is charged above, and received nothing for it : viz. at Glasnevin.

Also he claims allowance of 8*s*. 3*d*. of the rent of Thomas Balle, there, for same term, because he received only 16*s*., and is charged above with 24*s*., because he will not pay the full rent to Spennyngs term next to come, and because half an acre was taken from him and given to Thomas Wauter, as appears by the indenture.

Also he claims allowance of 10*s*. of the rent of John Whyt, of Tipperstown, which brother Thomas de Beuley received for the expenses of the harvest, and whereof he is above charged.

(Item in decasu redditus Margarete Ketyngg de uno termino ii s., quia defficiunt vi acre per mensuram.)[1]

Item in decasu redditus Stephani Olyn de dicto termino xviii d., quia iii acre terre de terra quam tenuit jascent frisce.

Summa xxxii s. viii d.   Probata.

Item idem computat in cervisia empta pro Priore & Conventu, ob deffectum Celarii, die dominica proxima ante festum Omnium Sanctorum, xi d.

Item in pane empto pro eisdem Priore & Conventu, die Sabbati proxima ante festum Sancti Luce, iii d.

Item in pane empto pro eisdem, die Dominica proxima sequente, xvii d.

Item in expensis diversimode factis in camera domini Prioris a tempore quo Petrus Camerarius se non intromisit de expensis camere Prioris, usque diem Lune in vigilia Epiphanie Domini, anno Domini mcccxliii., xxvii s. iiii d. ob., ut patet in uno rotulo inde.

(Also in loss of rent of Margaret Ketyng, for one term, 2*s.*, because 6 acres, by admeasurement, are wanting.)

Also in loss of rent of Stephen Olyn, of said term, 18*d.*, because 3 acres of the land which he held, lie uncultivated.

Total, 32*s.* 8*d.*   Checked.

Also he accounts in ale bought for the Prior and Convent, owing to default of the cellarer, on Sunday next before the feast of All Saints, 11*d.*

Also in bread bought for the same Prior and Convent, on the Saturday next before the feast of S. Luke, 3*d.*

Also in bread bought for same, on Sunday next following, 17*d.*

Also in expenses incurred in different ways in the chamber of the lord Prior, from the time in which Peter the chamberlain did not interpose in the expenses of the Prior's chamber, to Monday, the vigil of the Epiphany of our Lord, A. D. 1343, 27*s.* 4½*d.*, as appears in a roll thereof.

---

[1] This entry struck out in original.

Item in expensis neccessariis emptis pro camera Prioris, per dictum
terminum, ut patet in dorso dicti rotuli, x s. ob. quad.

Summa xl s. quad.

SUMMA OMNIUM EXPENSARUM, lxxv li. xi s. ii d. ob. quad.

Et adhuc restant xlviii s. v d. ob. quad.   Unde oneratus est &
respondebit in compoto suo prox. subsequente.

EXITUS HAGARDI DE GORMAN DE GRANO AUTUMPNI ANNO
REGNI REGIS XVII° USQUE FESTUM OMNIUM SANCTORUM
PROX. SEQUENS.

In primis idem reddit compotum de xlv cran. v pᶜ frumenti
receptis de magistro Hugone de Calce, ex mutuo, videlicet
vii pᶜ cumul' pro cran., quod se extendit ad xl cran.
videlicet viii pᶜ cumul' pro cran.

Et de xlvi cran. receptis de exitu hagardi de novo grano, ut patet
per talliam Johannis de Pulesdon existentis ibidem, super
trituracionem, usque adventum Hugonis Belynges.

Et de i cran. i pᶜ receptis de Roberto de Houghton ex mutuo.

Also in expenses for necessaries bought for the Prior's chamber for the
said term, as appears on the back of said roll, 10s. 0¾d.

Total, 40s. 0¼d.

TOTAL OF ALL EXPENSES, £75 11s. 2¾d.

And there still remain 48s. 5¾d., with which he is charged, and will
answer in his account next following.

THE ISSUE OF THE HAGGARD OF GORMAN, OF THE GRAIN OF THE HARVEST
IN THE 17TH YEAR OF THE KING'S REIGN, TO THE FEAST OF ALL
SAINTS NEXT FOLLOWING.

In the first place he renders account of 45 crannocs 5 pecks of wheat
received from master Hugh de Calce as a loan, at 7 pecks, heaped
measure, to the crannoc, which extends to 40 crannocs, at 8 pecks,
heaped measure, to the crannoc.

And of 46 crannocs received of the issue of the haggard of the new grain,
as appears by the tally of John de Pulesdon, being there over the
threshing, until the coming of Hugh Belynges.

And of 1 crannoc 1 peck received from Robert de Houghton, as a loan.

E

Et de xii cran. di. p^e receptis de dicto exitu dicti hagardi per autumpnum.

Summa v^{xx} iiii cran. vi p^e di. videlicet vii p^e cumul' pro cran.

De quibus idem computat liberatum fratri Stephano Domus Sancte Trinitatis Dublin celerario per i talliam contra eundem, xxix cran. videlicet vii p^e cumul' pro cran. . . . est xxiii cran., viii. p^e cumul' pro cran.

Item liberatum Nicholao Chamburleyn ballivo de Glasnevyn per i talliam contra eundem, vii p^e.

Item in pane furnito per a[utumpnum] apud Gorman, iii cran. vi p^e videlicet vii p^e cumul' pro cran.

Item in liberationibus i servientis, unius carectarii, vi carucariorum, de Glasnevyn, a die Dominica proxima ante festum [Sancti] Dunstani usque festum Sancte Margarete virginis, per x septimanas, vii cran. i p^e videlicet vii p^e cumul' pro cran., & quilibet capit viii p^e rasa mensura per x septimanas quod est per [cumulum] vi p^e i sq'.

Item in liberationibus unius bercarii & unius janitoris ibidem per dictum terminum i cran. i p^e videlicet vii p^e cumul'

And of 12 crannocs half a peck received of the said issue of said haggard during the harvest.

     Total, 104 crannocs 6½ pecks, viz. 7 pecks, heaped measure, to the crannoc.

Of which he accounts, as delivered to brother Stephen, cellarer of the house of the Holy Trinity, Dublin, by one tally against him, 29 crannocs, at 7 pecks, heaped, to the crannoc [that] is, 23 crannocs, at 8 pecks, heaped, to the crannoc.

Also delivered to Nicholas Chamburleyn, bailiff of Glasnevin, by one tally against him, 7 pecks.

Also in bread baked during harvest at Gorman, 3 crannocs 6 pecks, at 7 pecks, heaped, to the crannoc.

Also in allowances of one serjeant, one carter, 6 ploughmen, of Glasnevin, from the Sunday (18 May) next before the feast of S. Dunstan to the feast of S. Margaret the virgin (20 July) for 10 weeks, 7 crannocs 1 peck, at 7 pecks, heaped, to the crannoc, and each takes 8 pecks, level measure, for 10 weeks, which is, by heaped measure, 6¼ pecks.

Also in allowances of one shepherd and one doorkeeper there for the said pro cran. & sic quilibet capit mediam liberationem per cumulum.

Item in liberatione unius ancille domus per dictum terminum, iii p^e per cumulum & capit mediam liberationem rasa mensura.

Item in liberationibus ii serviencium apud Gorman ii carectariorum, & vi carucariorum ibidem ab in crastino Apostolorum Petri & Pauli usque festum Nativitatis Beate Marie Virginis, per x septimanas viii cran. vi p^e di. (unde de novo grano i cran. iii p^e di.) & sic quilibet capit per x septimanas viii p^e rasa mensura, quod est per cumulum vi p^e sq'.

Item in semine, per talliam contra Johannem Chamburleyn messorem ibidem, xxxiiii cran. iii p^e.

Item liberatum fratri Nicholao de Barton celerario, per i talliam contra eundem v [cran.]

Item in liberationibus dictorum x famulorum, a festo Nativitatis Beate Marie Virginis usque in tercium diem post festum Omnium Sanctorum videlicet per viii septimanas vii cran. i p^e videlicet vii p^e cumul' pro [cran.]

---

term, 1 crannoc 1 peck, at 7 pecks, heaped, to the crannoc, and so each takes half his allowance by heaped measure.

Also in allowance of one housemaid for said term, 3 pecks, heaped, and she takes half her allowance by level measure.

Also in allowances of 2 serjeants, at Gorman, 2 carters, and 6 ploughmen, there, from the morrow (30 June) of the apostles Peter and Paul, to the feast of the Nativity of the Blessed Virgin Mary (8 Sept.), for 10 weeks, 8 crannoes 6½ pecks (whereof of new grain, 1 crannoc 3½ pecks), and so each takes for 10 weeks, 8 pecks, level measure, which is, by heaped measure, 6¼ pecks.

Also in seed, by tally against John Chamburleyn, messer there, 34 crannoes 3 pecks.

Also delivered to brother Nicholas de Barton, cellarer, by a tally against him, 5 crannoes.

Also in allowances of said 10 servants, from the feast of the Nativity of the Blessed Virgin Mary (8 Sept.) to the third day (1 Nov.) after the feast of All Saints, that is 8 weeks, 7 crannoes 1 peck, at 7 pecks, heaped, to the crannoc.

Item in liberatione unius ballivi ibidem a die Jovis proxima post
     festum Apostolorum Petri & Pauli usque diem Jovis prox.
     post festum Omnium Sanctorum per xviii septimanas ii
     cran. videlicet vii p^c cumul' pro cran.

Item liberatum Hugoni Belynges ballivo de Gorman per i talliam
     contra eundem ix cran. i p^c.

    Summa v^{xx} ix cran. i p^c di., unde de incremento iii cran.
     vi p^c videlicet vii p^c [cum.] pro cran. De quibus . . .

Hastiuell. Item reddit compotum de xvi cran. ii p^c hastiuell receptis de
     exitu dicti hagardi.

    Summa xvi cran. ii p^c patet.

In semine, liberatum per i talliam contra Johannem Chamburleyn
     ibidem messorem, ii cran.

Item cuidam garcioni custodienti dictum hastiuell in campo, ii p^c

Item in liberationibus ii serviencium ibidem ii carectariorum & vi
     carucariorum, a festo Sancti Augustini usque festum Apos-
     tolorum Petri & Pauli prox. sequens, per v septimanas,
     vi cran. ii p^c : cuilibet per v septimanas, v p^c.

Also in allowance of one bailiff there from Thursday (3 July) next after
     the feast of the apostles Peter and Paul to Thursday (6 Nov.) next
     after the feast of All Saints for 18 weeks, 2 crannocs, at 7 pecks,
     heaped, to the crannoc.

Also delivered to Hugh Belynges, bailiff of Gorman, by one tally against
     him, 9 crannocs 1 peck.

    Total, 109 crannocs 1½ peck, of which 3 crannocs 6 pecks,
     at 7 pecks to the crannoc, are in excess of what is to be
     accounted for. Of which . . .

Hastiuell. Also he renders account of 16 crannocs 2 pecks hastiuell received of the
     issue of said haggard.

    Total, 16 crannocs 2 pecks, is manifest.

In seed, delivered by 1 tally against John Chamburleyn, messer there,
     2 crannocs.

Also to a certain serving man guarding the said hastiuell in the field,
     2 pecks.

Also in allowances of 2 serjeants there, 2 carters, and 6 ploughmen, from
     the feast of S. Augustine (26 May) to the feast of the apostles
     Peter and Paul (29 June) next following, for 5 weeks, 6 crannocs
     2 pecks ; to each for 5 weeks, 5 pecks.

Item liberatum Hugoni ballivo ibidem, per i talliam contra eundem, vi cran. vi p^e.

Item liberatum Johanni Chamburleyn ballivo de Clonken, per i [talliam] contra eundem, i cran.

      Summa ut supra.   Et nihil remanet.

Item idem reddit compotum de xi p^e avenarum receptis ibidem   Avene. post tempus fratrum Willelmi de Assheburne & Stephani Derby ad stallamentum Prioris.

Et de vii p^e avenarum receptis de empcione ut infra.

Et de iiii cran. di. receptis de novo grano de exitu grangie, de hagardo supradicto.

      Summa v cran. xi p^e.

De quibus idem computat liberatum Henrico Hay palefridario Prioris, per i talliam contra eundem, post adventum suum videlicet ad festum Sancti Petri Advincula, x p^e di.

Item in prebenda palefridi Prioris & haken brunei, a stallamento Prioris usque festum Sancti Petri Advincula, iiii p^e di.

Also delivered to Hugh, the bailiff there, by one tally against him, 6 crannocs 6 pecks.

Also delivered to John Chamburleyn, bailiff of Clonken, by one tally against him, 1 crannoc.

      Total as above, and nothing remains.

Also he renders account of 11 pecks of oats received there after the time Oats. of brothers William de Assheburne and Stephen Derby at the installation of the Prior.

And of 7 pecks of oats received by purchase, as inside the roll.

And of 4 crannocs and a-half received of new grain of the issue of the grange, of the haggard abovesaid.

      Total, 5 crannocs 11 pecks.

Of which he accounts as delivered to Henry Hay, palfreykeeper of the Prior, by one tally against him after his coming, at the feast of S. Peter ad Vincula, 10½ pecks.

Also in provender of the Prior's palfrey and the brown hackney, from the installation of the Prior to the feast of S. Peter ad Vincula, 4½ pecks.

Item liberatum Leticie Marcold siccatrici brasii ibidem, pro brasio
    inde faciendo per unam talliam contra eandem, iiii cran. x
    p^{c}

        Summa ut supra.   Et nihil remanet.

Also delivered to Leticia Marcold, the woman drying malt there, to
    make malt of it, by one tally against her, 4 crannocs 10 pecks.

        Total as above, and nothing remains.

III.

COMPOTUS JOHANNIS CHAMBURLEYN BALLIVI DE CLONKEN de omnibus recepcionibus misis expensis & liberationibus ibidem per ipsum factis, a festo Sancti Petri Ad vincula, anno Domini Millesimo ccc^mo. xliiii^to, usque idem festum proximum sequens, anno revoluto.

In primis idem reddit compotum de xiii s. ii d. receptis de placitis & perquisitionibus curiarum per tempus compoti tentarum ut patet per iii extractas super compotum prolatas.   *Perquisitiones Curiarum.*

   Summa xiii s. ii d. patet.

Item idem reddit compotum de iiii s. ii d. receptis de minutis decimis hoc anno receptis.   *Minute Decime.*

Et de iii s. i d. receptis de turbis venditis hoc anno.

   Summa vii s. iii d.

Item idem reddit compotum de iiii s.¹ receptis de argilla pro ollis luteis inde faciendis vendita, per manus Dowenild Ohelyn.   *Venditio Argille.*

   Summa iiii s. patet.

ACCOUNT OF JOHN CHAMBURLEYN, BAILIFF OF CLONKEN, of all receipts, disbursements, expenses, and payments there made by him, from the feast of Saint Peter ad Vincula (1st Aug.) A.D. 1344, to the same feast next following in the succeeding year.

In the first place he renders account of 13s. 2d. received of the pleas and profits of the courts held during the time of the account, as appears by 3 estreats produced upon the account.   *Profits of Courts.*

   Total 13s. 2d., is manifest.

Also he renders account of 4s. 2d. received for small tithes received this year.   *Small Tithes.*

And of 3s. 1d. received for turf sold this year.

   Total 7s. 3d.

Also he renders account of 4s. received for clay sold by the hands of Dowenild OHelyn, for making earthenware pots.   *Sale of Clay.*

   Total 4s., is manifest.

----

¹ Written over xxii d. struck out.

Venditio Lane. Item idem reddit compotum de xvii s. vi d. receptis de vii petris & di. lane venditis, de tonsura de termino Omnium, precium petre ii s. iiii d.

Et de xiiii s. vi d. receptis de vii petris & 1 quart. lane venditis de tonsura de termino Apostolorum Philippi & Jacobi, precium petre ii s.

Et de vii s. vi d. receptis de iii petris lane agnine venditis de tonsura Nativitatis Beati Johannis, precium petre ii s.

Summa xxxix s. vi d.

[Venditio] frumenti. Item idem reddit compotum de xix s. vii d. receptis de vi cran. v p^c. frumenti venditis, precium cran. ii s. xi d.

Et de iii s. ii d. ob. receptis de i cran. vendito, precium p^c. v d. ob.

Summa xxii s. ix d. ob.

Venditio Stauri. Item idem reddit compotum de x s. receptis de ii bobus venditis, pro debilitate & senectute, per visum fratris Johannis Comyn senescalli.

Et de ii s. receptis de i porco vendito.

Et de xx d. receptis de uno alio minori vendito.

Sale of Wool. Also he renders account of 17s. 6d. received for 7½ stones of wool sold, of the shearing of the term of All [Saints, Nov. 1]: price 2s. 4d. a stone.

And of 14s. 6d. received for 7¼ stones of wool sold, of the shearing of the term of the apostles Philip and James (May 1): price 2s. a stone.

And of 7s. 6d. received for 3 stones of lambs' wool sold, of the shearing at the time of the Nativity of Saint John (June 24): price 2s. a stone.

Total 39s. 6d.

Sale of Wheat. Also he renders account of 19s. 7d. received for 6 crannocs 5 pecks of wheat sold: price 2s. 11d. a crannoc.

And of 3s. 2¼d. received for one crannoc sold: price 5½d. a peck.

Total 22s. 9½d.

Sale of Stock. Also he renders account of 10s. received for 2 oxen sold on account of weakness and old age, by direction of brother John Comyn the seneschal.

And of 2s. received for 1 hog sold.

And of 20d. received for another smaller sold.

Et de iii d. receptis de i coreo affrino vendito, mortuo de morina. Coria.

Et de v d. receptis de i alio coreo equino vendito de morina.

Et de iiii d. de i alio coreo affrino vendito de morina.

Et de xiiii d. receptis de uno coreo vaccino vendito de morina.

Et de ii s. receptis de viii pellibus lanutis venditis, de multon’ missis de Glasnevin, apud Clonken, ad dominum Archiepiscopum & ad Priorem.

Summa xvii s. x d.

Item idem reddit compotum de c iii s. v d. receptis de fratre Rec’ for’. Johanne Comyn senescallo per i talliam contra eundem, pro diversis rebus & husbonderia ibidem ordi[nanda] ante Natalem Domini.

Et de xxxiii s. v d. ob. receptis de eodem Johanne per i aliam talliam contra eundem.

Summa, vi li. xvi s. x d. ob.

SUMMA TOCIUS RECEPT’, xii li. xvii d.

Item idem computat in meremio empto pro xii carucis novis inde Custus faciendis pro stauro habendo, de quodam hibernico, iii s. Caruca-
rum.

Item in uno scem’ virga[rum] pro hartis & themes inde faciendis, pro carucis, iii d.

And of 3*d.* received for one hide sold of an affer that died of murrain. Hides.

And of 5*d.* received for a horse hide sold, that died of murrain.

And of 4*d.* received for au affer hide sold, that died of murrain.

And of 14*d.* received for a cow hide sold, that died of murrain.

And of 2*s.* received of 8 woolfells sold, of sheep sent from Glasnevin to Clonken for the lord Archbishop and the Prior.

Total, 17*s.* 10*d.*

Also he renders account of 103*s.* 5*d.* received from brother John Comyn, Extern seneschal, as by one tally against him for divers things and for receipts. conducting the farming there before Christmas.

And of 33*s.* 5½*d.* received from the same John, as by one other tally against him.

Total, £6 16*s.* 10½*d.*

TOTAL OF ALL RECEIPTS, £12 1*s.* 5*d.*

Also he renders account in timber bought for making 12 new ploughs, to Cost of have in stock, of a certain Irishman, 3*s.* Ploughs.

Also in one load of rods to make handles and themes for the ploughs, 3*d.*

Item in duabus bendis & di. ferri pro ferro carucali inde sustinendo & faciendo per tempus compoti, x s.

Item in stipendio fabri pro dictis ferris carucalibus faciendis &
fabricandis, per tempus supradictum, ex certa convencione, vi s.
viii. d.

Item in iiii°ʳ vomeribus emptis, ii s.

Summa xxi s. xi d.

Arura
Carucarum
ex Consue-
tudine.
Item idem computat in pane furnito ut extra pro xiiii carucis ex
consuetudine ad semen yemale ad quas fuerunt xxviii viri, ii
pᶜ. frumenti. Item in cervisia xii d. Et de stauro unus porcus.[1]

Item in pane furnito pro arura alia, de xiiii carucis, ad quas
fuerunt xxviii viri, ii pᶜ frumenti ut extra. In cervisia empta
xiii d., in pisce empto, ix d.

Summa ii s. x d.

Custos
Carecta-
rum.
Item idem computat in una corda empta de canabo pro carecta
liganda, iiii d.

Item in ii paribus de tractibus de canabo emptis, iiii d.

Item in uno pare rotarum empto, ii s. v d.

Item in i alio pare rotarum empto, ii s. ii d.

Also in two bends and a half of iron, to maintain and to make plough
iron during the time of account, 10s.

Also in wages of a smith to make and forge the said plough irons during
the aforesaid time, by a fixed agreement, 6s. 8d.

Also in 4 ploughshares bought, 2s.

Total 21s. 11d.

Ploughing
of the cus-
tomary
ploughs.
Also he accounts in bread baked as on the outer side (of the roll) for 14
ploughs by custom at winter seed time, to which were 28 men, 2
pecks of wheat. Also in ale 12d. And from the stock 1 hog.

Also in bread baked for another ploughing of 14 ploughs, to which were
28 men, 2 pecks of wheat, as on the other side. In ale bought
13d., in fish bought, 9d.

Total, 2s. 10d.

Cost of
arts.
Also he accounts in one cord of hemp bought for binding a cart, 4d.

Also in 2 pairs of traces of hemp bought, 4d.

Also in one pair of wheels bought, 2s. 5d.

Also in another pair of wheels bought, 2s. 2d.

---

[1] Porco in the original.

Item in i alio pare rotarum empto, ii s. i d.

Item in i arbore empto pro i pare de razes pro carectis faciendo, i. d.

Item in conduccione unius carpentarii pro dictis razes pro carectis faciendis, & ad inponendos duos axes, per ii dies ad mensam in autumpno, ii d.

Item in unguento empto ad carectas, ii d.

Item in duobus cartobaas emptis per visum Johannis Comyn, xii d.

Item in uno stradul empto ad carectam, i d.

Item in i carre empto ad tractandas decimas de Thillagh, ii d. ob.

Item in i corda de canabo empta pro dicto carre ligando, i d.

Item in clut' ferreis & clavis emptis pro eisdem firmandis, v d.

Item in i axe empto, i d. ob.

Item in ferura iii equorum ad carectam per tempus compoti, iiii s.

Item in ferura equi super quem frater Thomas de Beuley equitavit in autumpno, xii d.

Item in ii paribus rotarum lanearum emptis contra autumpnum, iiii s. iiii d.

Item in ii axibus emptis pro carecta unacum imposicione & aptacione eorundem, iiii d. ob.

Also in another pair of wheels bought, 2s. 1d.

Also in one tree bought for making one pair of razes for carts, 1d.

Also in hire of one carpenter for making said razes for carts, and putting on two axles, for 2 days, at board, in harvest time, 2d.

Also in grease bought for the carts, 2d.

Also in two cartbass bought by direction of John Comyn, 12d.

Also in one straddle bought for a cart, 1d.

Also in one car bought to draw the tithes from Tully, 2½d.

Also in one cord of hemp bought to bind the said car, 1d.

Also in iron clouts, and nails bought to secure them, 5d.

Also in one axle bought, 1½d.

Also in shoeing of 3 cart horses during the time of account, 4s.

Also in shoeing of the horse which brother Thomas de Beuley rode in harvest, 12d.

Also in 2 pairs of woollen wheels bought against harvest, 4s. 4d.

Also in 2 axles bought for a cart, together with the putting on and fitting of them, 4½d.

Item in clut' emptis, & clavis pro eisdem firmandis, v d. ob.

Summa xix s. x d.

Emendacio Domorum. Item idem computat in factura parietum domus torelli ex longitudine quatuor perticat' ii s. iiii d. : pro qualibet pertic', vii d.

Item in conduccione cuiusdam carpentarii scarpilantis aptantis & levantis ii copulas pro eadem per iii dies ad mensam, vi d.

Item in clathes emptis pro eadem, iii d.

Item cuidam homini colligenti watul pro eodem, i d.

Item in conduccione unius coopertorii, cooperientis dictam domum per x dies ad tascham, ii s. i d., per diem ii d. ob.

Item in conduccione duorum garcionum deserviencium eidem per dictos x dies ad tascham, xx d., cuilibet per diem i d.

Item in conduccione dicti coopertorii cooperientis super bostar' per iiii^{or}. dies ad tascham x d., per diem ut supra.

Item duobus eidem deservientibus per dictos iiii^{or} dies ad tascham, viii d., cuilibet per diem i d.

Item in conduccione eiusdem coopertorii cooperientis super grangiam per ii dies ad tascham, v d., per diem ut supra.

Also in clouts bought, and nails for securing them, 5½d.

Total 19s. 10d.

Repair of houses. Also he accounts in making the walls of the kiln house of the length of 4 perches, 2s. 4d. ; for each perch, 7d.

Also in hire of a carpenter cutting, fitting, and putting up two roof couples for the same, for 3 days at board, 6d.

Also in hurdles bought for same, 3d.

Also to a man collecting wattle for same, 1d.

Also in hire of a thatcher roofing said house for 10 days at full wages, 2s. 1d. ; by the day, 2½d.

Also in hire of two serving men helping him for the said 10 days, at full wages, 20d. ; to each by the day, 1d.

Also in hire of said thatcher roofing the ox house for 4 days, at full wages, 10d. ; by the day as above.

Also to two men helping him for said 4 days at full wages, 8d. ; to each by the day, 1d.

Also in hire of the same thatcher roofing over the grange for 2 days, at full wages, 5d. ; by the day as above.

Item dictis duobus eidem coopertorio deservientibus per dictos ii dies, iiii d.

Item in C. de draghtbord emptis, ad Hibernicos, v s.

Item in meremio empto, per Ricardum Taloun, in Glenwhery, pro domo vaccarum de novo edificanda, iii s. vi d.

Item in conduccione Ricardi Taloun carpentarii, dictum meremium aptantis & levantis per octo dies ad tascham, xx d., per diem ii d. ob.

Item in factura murorum eiusdem domus ex longitudine iiij" perticatarum, ii s. viii d., pro pertica ad tascham viii d.

Item in factura unius parve serure ad le wyket magne porte, ii d.

Item liberavit pro meremio supradicto cariando de Glewhery, die Sancti Nicholai, iiii d.

Item in uno spochour empto ad iactandam aquam, ad muros faciendos, i d. ob.

Item in meremio empto videlicet xxvi spyres pro dicta domo adimplenda, ii s. ii. d.

Item cuidam carpentario facienti hostium & adimplenti dictam domum, per ii dies ad tascham, v d.

Summa cum cedula xxix s. ii d.

Also to said two helping the same thatcher for said 2 days, 4*d*.

Also in 100 of draughtboard bought among the Irish, 5*s*.

Also in timber, bought by Richard Taloun in Glenwhery to build anew the cow house, 3*s*. 6*d*.

Also in hire of Richard Taloun, carpenter, fitting and putting up the said timber for 8 days at full wages, 20*d*.; by the day, 2½*d*.

Also in making the walls of same house of the length of four perches 2*s*. 8*d*.; by the perch, at full wages, 8*d*.

Also in making of a small lock for the wicket of the great gate, 2*d*.

Also he paid for carrying the said timber from Glenwhery, on Saint Nicholas' day (Dec. 6), 4*d*.

Also in a spochour, bought to throw water for making the walls, 1½*d*.

Also in timber bought, viz. 26 beams to complete the said house, 2*s*. 2*d*.

Also to a carpenter making the door and completing the said house, for 2 days at full wages, 5*d*.

Total, with the schedule, 29*s*. 2*d*.

[Stipen] dia famu- lorum.

Item idem computat in stipendio Johannis Chamburleyn ibidem ballivi, per annum, vi s. viii d.

Item in stipendio unius servientis, unius carectarii & duorum ten- torum carucarum per annum xx s., cuilibet per annum, v s. pro eodem.

Item liberatum duobus fugatoribus carucarum pro eodem per annum, & uni janitori, xii s., cuilibet per annum iiii s.

Item cuidam mulieri siccanti brasium & facienti alia necessaria infra manerium, a festo Sancti Petri Advincula usque in diem dominicam proximam ante festum Sancti Dunstani pro salario suo, iii s.

Item cuidam vaccario, pro eodem, a festo Sancti Andree Apostoli usque dictam diem dominicam proximam ante festum Sancti Dunstani, ii s.

Summa xliii s. viii d.

Empcio Stauri.

In i equo empto pro carecta, ix s.

Item in i boviculo empto pro caruca, iiii s.

Summa xiii s.

Expense Minute & necessarie.

Item idem computat in i pᶜ salis empto, iii d.

In discis & platellis contra autumpnum, ii d.

Wages of servants.

Also he accounts in the wages of John Chamburleyn the bailiff there, for a year, 6*s.* 8*d.*

Also in wages of 1 serjeant, 1 carter, and two ploughmen, for a year, 20*s.* ; to each by the year, 5*s.*

Also paid to two drivers of ploughs for the same (wages) by the year, and to 1 door keeper, 12*s.* ; to each by the year, 4*s.*

Also to a woman drying malt and doing other necessary work within the manor, from the feast of Saint Peter ad Vincula (Aug. 1), to the Sunday next before the feast of Saint Dunstan, for her salary, 3*s.*

Also to a cowherd for same from the feast of Saint Andrew the apostle (Nov. 30) to the said Sunday (May 15) next before the feast of Saint Dunstan, 2*s.*

Total, 43*s.* 8*d.*

Buying of Stock.

In 1 horse bought for the cart, 9*s.*

Also in 1 bullock bought for the plough, 4*s.*

Total, 13*s.*

Small ex- penses and necessaries.

Also he accounts in 1 peck of salt bought, 3*d.*

In dishes and plates against harvest, 2*d.*

Item in ciphis de fraxino emptis, ob.

Item in meremio empto pro circulis inde faciendis iii d.

Item in conduccione unius cuparii, facientis & emendantis vasa diversa, per iiii^{or} dies ad mensam, iiii d.

Item alia vice eidem cupario emendanti vasa domus in autumpno per i diem & dimidiam diem iii d. ad mensam.

Item in i patella enea empta per visum fratris Johannis Comyn, ii s. viii d.

Item in factura unius novi cornu, in[1] i zona nova empta pro eodem v d.

Item in uno ventilabro empto ii s. viii d.

Item in uno sacco novo empto x d.

Item in emendacione del ffurneys ii d.

Item in cribro empto, iii d.

Item in pyk ferro empto pro garbis levandis & in iii magnis corulis, pro schaftus videlicet stelus i d.

Item in ventilatione ix^{xx} xvii. cran. iiii p^c frumenti, vi cran. hastiuell, xiiii cran. ordei, xix cran. iii p^c. fabarum & pisarum &

Also in cups of ashwood bought, ½d.

Also in timber bought for making barrel hoops, 3d.

Also in hire of a cooper making and mending divers vessels, for 4 days at board, 4d.

Also another time to same cooper mending vessels of the house in harvest time for 1 day and a-half, 3d. at board.

Also in 1 brass pan bought by direction of brother John Comyn, 2s. 8d.

Also in making of 1 new horn, and 1 new belt bought for same, 5d.

Also in a winnowing fan bought, 2s. 8d.

Also in a new sack bought, 10d.

Also in repair of the furnace, 2d.

Also in a sieve bought, 3d.

Also in an iron fork bought for lifting sheaves, and three large hazel trees for shafts or handles, 1d.

Also in winnowing 197 crannocs, 4 pecks of wheat, 6 crannocs of hastiuell, 14 crannocs of barley, 19 crannocs, 3 pecks of beans and peas, and

---

[1] *in* is repeated in original.

v^{xx} xiii cran. & xiii p^c. avene, vii s. iii d. ob. quad., videlicet
pro ventilatione quatuor cran. i d.

Item in conduccione ii hominum amputancium subboscum in bosco
de Clonken, per xiiii dies in autumpno ad mensam, ad bras'
& furn' ad Abbatiam in autumpno, ii s. iiii d., cuilibet per
diem i d.

Item in conduccione ii hominum flagencium sive triturancium
diversa blada in autumpno, per xi dies ad mensam, xxii d.,
cuilibet per diem ad mensam i d.

Item duobus vigilantibus supra cacumina moncium pre timore
Hibernicorum, per ii noctes, iiii d.

Summa xxi s. quad. cum cedula.

Falcacio.   Item in v acris iii stangnis prati falcandis iii s. iii d. ob., pro acra
vii d.

Summa iii s. iii d. ob.

Expense
Autump-
nales ut in   In conduccione vi metentium hastiuell, vi d.
conduc-
cione di-   Die Jovis proxima post festum Sancti Petri Advincula in con-
versorum   duccione iiii^{xx} viii metencium blada, ad cibum, vii s. iiii d.,
metencium   cuilibet per diem i d.
blada.

---

113 crannocs, 13 pecks of oats, 7s. 3¾d., viz. for winnowing 4
crannocs, 1d.

Also in hire of 2 men cutting underwood in the wood of Clonken for 14
days in autumn at board, for brewing and baking for the abbey in
autumn, 2s. 4d. ; to each by the day, 1d.

Also in hire of 2 men threshing different kinds of grain in harvest time,
for 11 days at board, 22d. ; to each by the day at board, 1d.

Also to 2 men watching upon the tops of the mountains through fear of
the Irish, for 2 nights, 4d.

Total, 21s 0¼d., with a schedule.

Mowing.   Also in mowing 5 acres, 3 stangs, of meadow, 3s. 3½d. ; for an acre, 7d.

Total, 3s. 3½d.

Harvest
expenses :   In hire of 6 men reaping hastiuell, 6d.
as in hire   On Thursday (August 5) next after the feast of S. Peter ad Vincula in hire
of divers   of 88 men reaping corn, with food, 7s. 4d. ; to each by the day, 1d.
reaping
corn.

Die Veneris proxima sequente, in conduccione xxxiiii metencium
ad cibum, ii s. x d., cuilibet per diem i d.

Item die Mercurii proxima post festum Sancti Laurencii, in conduccione xxv hominum ad cibum, ii s. i d., cuilibet per diem ut
supra.

Die Jovis proxima sequente in conduccione xxx hominum metencium ad cibum, ii s. vi. d., cuilibet ut supra.

Die Veneris proxima sequente in conduccione xxxiiii hominum
metencium ad mensam, ii s. x d.; cuilibet ut supra.

Die Lune proxima post festum Assumpcionis Beate Marie Virginis,
in conduccione xix metencium ad mensam, xix d.; cuilibet
ut supra.

Die Jovis proxima sequente in conduccione xx metencium ad
mensam, xx d., cuilibet ut supra.

Item eodem die fuerunt ibidem metentes de custumariis, xv de
Kyllenyn, pro quibus computat, pane & cervisia de stauro.
In carnibus emptis pro eisdem, iii d.

Die Veneris proxima sequente in conduccione xxi metencium ad
mensam, xxi d., cuilibet ut supra.

Friday next following, in hire of 34 reapers, with food, 2*s.* 10*d.*; to each
by the day, 1*d.*

Also on Wednesday next after the feast of S. Laurence, in hire of 25 men,
with food, 2*s.* 1*d.*; to each by the day as above.

Thursday next following, in hire of 30 men reaping, with food, 2*s.* 6*d.*;
to each as above.

Friday next following, in hire of 34 men reaping at board, 2*s.* 10*d.*;
to each as above.

Monday (Aug. 16) next after the feast of the Assumption of the Blessed
Virgin Mary, in hire of 19 reapers, at board, 19*d.*; to each as
above.

Thursday next following, in hire of 20 reapers, at board, 20*d.*; to each
as above.

Also on same day there were reapers there of the customary tenants,
15 from Killiney, for whom he accounts in bread and ale from
stock. In flesh bought for the same, 3*d.*

Friday next following, in hire of 21 reapers, at board, 21*d.*; to each as
above.

F

Die Lune proxima sequente in couduccione xvii metencium ad mensam, xvii d., cuilibet ut supra.

Die Jovis proxima sequente in conduccione iiii hominum metencium ad mensam, iiii d., cuilibet eorum ut supra.

Et fuerunt ibi eodem die lx metentes de custumariis ad mensam. Panis & cervisia pro eisdem de stauro, in allece i d., et de stauro i porcus.

Die Veneris proxima sequente in conduccione ix metencium, ad cibum, ix d., cuilibet ut supra.

Die Sabbati proxima sequente in conduccione xxxi metencium per dimidiam diem ad tascham, ii s. vii d.: cuilibet i d.

Die Lune proxima post festum decollationis Beati Johannis Bapthiste, in conduccione xiiii hominum metencium ad cibum, xiiii d., cuilibet ad cibum ut supra.

Et eodem die fuerunt ibidem xvi custumarii metentes pro quibus panis & cervisia de stauro, in carnibus emptis ii d.

Die Martis proxima sequente, in conduccione xxiiii metencium ad mensam, ii s., cuilibet ut supra.

Monday next following, in hire of 17 reapers, at board, 17*d.*; to each as above.

Thursday next following, in hire of 4 men reaping, at board, 4*d.*; to each of them as above.

And there were there on the same day 60 reapers of the customary tenants, at board. Bread and ale for the same from stock, in herrings, 1*d.*, and from stock 1 hog.

Friday next following, in hire of 9 reapers, with food, 9*d.*; to each as above.

Saturday next following, in hire of 31 reapers for half a day, at full wages, 2*s.* 7*d.*; to each 1*d.*

Monday (Aug. 30) next after the feast of the beheading of S. John the Baptist, in hire of 14 men reaping, with food, 14*d.*; to each with food, as above.

And the same day there were there 16 customary reapers, for whom bread and ale from stock; in flesh bought, 2*d.*

Tuesday next following, in hire of 24 reapers, at board, 2*s.*; to each as above.

Die Mercurii proxima sequente, in conduccione xxv metencium ad
   mensam, ii s. i d., cuilibet ut supra.

Die Jovis proxima sequente in conduccione xvi hominum metencium ad mensam, xvi d., cuilibet ut supra.

Die Veneris proxima sequente in conduccione xlv hominum
   metencium ad mensam, iii s. ix d. cuilibet i d. ut supra.
   Item in allece pro eisdem ii d.

Die Sabbati proxima sequente, in conduccione ix metencium, ad
   mensam, ix d., cuilibet ut supra.   Et tunc finit messio.

Summa xxxix s. xi d.

Conduccio operariorum in haggardo.

Item idem computat unius vocati Walteri Harald tassantis in
   hagardo, per dies Veneris & Sabbati proximas post festum
   Sancti Bartholomei ad mensam, ii d.

Item in conduccione unius tassatoris per unam septimanam post
   festum Decollationis Beati Johannis, ex certa convencione ad
   mensam, v d.

Item in conduccione dictorum duorum, per unam septimanam
   proximam sequentem, per certam convencionem ad mensam
   x d., cuilibet per septimanam v d.

Wednesday, in hire of 25 reapers, at board, 2*s.* 1*d.*; to each as above.

Thursday, in hire of 16 men reaping, at board, 16*d.*; to each as above.

Friday, in hire of 45 men reaping, at board, 3*s.* 9*d.*; to each 1*d.* as
   above.   Also in herrings for them, 2*d.*

Saturday next following (Sept. 4), in hire of 9 reapers, at board, 9*d.*
And then the reaping ends.

Total, 39*s.* 11*d.*

Hire of workmen in the haggard :—

Also he accounts [in hire] of one called Walter Harald stacking in the
   haggard for Friday and Saturday (August 27 and 28) next after the
   feast of S. Bartholomew, at board, 2*d.*

Also in hire of a stacker for 1 week after the feast of the beheading of
   S. John (Aug. 29), by agreement, at board, 5*d.*

Also in hire of said 2 men for 1 week next following, by agreement, at
   board, 10*d.*; to each for the week, 5*d.*

F 2

Item in conduccione ii hominum picchantium[1] blada in hagardo, per ii dies ad mensam, ii d.

Item in conduccione duorum tassatorum in hagardo per unam septimanam proximam sequentem, ad mensam, x d., ex certa convencione.

Item in conduccione unius mulieris ligantis garbas in hagardo per xii dies ad mensam, vi d., per diem ob.

Item in conduccione Walteri Harald tassantis decimas & cooperientis tassos, per iii septimanas, ad mensam ex certa convencione, xii d., per septimanam iiii d.

Summa iii s. xi d.

Conduccio collectorum Decimarum & custodum.

In primis idem computat liberatum clerico de Tyllagh, tractanti decimas de Tyllagh, cum equo suo proprio, xii d.

Item Philippo Hogheryn tractanti decimas pariter de Tyllagh, cum equo domini, ad mensam, xv d.

Item garcioni domini Thome capellani de Tyllagh, custodienti [decimas] de Dengen, iii d.

Item garcioni Oliveri Haket custodienti decimas de Kyllenyn & Balylaghnan, ii s.

Also in hire of 2 men forking corn in the haggard for 2 days, at board, 2d.

Also in hire of 2 stackers in the haggard for 1 week next following, at board, 10d. by agreement.

Also in hire of 1 woman binding sheaves in the haggard for 12 days, at board, 6d.; by the day, ½d.

Also in hire of Walter Harald stacking tithes and thatching stacks for 3 weeks, at board, by agreement, 12d.; by the week, 4d.

Total, 3s. 11d.

Hire of collectors and watchmen of tithes :—

In the first place he accounts as paid to the clerk of Tully drawing the tithes of Tully with his own horse, 12d.

Also to Philip Hogheryn likewise drawing tithes from Tully with a horse of the lord, at board, 15d.

Also to the serving man of sir Thomas, chaplain of Tully, watching tithes of Dengen, 3d.

Also to the serving man of Oliver Haket watching the tithes of Killiney and Loughlinstown, 2s.

---

[1] Picchantibus in original.

Item cuidam C. . . . ken custodienti decimas de villa Roch, & de illis partibus, ii s. iii d.

Item Simoni Harald custodienti decimas de Baly . . . & Fernecost, xviii d.

Item Johanni Punchard furnienti & bracianti ibidem per autumpnum & facienti alia necessaria, ii s.

Item Thome Haket pro sotularibus, iii d.

Item Willelmo Haket pro sotularibus, iii d.

Item Johanni Notyngham pro sotularibus, iiii d.

Item Johanni de Burton clerico pro sotularibus, iiii d.

Item Philippo Taunton pro sotularibus, ii d.

Item Roberto de Taunton custodienti decimas de Dengen, per modicum tempus, iiii d.

Item in cirotecis emptis pro Thoma de Beuley & tota familia in hagardo, xii d.

Item Johanni Haket pro cirotecis secundum consuetudinem, xii d.

Item hominibus Johannis Balygodman ex curialitate, xii d. *Ex curialitate.*

Item hominibus Margarete Ketyngg, ex curialitate, xii d.

Also to a certain . . . . watching the tithes of Rochestown and those parts, 2*s*. 3*d*.

Also to Simon Harald watching the tithes of Baly . . . . and Fernecost, 18*d*.

Also to John Punchard baking and brewing there during the harvest time, and doing other necessary things, 2*s*.

Also to Thomas Haket for shoes, 3*d*.

Also to William Haket for shoes, 3*d*.

Also to John Notyngham for shoes, 4*d*.

Also to John de Burton, clerk, for shoes, 4*d*.

Also to Philip Taunton for shoes, 2*d*.

Also to Robert de Taunton watching tithes of Dengen for a short time, 4*d*.

Also in gloves bought for Thomas de Beuley and the whole household in the haggard, 12*d*.

Also to John Haket for gloves according to custom, 12*d*. *Gratuity.*

Also to the men of John Balygodman, as a gratuity, 12*d*.

Also to the men of Margaret Ketyng, as a gratuity, 12*d*.

Item hominibus Gregorii Taunton ex curialitate, vi d.

Summa xvi s. v d.

Expense autupnales ut pro mensa tenenda.

Die Mercurii proxima post festum Sancti Petri quod dicitur Advincula in pane furnito pro metentibus blada, vii pᶜ frumenti.

Item in cervisia braciata, eodem die, i pᵒ brasii frumenti, & x pᵉ brasii avene.

Item eodem die in carnibus emptis pro Johanne ballivo, ad mensam Johanne Punchard, uno carpentario emendanti vasa, parvo Stephano ibidem clavigero, ii d.

Die Jovis omnia de stauro.

Die Veneris proxima sequente panis & cervisia de stauro, in allece pro eisdem, i d.

Diebus Sabbati, Dominice, Lune, & Martis, omnia de stauro.

Die Mercurii proxima [sequente] in pane furnito i cran. frumenti, in cervisia empta viii d., quo die fuerunt ad mensam, frater Thomas de Beul[ey, Johannes] Notyngham, Johannes

---

Also to the men of Gregory Taunton, as a gratuity, 6*d*.

Total, 16*s*. 5*d*.

Harvest expenses, as for maintaining the table :—

On Wednesday (August 4) next after the feast of S. Peter which is called Ad Vincula, in bread baked for the reapers of the corn, 7 pecks of wheat.

Also in ale brewed on same day, 1 peck of wheat malt, and 10 pecks of oat malt.

Also on same day, in flesh bought for John the bailiff, there being at board John Punchard, a carpenter employed mending vessels, and little Stephen, the doorkeeper, 2*d*.

Thursday.   All from stock.

Friday next following.   Bread and ale from stock ; in herrings for same, 1*d*.

Saturday, Sunday, Monday, and Tuesday.   All from stock.

Wednesday next following.   In bread baked, 1 crannoc of wheat ; in ale bought. 8*d*. On which day there were at table brother Thomas de Beuley, John Notyngham, John Burton, clerks, Thomas

Burton, clerici, Thomas Haket, Willelmus Haket filius Oliveri Haket, Philippus Taunto, garcio . . . una cum supradictis, in carnibus emptis, vi d.

Die Jovis proxima sequente, omnia de stauro.

Die Veneris proxima sequente panis de stauro, in cervisia braciata i pᶜ brasii frumenti & i cran. brasii avene, in allece, ii d.

Die Sabbati proxima sequente, omnia de stauro.

Die Dominica proxima sequente, panis & cervisia de stauro, in carn' empt' xi d.

Die Lune proxima sequente, videlicet in festo Assumpcionis Beate Marie Virginis, omnia de stauro, preter in pullis, i d.

Die Martis proxima sequente in pane furnito, i cran. frumenti.

Die Mercurii proxima sequente, omnia de stauro.

Die Jovis proxima sequente, panis & cervisia de stauro, in carn' empt' iiii d. ob.

Die Veneris panis & cervisia de stauro, in allece, iii d.

Die Sabbati in pane furnito i cran. iii pᶜ frumenti, in cervisia braciata i pᶜ brasii frumenti, & i cran. brasii avene, &c., de stauro.

Haket, William Haket son of Oliver Haket, Philip Taunton, the serving man . . . . together with the above named. In flesh bought, 6*d*.

Thursday next following. All from stock.

Friday. Bread from stock; in ale brewed, 1 peck of wheat malt and 1 crannoc of oat malt; in herrings, 2*d*.

Saturday. All from stock.

Sunday. Bread and ale from stock; in flesh bought, 11*d*.

Monday next following, viz. in the feast of the Assumption of the Blessed Virgin Mary. All from stock, except in chickens, 1*d*.

Tuesday next following. In bread baked, 1 crannoc of wheat.

Wednesday. All from stock.

Thursday. Bread and ale from stock; in flesh bought, 4½*d*.

Friday. Bread and ale from stock; in herrings, 3*d*.

Saturday. In bread baked, 1 crannoc, 3 pecks of wheat; in ale brewed, 1 peck of wheat malt and 1 crannoc of oat malt, &c., from stock.

Die Dominica proxima sequente panis & cervisia de stauro, in carnibus xii d., in pulcin' i d.

Die Lune in vigilia Sancti Bartholomei panis & cervisia de stauro, in allece, ii d.

Diebus Martis & Mercurii, omnia de stauro.

Die Jovis, omnia de stauro.

Die Veneris, panis & cervisia de stauro, in allece ii d., in candelis, ii d.

Die Sabbati proxima sequente panis de stauro, in cervisia braciata i p^e brasii frumenti, i cran. brasii avene, item in pane furnito i cran. iii p^e frumenti.

Die Dominica in festo Decollacionis Sancti Johannis, panis & cervisia de stauro, in carn' . . . xiiii d.

Diebus Lune & Martis omnia de stauro.

Die Mercurii panis & cervisia de stauro, in allece, i d.

Die Jovis omnia de stauro.

Die Veneris panis de stauro, in cervisia empta, pro familia & metentibus, ii s., in allece, ii d.

Sunday. Bread and ale from stock ; in flesh 12*d.* ; in chickens, 1*d.*

Monday, the vigil of S. Bartholomew. Bread and ale from stock ; in herrings, 2*d.*

Tuesday and Wednesday. All from stock.

Thursday. All from stock.

Friday. Bread and ale from stock ; in herrings, 2*d.* ; in candles, 2*d.*

Saturday. Bread and ale from stock ; in ale brewed, 1 peck of wheat malt, 1 crannoc of oat malt. Also in bread baked, 1 crannoc, 3 pecks of wheat.

Sunday, the feast of the beheading of S. John. Bread and ale from stock ; in flesh . . . . 14*d.*

Monday and Tuesday. All from stock.

Wednesday. Bread and ale from stock ; in herrings, 1*d.*

Thursday. All from stock.

Friday. Bread from stock ; in ale bought for the household and reapers, 2*s.* ; in herrings, 2*d.*

Die Sabbati proxima sequente, in pane furnito, i cran. iii pᵉ fru-
    menti, in cervisia braciata i pᵉ brasii frumenti, di. cran.
    brasii avene & i cran. brasii hastiuell.

Die Dominica proxima ante festum Nativitatis Beate Marie
    Virginis pro Priore, fratribus Willelmo de Assheborne,
    Robert de Sancto Neoto & Johanne Comyn, cum eorum
    sequela venientibus ibidem, panis & cervisia de stauro, in
    carn' bovin' empta x d., iu i multone empto xii d., in vino vii d.
    ob., et de stauro ii auce.

Die Lune in vigilia Nativitatis Beate Marie Virginis panis &
    cervisia de stauro, in allece pro familia, ii d.

Die Martis, omnia de stauro.

Die Mercurii proxima sequente, panis de stauro, iu cervisia bra-
    ciata di. pᵉ brasii frumenti, i cran. brasii hastiuell, iu carn'
    boviu', iiii d., et de stauro i porcus.

Die Jovis proxima sequente, omnia de stauro.

Die Veneris omnia de stauro, preter in allece ii d.

Die Sabbati in pane furnito, i cran. iiii pᵉ frumenti, &c., de stauro.

Saturday. In bread baked, 1 crannoc, 3 pecks of wheat; in ale brewed,
    1 peck of wheat malt, half a crannoc of oat malt, and 1 crannoc of
    hastiuell malt.

Sunday next before the feast of the Nativity of the Blessed Virgin
    Mary. For the Prior, brothers William de Assheborne, Robert de
    S. Neot, and John Comyn, with their following coming there,
    bread and ale from the stock; in beef bought 10*d.*; in 1 mutton
    bought, 12*d.*; in wine, 7½*d.*; and from stock 2 geese.

Monday, the vigil of the Nativity of the Blessed Virgin Mary. Bread
    and ale from stock; in herrings for the household, 2*d.*

Tuesday. All from stock.

Wednesday. Bread from stock; in ale brewed, half a peck of wheat
    malt, 1 crannoc of hastiuell malt; in beef 4*d.*; and from stock, 1
    hog.

Thursday. All from stock.

Friday. All from stock, except in herrings, 2*d.*

Saturday. In bread baked, 1 crannoc, 4 pecks of wheat, &c., from
    stock.

Die Dominica proxima sequente, panis & cervisia de stauro, in
carn' multon' pro Gregorio T[aunton], Simone Archebold
cum iiii fratribus, iiii d., et de stauro i porcus, & i auca.

Diebus Lune & Martis in festo Exaltacionis Sancte Crucis, omnia
de stauro.

Die Mercurii proxima sequente, panis de stauro, in cervisia
braciata contra adventum Prioris ii pᶜ brasii frumenti, i
cran. brasii hastiuell & x pᶜ brasii avene, iu i pᶜ salis, iii d.

Die Jovis omnia de stauro, preter in carn' multon', vi d.

De Veneris omnia de stauro preter in cc allecibus emptis de
Johanne Kendal, xvi d., item iu vino empto, v d.

Die Sabbati proxima sequente, in pane furuito contra adventum
domini Archiepiscopi, i cran. iii pᶜ frumenti, in cervisia
braciata ii pᵉ brasii frumenti, i cran. brasii avene, &c. de
stauro.

Die Dominica ante festum Sancti Mathei Apostoli pro domino
Archiepiscopo veniente ibidem, Priore & ejus sequela, panis de
stauro, iu cervisia empta causa Archiepiscopi ii s. i d., iu

Sunday. Bread and ale from stock ; in mutton for Gregory Taunton,
Simon Archebold, with 4 brethren, 4*d.* ; and from stock 1 hog,
and 1 goose.

Monday and Tuesday in feast of Exaltation of the Holy Cross. All from
stock.

Wednesday next following. Bread from stock ; in ale brewed against
the coming of the Prior, 2 pecks of wheat malt, 1 crannoc of
hastiuell malt, and 10 pecks of oat malt ; in 1 peck of salt, 3*d.*

Thursday. All from stock, except in mutton, 6*d.*

Friday. All from stock, except in 200 herrings bought of John Kendal,
16*d.* ; also in wine bought, 5*d.*

Saturday. In bread baked against the coming of the lord Archbishop, 1
crannoc, 3 pecks of wheat ; in ale brewed, 2 pecks of wheat malt,
1 crannoc of oat malt, &c., from stock.

Sunday before the feast of S. Matthew the Apostle. For the lord Archbishop coming there, the Prior and his retinue ; bread from stock ;
in ale bought on account of the Archbishop, 2*s.* 1*d.* ; in fuel

focali empto pro eodem x d., iu vino empto x d., et in ex-
hennio eidem ii multou' de stauro, et in prebenda pro eodem
per ii noctes, ii cran. i pᵉ avene.

Die Lune in vigilia Sancti Mathei, omnia de stauro, preter in
vino pro Archiepiscopo, x d.

Diebus Martis, Mercurii, Jovis, & Veneris, omnia de stauro, cum
lib' Prioris.

Die Sabbati [in] pane furnito, i cran. iiii pᵉ frumenti, in cervisia
braciata i pᵉ brasii frumenti, i cran. brasii avene.

Die Dominica proxima sequente, panis & cervisia de stauro, in
focali pro Priore v d., in pulcin' & ovis emptis ii d., et de
stauro ii multon'.

Diebus Lune & Martis, omnia de stauro.

Die Mercurii in festo Sancti Michaelis, omnia de stauro, preter in
pulcin' i d., et in vino vii d. ob., et de stauro unus porcus.

Die Jovis omnia de stauro, preter in vino pro Priore, v d.

Die Veneris, in pane furnito i cran. iii pᵉ frumenti, in cervisia
braciata i pᵉ brasii frumenti, i cran. brasii hastiuell & v pᵉ
brasii avene, in allece iiii d.

-----

bought for him, 10*d.*; in wine bought, 10*d.*; and as a present to
him, two muttons from stock; and in provender for the same for
two nights, 2 crannocs, 1 peck of oats.

Monday, the vigil of S. Matthew. All from stock, except in wine for the
Archbishop, 10*d.*

Tuesday, Wednesday, Thursday, and Friday. All from stock with the
approval of the Prior.

Saturday. In bread baked, 1 crannoc, 4 pecks of wheat; in ale brewed,
1 peck of wheat malt, 1 crannoc of oat malt.

Sunday. Bread and ale from stock; in fuel for the Prior, 5*d.*; in
chickens and eggs bought, 2*d.*; and from stock, 2 muttons.

Monday and Tuesday. All from stock.

Wednesday the feast of S. Michael. All from stock, except in chickens,
1*d.*; and in wine 7½*d.*; and from stock, 1 hog.

Thursday. All from stock, except in wine for the Prior, 5*d.*

Friday. In bread baked, 1 crannoc, 3 pecks of wheat; in ale brewed,
1 peck of wheat malt, 1 crannoc hastiuell malt, and 5 pecks oat
malt; in herrings, 4*d.*

Die Sabbati sequente, omnia de stauro.

Die Dominica proxima sequente, panis &c. de stauro, in carn' bovin' empt' iiii d. ob., et de stauro ii multon' pro vicecomite, Johanne Haket & eorum sequela, in prebenda iii p^c avene, in vino vi d. quad.

Die Lune proxima sequente, panis de stauro, in cervisia braciata i p^c brasii frumenti, i cran. brasii hastiuell di. cran. brasii avene.

Die Martis proxima ante festum Apostolorum Simonis & Jude, panis de stauro, in cervisia braciata i p^c brasii frumenti, i cran. brasii hastiuell, ix p^c brasii avene, in vino pro Priore veniente ibidem & domino Archiepiscopo, de Novo Castro, x d., in carn' bovin' vi [d.], et de stauro ii multon'.

Die Mercurii in vigilia Simonis & Jude, panis & cervisia de stauro, in vino vi d. quad., in pisse iiii d.

Die Jovis proxima sequente, omnia de stauro, preter in carne v d.

Die Veneris, omnia de stauro, quo die Prior euillavit apud Dublin.

Die Lune in vigilia Sancti Clementis in pane furnito pro Priore veniente ibidem vi p^c frumenti, in cervisia braciata iii p^c

---

Saturday following. All from stock.

Sunday. Bread, &c., from stock; in beef bought, $4\frac{1}{2}d.$; and from the stock, 2 muttons, for the sheriff, John Haket, and their retinue; in provender 3 pecks of oats; in wine, $6\frac{1}{4}d.$

Monday. Bread from stock; for brewing ale, 1 peck of wheat malt, 1 crannoc of hastiuell malt, half a crannoc of oat malt.

Tuesday next before the feast of the Apostles Simon and Jude. Bread from stock; for brewing ale, 1 peck of wheat malt, 1 crannoc of hastiuell malt, 9 pecks of oat malt; in wine for the Prior coming there, and the lord Archbishop from New Castle, 10$d.$; in beef, 6$d.$; and from stock, 2 muttons.

Wednesday, the vigil of Simon and Jude. Bread and ale from stock; in wine, $6\frac{1}{4}d.$; in fish, 4$d.$

Thursday next following. All from stock, except in flesh, 5$d.$

Friday (Oct. 8). All from stock, on which day the Prior went away to Dublin.

Monday (Nov. 22), the vigil of S. Clement. In bread baked for the Prior coming there, 6 pecks of wheat; in ale brewed, 3 pecks of

brasii frumenti, xix p^e brasii avene, iu focali iii d., in vino
viii d. ob., et de stauro v galline.

Summa xxv s. iii d.

SUMMA OMNIUM MISARUM & EXPENSARUM xii li. iii s. ix d. ob. quad.
Et sic superexpendit ii s. iiii d. ob. quad.
Et aquietabit Priorem & Conventum versus quoscunque deomni-
bus compotum supradictum contentis.

[*A slip attached here contains the following three items :—*]

Item computat in pane furnito pro lxiiii sarclantibus ex consuetu- Sarclacio.
dine ut extra ii p^e di. frumenti.

It[em] . . . empta pro eisdem xiii d.

Summa xiii d.

Item computat in iiii^{or} acris prati & i stanguo falcandis ii s. vi d. Falcacio.
pro acra vii d.

Summa ii s. vi d.

EXITUS HAGARDI DE CLONKEN de grano Autumpni, Anno
Regui Regis Edwardi tercii post Conquestum Decimo octavo.
In primis idem reddit compotum de iii cran. v p^e iii sq. receptis Frumen-
tum.

---

wheat malt, 19 pecks of oat malt; in fuel, 3d.; in wine, 8$\frac{1}{2}d$.;
and from stock, 5 hens.

Total, 25s. 3d.

TOTAL of ALL PAYMENTS and EXPENSES, £12 3s. 9$\frac{3}{4}d$.

And so he spent beyond receipts 2s. 4$\frac{3}{4}d$.
And he will secure the Prior and Convent against every person as to all
things contained in the above account.

Also he accounts in bread baked for 64 persons hoeing, by custom as Hoeing.
outside (the roll), 2$\frac{1}{2}$ pecks of wheat.

Also . . . . bought for same, 13d.

Total, 13d.

Also he accounts in mowing 4 acres and 1 staug of meadow, 2s. 6d.; for Mowing.
an acre, 7d.

Total, 2s. 6d.

ISSUE OF THE HAGGARD OF CLONKEN of grain of the Harvest in the
eighteenth year of the reign of King Edward the third since the
Conquest.

In the first place he renders account of 3 crannoes, 5$\frac{3}{4}$ pecks, received of Wheat.

de remanenti compoti precedentis.   Et de iii cran. receptis de
fratre Ricardo . . . celerario per unam talliam contra eundem.

Dominic'.   Item idem reddit compotum de v^{xx} xiii cran. iii p^c receptis de
exitu hagardi supradicti de dominicis ibidem, per unam talliam
contra Johannem Punchard trituratorem.

Decim'.   Item de iiii^{xx} vii cran. ii p^c receptis de exitu de hagardo de decimis
per unam talliam contra dictum Johannem.

Et de iiii cran. iiii p^c receptis de Petro Howell prodecim is de
Balymolewhan.

Summa x^{xx} xi cran. vi p^c iii sq.

. . . Rogero   De quibus idem computat liberatum Nicholao Taunton servienti
de Pu[le]s-
don cong-   pro semine per talliam contra eundem, xxvii cran. i p^c di.
nato Prioris
. . . precep-   Item liberatum fratri Roberto de Sancto Neot' celerario per unam
to eiusdem.   talliam contra eundem, v^{xx} ix cran.

Item in pane furnito pro duobus . . . videlicet pro uno ad semen
yemale & [alio] ad semen quadragesimale, & quod erat de
xiiii carucis ad quas fuerunt xxviii viri, iiii p^c.

----

the balance remaining from the preceding account.   And of 3
crannocs received of brother Richard [de S. Neot] cellarer as by a
tally against him.

Demesne.   Also he renders account of 113 crannocs, 3 pecks, received of the issue of
the abovesaid haggard, of the demesnes there, as by a tally against
John Punchard the thresher.

Tithes.   Also of 87 crannocs, 2 pecks, received of the issue of the haggard, of the
tithes, as by a tally against said John

And of 4 crannocs, 4 pecks received of Peter Howell for the tithes of
Murphystown.

Total 211 crannocs, 6¾ pecks.

[Delivered]   Of which he accounts as delivered to Nicholas Taunton serjeant, for seed,
to Roger de
Pulesdon,   as by tally against him, 27 crannocs, 1½ peck.
kinsman of   Also delivered to brother Richard de S. Neot, cellarer, as by one tally
the Prior,   against him, 109 crannocs.
by his com-
mand. . . .   Also in bread baked for two [customary ploughings], viz. for one at
winter seedtime, and another at Lent seedtime, and which was
of 14 ploughs to which were 28 men, 4 pecks.

Item in brasio fuso unde respondebit inferius, xiii cran. & di p^c.

Item liberatum per preceptum domini Prioris ex dono eiusdem, ut patet per sex precepta sub sigillo eiusdem, v cran i p^c.

Item in mixtura ad poturam famulorum ut inferius, xxix cran. v p^c & sq.

Item cuidam garcioni custodienti agnos de decima ii p^c.

Item cuidam custodienti porcos domini ne forirent ad nocumentum vicinorum, ii p^c.

Item in pane furnito pro domino Priore cum ejus sequela veniente ibidem per autumpnum, domino Archiepiscopo veniente ibidem diversimode de Novo Castro, & de patria, & pro diversa familia & operariis per autumpnum, xiiii cran. i p^c.

Item in venditione ut infra, vii cran. v. p^c.

Item Willelmo Frankan pro capite suo sanando quod frangebatur quando domus vaccarum cecidit, precepto Senescalli ii p^c.

Item lxiiii sarclatoribus ex consuetudine, in pane furnito, ii p^c di.

Summa x^xx xii cran. iii sq. Et sic incremento i p^c.

Item reddit compotum de iiii cran. receptis de exitu Hagardi de dominicis per i talliam contra Johannem Punchard.

Marginal notes:
Item liberatum Carragh olyn hibernico ex dono Prioris, iiii p'. Item fratri J. de Castro per preceptum i cran. i p^c.

Hastinell. Dominic'.

Also malted, whereof he will answer below, 13 crannocs and half a peck.

Also delivered by command of the lord Prior as his gift, as appears by six orders under his seal, 5 crannocs, 1 peck.

Also in mixed corn for the food of the servants as below, 29 crannocs, 5¼ pecks.

Also to a serving man keeping the tithe lambs, 2 pecks.

Also a certain man keeping the pigs of the lord (Prior) lest they should be an injury of the neighbours, 2 pecks.

Also in bread baked for the lord Prior with his retinue coming there for the harvest, the lord Archbishop coming there at different times from New Castle, and from the country, and different domestics and workmen during the harvest, 14 crannocs, 1 peck.

Also in sales as within, 7 crannocs, 5 pecks.

Also to William Frankan for healing his head which was broken when the cow house fell, by command of the seneschal, 2 pecks.

Also 64 hoers by custom, in bread baked, 2½ pecks.

Total, 212 crannocs, ¾ peck, and so of increase, 1 peck.

Also he renders account of 4 crannocs received of the issue of the haggard of the demesnes, as by 1 tally against John Punchard.

Marginal notes:
Also delivered to Carragh Olyn, an Irishman, of the gift of the Prior, 4 pecks. Also to brother J. de Castro by command 1 crannoc 1 peck.

Hastinell. demesnes.

Decim'.   Et de ii cran. receptis de exitu hagardi de decimis per i talliam contra dictum Johannem.

Summa vi cran.

Quos computat in brasio fuso unde respondebit inferius. Et nihil remanet.

Ordium.   Item idem reddit compotum de iiii cran. receptis de dicto exitu de dominicis per unam talliam contra dictum Johannem Punchard.

Et de x cran. receptis de dicto exitu videlicet de decimis per i talliam contra eundem.

Summa xiiii cran.

De quibus idem computat liberatum Nicholao Taunton servienti pro semine per i talliam contra eundem i cran vi p^c.

Item in brasio fuso, unde respond[ebit] xii cran. ii p^c.

Summa ut supra. Et nihil remanet.

Fabe & pise.   Item idem reddit compotum de ii cran. v p^c receptis de remanenti compoti precedentis.

Dominic'.   Et de v. cran. vii p^c receptis de dicto exitu de dominicis per i talliam contra dictum Johannem Punchard.

Tithes.   And of 2 crannocs received of the issue of the haggard, from tithes, as by one tally against said John.

Total, 6 crannocs.

Which he accounts for as malted, whereof he will answer below. And nothing remains.

Barley.   Also he renders account of 4 crannocs received of said issue of the demesnes, as by 1 tally against said John Punchard.

And of 10 crannocs received of the said issue, viz. of the tithes, as by 1 tally against the same.

Total, 14 crannocs.

Of which he accounts as delivered to Nicholas Taunton, serjeant, for seed, by 1 tally against him, 1 crannoc, 6 pecks.

Also malted, whereof he will answer, 12 crannocs, 2 pecks.

Total as above, and nothing remains.

Beans and Peas.   Also he renders account of 2 crannocs, 5 pecks, received of the balance of preceding account.

Demesnes.   And of 5 crannocs, 7 pecks of said issue of the demesnes, as by 1 tally against said John Punchard.

Et de xiii cran. i p^c de dicto exitu de decimis per i talliam contra Decim'.
     dictum Johannem Punchard.

Summa xxi cran. v p^c.

De quibus idem computat liberatum Nicholao Chamburleyn
     ballivo de Glasnevyn, per unam talliam contra eundem, iii
     cran. ii p^c.

Item liberatum Hugoni [Belyng] ballivo de Gorman per unam
     talliam contra eundem vi cran.

Item in mixtura ad poturam famulorum ut inferius, xi cran. vii p^c.

Item liberatum fratri Johanni Comyn pro pane pro equo suo inde
     furniendo iiii p^c.

Summa ut supra.   Et nihil remanet.

Item idem reddit compotum de lvii cran. ix. p^c receptis de dicto Avene.
     exitu de dominicis per talliam contra dictum Johannem Dominic.
     Punchard.

Et de lv cran. iiii p^c receptis de dicto exitu de decimis per talliam Decim'.
     contra dictum Johannem Punchard.

Et de iiii cran. receptis de Petro Howell pro decimis de Balymol-
     whan.

Summa v^{xx} xvi cran. xiii p^c.

And of 13 crannocs, 1 peck, of said issue, of the tithes, as by a tally Tithes.
     against said John Punchard.

Total, 21 crannocs, 5 pecks.

Of which he accounts as delivered to Nicholas Chamburleyn, bailiff of
     Glasnevin, as by a tally against him, 3 crannocs, 2 pecks.

Also delivered to Hugh Belyng, bailiff of Gorman, as by a tally against
     him, 6 crannocs.

Also in mixed corn for food of the servants as below, 11 crannocs,
     7 pecks.

Also delivered to brother John Comyn to bake bread for his horse,
     4 pecks.

Total as above, and nothing remains.

Also he renders account of 57 crannocs, 9 pecks, received of said issue, of Oats.
     the demesnes, as by tally against said John Punchard. Demesnes.

And of 55 crannocs, 4 pecks, received of said issue, of tithes, as by tally Tithes.
     against said John Punchard.

And of 4 crannocs received of Peter Howell for tithes of Murphystown.

Total, 116 crannocs, 13 pecks.

De quibus idem computat liberatum Nicholao **Taunton** servienti pro semine ibidem per talliam contra eundem, xxii cran. **v** p^c.

Item liberatum Sarre siccatrici brasii apud Gorman pro brasio inde faciendo, vii cran. vi p^c.

Item liberatum Ricardo Palefridario domini Prioris pro prebenda palefridi sui & aliorum equorum diversimode ibidem cum ipso venientium, per talliam contra dictum Ricardum, iii cran. ii p^c.

Item Johanni carectario de celario pro prebenda equorum de celar[io] per diversas vices ix p^c.

Item liberatum Gilberto Lomp, pro prebenda equorum ad carectam, per talliam contra eundem, i cran.

Item liberatum Johanni Mar . . . [ave]nario domini Archiepiscopi, pro prebenda equorum dicti domini Archiepiscopi, per i talliam contra dictum Avenarium per diversas vices, **v** cran. xi p^c.

Item liberatum . . . Comyn pro farina pro legumine i cran.

Item in prebenda equorum Wlfranni de Berneuall, venientis ibidem cum pluribus eius de exercitu . . .

Of which he accounts as delivered to Nicholas Taunton, serjeant, for seed there, as by tally against him, 22 crannocs, 5 pecks.

Also delivered to Sarra, the woman drying malt at Gorman, to make malt, 7 crannocs, 6 pecks.

Also delivered to Richard, palfreykeeper of the lord Prior, for provender of his palfrey and other horses coming there occasionally with him, as by tally against said Richard, 3 crannocs, 2 pecks.

Also to John carter of the cellar, for provender of the horses of the cellar on several occasions, 9 pecks.

Also delivered to Gilbert Lomp, for provender of the cart horses, as by tally against him, 1 crannoc.

Also delivered to John Mar . . ., avener of the lord archbishop, for provender of the horses of the said lord archbishop, as by a tally against the said avener, on several occasions, 5 crannocs, 11 pecks,

Also delivered to . . . . Comyn for meal for pottage, 1 crannoc.

Also in provender of horses of Wulfran de Bernevall, coming there with many of his men of the army . . . .

[Item] liberatum Michaeli Mongomery, vicecomiti per preceptum sub sigillo domini, di. cran.

Item in farina pro legumine in autumpno, & pro diversis advent . . . . v p^c.

Item in brasio fuso unde respondebit inferius, lxxiiii cran. iii p^c.

> Summa v^{xx} xvi cran. viii p^c. Et rem[anent v p^c de quibus idem] computat in prebenda equorum Senescalli diversimode ibidem venientis pro curia tenenda & aliis necessariis faciendis. Et sic . . .

Tolnetum Molendini.

Item idem reddit compotum de ii cran. v p^c receptis de tolneto molendini Johannis Haket. Quod [computat in] mixtura ad poturam famulorum ut inferius. Et nihil remanet.

Mixtura ad poturam famulorum.

Item idem reddit compotum de xxix cran. v p^c & sq. frumenti receptis ut supra ad poturam famulorum.

Et de xi cran. vii p^c fabarum & pisarum receptis ut supra pro eodem.

Also delivered to Michael Mongomery, sheriff, by command under seal of the lord (Prior), half a crannoc.

Also in meal for pottage in harvest, and for different visits . . . . 5 pecks.

Also malted, whereof he will answer below, 74 crannocs, 3 pecks.

> Total, 116 crannocs, 8 pecks; and there remain 5 pecks, as to which he accounts in provender of horses of the seneschal coming there occasionally to hold court, and transact other necessary business. And so . . . .

Tolls of the Mill:—

Also he renders account of 2 crannocs, 5 pecks, received of the toll of the mill of John Haket. Which he accounts for in mixed corn for food of the servants as below. And nothing remains.

Mixed corn for food of the servants:—

Also he renders account of 29 crannocs, 5½ pecks of wheat received as above for food of the servants.

And of 11 crannocs, 7 pecks of beans and peas received as above for same.

Et de ii cran. v p^c receptis de tolueto molendini ut supra pro eodem.

Summa xliiii cran. i p^c i sq.

De quibus idem computat in potura unius ballivi videlicet Johannis Chamburleyn, ab in crastino Sancti Dunstani, usque festum Sancti Petri Advincula proximum sequens videlicet per xlii septimanas iiii cran. v p^c di. & sic capit viii p^c cumul' per x septimanas.

Item in potura unius servientis, unius janitoris, unius carectarii, & quatuor carucariorum, a festo Sancti Petri Advincula, usque idem festum proximum sequens, anno revoluto, per lii septimanas, xix cran. iii p^c di. & sq. frumenti, x cran. & iiii p^c fabarum & pisarum, & ii cran. v p^c bladi de tolueto molendini, & sic quilibet capit viii p^c frumenti rasa mensura per x septimanas, quod est per cumulum, vi p^c sq. frumenti, & quilibet capit de fabis pisis & blado de tolueto viii p^c cumul' pro cran., per x septimanas.

Item in potura Mariote siccantis & facientis brasium ibidem a festo Sancti Petri Advincula, usque in diem dominicam

---

And of 2 crannocs, 5 pecks, received of the toll of the mill as above for same.

Total, 44 crannocs, 1¼ peck.

Of which he accounts in food of 1 bailiff, viz. John Chamburleyn, from the morrow of S. Dunstan to the feast of S. Peter ad Vincula (Aug. 1) next following, viz. for 42 weeks, 4 crannocs, 5½ pecks, and so he takes 8 pecks heaped measure for 10 weeks.

Also in food of 1 serjeant, 1 door-keeper, 1 carter, and 4 ploughmen, from the feast of S. Peter ad Vincula to the same feast next following in the succeeding year, for 52 weeks, 19 crannocs, 3¾ pecks of wheat, 10 crannocs, 4 pecks of beans and peas, and 2 crannocs, 5 pecks of corn from the toll of the mill, and so each takes 8 pecks of wheat level measure for 10 weeks, which is by heaped measure 6¼ pecks of wheat, and each takes of beans, peas, and corn from the toll, 8 pecks heaped for a crannoc for 10 weeks.

Also in food of Mariota drying and making malt there from the feast of S. Peter ad Vincula to the Sunday (May 15) next before the feast of proximam ante festum Sancti Duustani per xli septimanas, iii cran. frumenti & vi pᵉ fabarum & pisarum, & capit viii pᵃ frumenti rasa mensura, ut supra, & viii pᵉ fabarum & pisarum ut supra.

Item in potura unius vaccarii a festo Sancti Andree Apostoli usque diem dominicam proximam ante festum Sancti Duustani per xxiii septimanas & iii dies i cran. iii pᵉ di. frumenti, & v pᵉ fabarum & pisarum & capit ut supra.

Item in potura unius custodientis vaccas & agnos a festo Pentecostes usque festum Sancti Petri quod dicitur Advincula proximum sequens, videlicet per xi septimanas vi pᵉ & di. frumenti, per cumulum & capit cran., ut supra.

Summa ut supra. Et nihil remanet.

In primis idem reddit compotum de iiii pᵉ receptis de remanenti Brasium frumenti. compoti precedentis.

Et de iii pᵉ receptis de Alicia Raggeley ex mutuo.

Et de xiii cran. & di. pᵉ receptis de frumento, ut supra in brasio fuso.

Summa xiiii cran. di. pᵉ.

S. Dunstan, for 41 weeks, 3 crannocs of wheat, and 6 pecks of beans and peas, and she takes 8 pecks of wheat level measure as above, and 8 pecks of beans and peas as above.

Also in food of one cowherd from the feast of S. Andrew the apostle (Nov. 30) to the Sunday (May 15) next before the feast of S. Dunstan, for 23 weeks and 3 days, 1 crannoc, 3½ pecks of wheat, and 5 pecks of beans and peas, and he takes as above.

Also in food of one keeper of cows and lambs from the feast of Pentecost (May 15) to the feast of S. Peter which is called Ad Vincula next following, viz. for 11 weeks, 6½ pecks of wheat by heaped measure, and he takes the crannoc as above.

Total as above. And nothing remains.

In the first place he renders account of 4 pecks received of the balance Malt of Wheat. of preceding account.

And of 3 pecks received of Alice Raggeley as a loan.

And of 13 crannocs and half a peck received as above from the wheat malted.

Total 14 crannocs, half a peck.

De quibus in cervisia braciata pro diversa familia pro blado intrando in autumpno & pro diversis adventibus domini Archiepiscopi & Prioris cum eorum sequel' diversimode ut patet in
uno rotulo inde confecto, ii cran. ii p⁴ di.

Item liberatum fratri Roberto de Sancto Neoto per i talliam contra
eundem xi cran. ii p⁴.

> Summa xiii cran. iiii p⁴ di.   Et remanent in granario iii [p⁴],
> unde respondebit in compoto suo proximo subsequente.

Brasium
hastiuell.

Item idem reddit compotum de vi cran. receptis ut de hastiuell
in brasio fuso.

Quod computat in cervisia [bra]ciata pro cust' autumpni, adventibus dictorum domini Archiepiscopi & domini Prioris ut patet
in supradicto rotulo.   Et nihil remauet.

Brasium
ordei.

Item idem reddit compotum de xii cran. ii p⁴ receptis ut supra,
de ordeo fuso.

De quibus idem computat liberatum fratri Roberto de Sancto
Neoto per unam talliam contra eundem, xi cran. ii p⁴.

> Summa xi cran. ii p⁴.   Et remanet i cran.

Of which in ale brewed for divers servants for bringing in corn in
harvest, and for divers visits of the lord Archbishop and Prior
with their retinues occasionally, as appears in a roll made of them, ·
2 crannoes, 2½ pecks.

Also delivered to brother Robert de S. Neot, as by one tally against him,
11 crannoes, 2 pecks.

> Total 13 crannoes, 4½ pecks.   And there remain in the barn
> 3 pecks, whereof he will answer in his account next fol-
> lowing.

Malt of
Hastiuell.

Also he renders account of 6 crannoes received of hastiuell malted.
Which he accounts for in ale brewed for expenditure in harvest, visits of
the said lord archbishop and lord Prior, as appears in the aforesaid
roll.   And nothing remains.

Malt of
Barley.

Also he renders account of 12 crannoes, 2 pecks, received as above, of
barley malted.

Of which he accounts as delivered to brother Robert de S. Neot, as by
one tally against him, 11 crannoes, 2 pecks.

> Total, 11 crannoes, 2 pecks.   And there remains 1 crannoe.

Item idem reddit compotum de ii cran. v p^c receptis de re- <small>Brasium.</small>
manenti compoti precedentis. <small>Avene.</small>

Et de iii cran. di. receptis de Alicia Raggeley ex mutuo.

Et de iiii p^c receptis de tolneto molendini Johannis Haket.

Et de lxxiiii cran. iii p^c receptis ut supra do avena in brasio fuso.

Summa iiii^{xx} cran. v p^c.

De quibus idem computat in cervisia braciata pro cus . . . autumpni & pro supradictis . . . diversimode venientibus, ut
patet in eodem rotulo, ix cran. xi p^c.

Item liberatum fratri Roberto de Sancto Neoto celerario per unam
talliam contra eundem lxvi cran. di.

> Summa lxxvi cran. iiii p^c. Et remanent in granario iiii
> cran. i p^c unde respondebit in compoto suo proximo
> subsequente.

Also he renders account of 2 crannocs, 5 pecks, received of the balance of <small>Malt of</small>
preceding account. <small>Oats.</small>

And of 3½ crannocs received of Alice Raggeley as a loan.

And of 4 pecks received of the mill toll of John Haket.

And of 74 crannocs, 3 pecks, received as above, of oats malted.

> Total, 80 crannocs. 5 pecks.

Of which he accounts in ale brewed for expenditure in harvest and for
the aforesaid . . . . at different times coming, as appears in the
same roll, 9 crannocs, 11 pecks.

Also delivered to brother Robert de S. Neot, cellarer, by one tally against
him, 66½ crannocs.

> Total, 76 crannocs, 4 pecks. And there remain in the barn, 4
> crannocs, 1 peck, for which he will answer in his account
> next following.

IV.

Expense Fratris Johannis Comyn de Officio Senescalli a
Natale Domini Anno Domini m⁰. ccc^{mo}. xliiii^{to} usque ——.

Expense necessarie ad usum Prioris a festo Circumcisionis Domini.

In primis idem computat in una pellura empta pro capa Prioris,
      iii s.

Item in duabus pelluris emptis pro armigeris Prioris precepto
      ejusdem, iiii s.

Item in una pellura empta pro capucio Prioris, xii d.

Item in una pellura empta precepto Prioris & lib. Johanni de
      Evesham, ii s. iii d.

Item lib. Johanni Newrk cissori pro ii robis aptandis ad usum
      Prioris una videlicet contra Natalem Domini & una contra
      Pascham, xvi d.

Item eidem Johanni pro duabus amys aptandis pro Priore, vi d.

Item eidem pro aptacione unius tunice & unius capucii pro
      Laurencio consanguineo Prioris contra Natalem Domini &
      pro cindone & cerico, vii d.

———————————

Expenses of Brother John Comyn, in the office of Seneschal from
      Christmas a.d. 1344, to ——.

Necessary expenses for the use of the Prior, from the feast of the Circum-
      cision of the Lord.

In the first place he accounts in a skin with fur bought for the Prior's
      mantle, 3*s.*

Also in two skins bought for the esquires of the Prior, by his command,
      4*s.*

Also in one skin bought for the Prior's hood, 12*d.*

Also in one skin bought by command of the Prior and given to John de
      Evesham, 2*s.* 3*d.*

Also paid to John Newrk, tailor, for preparing two robes for the use of the
      Prior, one for Christmas and one for Easter, 16*d.*

Also to same John for preparing two amices for the Prior, 6*d.*

Also for preparing a coat and a hood for Laurence, kinsman of the Prior,
      for Christmas, and for fine linen and silk, 7*d.*

Item in iii paribus cirotecarum emptis pro domino Archiepiscopo, magistro Willelmo Broun & domino Priore, xxi d. ob.

Item lib. Waltero pellipario pro una pellura empta ad usum Prioris, xxi d.

Item in panno laneo empto pro capuciis & Amys ad usum Prioris faciendis, viii s.

Item in pellura empta pro magna amisia Prioris & una alia minori pro eodem, iii s. vi d.

Item in una pellura empta pro supertunica Prioris, ii s. ii d.

Item in i alia pellura empta pro una supertunica Prioris, iii s.

Item in calciamento empto pro Laurencio consanguineo Prioris, x d.

Item lib. Juliane Schipman pro factura duarum rochettarum ad usum Prioris, xii d.

Item in i duodeno salsariorum de peutreo, i duodeno discorum, i duodeno platellorum de peutreo & ii charjours ad usum Prioris, vii s.

Item in ii telis emptis pro gurthes & supercingulis inde faciendis, vi d.

Also in 3 pairs of gloves bought for the lord Archbishop, master William Broun, and the lord Prior, 21½*d.*

Also paid to Walter the skinner, for one skin bought for the use of the Prior, 21*d.*

Also in woollen cloth bought for making hoods and amices for the use of the Prior, 8*s.*

Also in a skin bought for the Prior's great amice, and another lesser one for him, 3*s.* 6*d.*

Also in a skin bought for a surcoat of the Prior, 2*s.* 2*d.*

Also in one other skin bought for a surcoat of the Prior, 3*s.*

Also in shoes bought for Laurence, kinsman of the Prior, 10*d.*

Also paid to Juliana Schipman for the making of two rochets for the use of the Prior, 12*d.*

Also in one dozen saucers of pewter (or tin), one dozen of dishes, one dozen plates of pewter, and two chargers, for the use of the Prior, 7*s.*

Also in two pieces of web bought for making girths and surcingles, 6*d.*

Item dat. Waltero aurifabro pro dictis vasis de peutreo signandis
  ex certa convencione, ix d.

Item in uno pare cirotecarum empto ad usum Prioris, v d.

Item in panno laneo empto pro duabus tunicis inde ad usum
  Prioris faciendis, ii s. xi d.

Item in una mensa empta pro camera Prioris, vi s. i d.

In aptacione iiii tunicarum pro Priore citra Pascham, xvi d.

Ferura.   Item computat in ferura haken a festo Sancti Michaelis usque
  festum Beati Patricii, xxiii d. quad.

Item in ferura eorundem ab illo festo usque diem Mercurii in festo
  Apostolorum Petri & Pauli, iii s. x d.

Item in ferura iii equorum de celario per primum tempus, iiii s.
  ii d. quad.

Item in ferura eorundem per ultimum tempus, xviii d.

Expense   In primis idem computat lib. pro quodam amerciamento in Thelo-
for'.   neo ad sectam Willelmi de Brendewode, vi d.

Item servienti de Theloneo pro feodo suo, i d.

Item cuidam garcioni portanti unam literam ad priorem de
  Holpatrik ex parte domini Prioris, i d.

————————

Also given to Walter the goldsmith for marking the said pewter vessels,
  by a settled agreement. 9*d*.

Also in one pair of gloves bought for the use of the Prior, 5*d*.

Also in woollen cloth bought for making two coats for the use of the
  Prior, 2*s*. 11*d*.

Also in one table bought for the Prior's chamber, 6*s*. 1*d*.

In preparing 4 coats for the Prior, since Easter, 16*d*.

Shoeing.   Also he accounts in shoeing the hackney from the feast of S. Michael
  (Sept. 29) to the feast of S. Patrick (March 17), 23¼*d*.

Also in shoeing the same from that feast to Wednesday, the feast of the
  Apostles Peter and Paul (June 29), 3*s*. 10*d*.

Also in shoeing 3 horses of the cellar during the first period, 4*s*. 2¼*d*.

Also in shoeing them for the last period, 18*d*.

Extern   In the first place he accounts as delivered for a certain amercement in the
expenses.   Tholsel court at the suit of William de Brendewode, 6*d*.

Also to the serjeant of the Tholsel, for his fee, 1*d*.

Also to a certain serving man carrying a letter to the prior of Holmpatrick, on behalf of the lord Prior, 1*d*.

Item cuidam garcioni eunti apud Balycor super negociis domini
videlicet pro pecunia petenda, i d.

Item lib. cuidam servienti ex dono Prioris, ii d.

Item cuidam nuncio Geraldi Obryn precepto Prioris, ii d.

Item uni garcioni eunti ad dominum Johannem Barby pro negociis domus, i d.

Item Willelmo cissori ex dono Prioris, iiii d.

Item cuidam garcioni eunti apud Kylcolyn & Kyldar super negociis Prioris, ii d.

Item cuidam garcioni de molendino molanti frumentum ex dono
Prioris, iiii d.

Item uni garcioni portanti unam literam ad magistrum Hugonem
de Saltu pro negociis domus, i d.

Item uni garcioni portanti unum breve videlicet breve prohibi-
cionis apud Kylkolyn, iiii d.

Item pro dicto brevi adquirendo, iii s. vi d.

Item lib. [ar]migeris & clericis domini Prioris pro oblacionibus
ad sepulturam Henrici nuper coci domini Archiepiscopi,
ii d.

Also to a certain serving man going to Ballycore, upon business of the lord
(Prior), to apply for money, 1*d.*

Also given to a certain serjeant, of the gift of the Prior, 2*d.*

Also to a certain messenger of Gerald Obryn, by command of the Prior,
2*d.*

Also to a certain serving man going to sir John Barby, on business of the
house, 1*d.*

Also to William the tailor, of the gift of the Prior, 4*d.*

Also to a certain serving man going to Kilcullen and Kildare upon
business of the Prior, 2*d.*

Also to a certain serving man of the mill grinding wheat, of the gift of
the Prior, 4*d.*

Also to a serving man carrying a letter to master Hugh de Saltu, on
business of the house, 1*d.*

Also to a serving man carrying a writ, viz. a writ of prohibition, to
Kilcullen, 4*d.*

Also for obtaining said writ, 3*s.* 6*d.*

Also given to the esquires and clerks of the lord Prior for oblations at the
burial of Henry, late cook of the lord Archbishop, 2*d.*

Item in panno empto & dato provisoribus Capitalis Justiciarii Hibernie ut nobis forent favorabiliores pro caligis sibi inde faciendis, ii s. viii d.

Item lib. servientibus majoris post Natalem Domini pro oblacionibus suis ex curialitate, xii d.

Item servientibus de Theloneo ex curialitate pro oblacionibus, vi d.

Item communibus servientibus, xii d.

Item servientibus in vigilia, vi d.

Item cuidam garcioni eunti apud Kylcolyn pro negociis ecclesiam eiusdem tangentibus eo tempore quo magister Thomas Giffard primo erat presentatus ad eandem, ii d.

Item lib. Rogero de Pulesdon armigero & consanguineo Prioris, precepto domini, xvi d.

Item cuidam garcioni eunti apud Kyldar pro oleo & crismate ibidem petendis, ii d.

Item lib. Petro camerario Prioris pro Priore & ejus sequela simul equitantibus apud Kyldar ad assisam in omnibus sumptibus ibidem & per viam eundo & redeundo, xiiii d.

Also in cloth bought and given to the purveyors of the Chief Justiciary of Ireland that they may be more favourable to us; to make hose of it for them, 2*s*. 8*d*.

Also given to the serjeants of the mayor, after Christmas, for their oblations, as a gratuity, 12*d*.

Also to the serjeants of the Tholsel, as a gratuity, for oblations, 6*d*.

Also to the common serjeants, 12*d*.

Also to the serjeants in the watch, 6*d*.

Also to a certain serving man going to Kilcullen, on business touching the church of that place, at the time when master Thomas Giffard first was presented to the same, 2*d*.

Also given to Roger de Pulesdon, esquire and kinsman of the Prior, by command of the lord (Prior), 16*d*.

Also to a certain serving man going to Kildare to procure oil and chrism there, 2*d*.

Also given to Peter the Prior's chamberlain, for the Prior and his retinue riding together to Kildare to the Assize, in all expenses there and by the way going and returning, 14*d*.

Item computat in expensis senescalli cum iii equis & iii hominibus equitantibus apud Kyldar pro diversis negociis ibidem expediendis ut pro rotis & aliis neccessariis ibidem providendis & emendis, per ii dies eundo & redeundo, xii d. ob.

Item in expensis eiusdem senescalli cum uno clerico & uno garcione cum iii equis equitantibus apud Droghda pro uno brevi de super modo & causa ad Cancellarium tunc ibidem petendo, a die dominica prima xlª e. usque diem Martis proximam sequentem & pro una curia apud Dromsalan tenenda die Lune in crastino dicte diei dominice. In pane cer[visia] vino & pisse emptis, ix d. In feno, pane, & avena emptis pro iii equis, vi d. ob.

Item in expensis supradictorum dicto die Martis apud Droghda & eodem die equitancium apud Balyscadan pro una curia ibidem tenenda & iterum eodem die redeuncium apud Droghda pro dicto brevi. In pane vino cervisia & pisse, emptis, xiii d. In pane, feno, & avena emptis pro equis, xi d. In ferura equorum eodem die, ii d. ob.

Item in expensis supradictorum commorancium apud Droghda diebus Mercurii & Jovis prox. sequentibus ad expectandum

---

Also he accounts in expenses of the seneschal with 3 horses and 3 men riding to Kildare to transact divers business there, as for providing and buying wheels and other necessaries there, for 2 days going and returning, 12½d.

Also in expenses of the same seneschal with one clerk and one serving man, with 3 horses, riding to Drogheda to the Chancellor, then being there, to procure a writ of "Super modo et causa," from the first Sunday of Lent to the Tuesday next following, and to hold a court at Drumshallon on Monday, the morrow of the said Sunday. In bread, ale, wine, and fish bought, 9d. ; in hay, bread, and oats bought for 3 horses, 6½d.

Also in expenses of the aforesaid on the said Tuesday at Drogheda, and on same day riding to Balscaddan to hold a court there, and again on same day returning to Drogheda for the said writ. In bread, wine, ale, and fish bought, 13d. ; in bread, hay, and oats bought for the horses, 11d. ; in shoeing of the horses on same day, 2½d.

Also in expenses of the aforesaid persons remaining at Drogheda, on Wednesday and Thursday next following, to await Roger de

Rogerum de Preston pro pecunia ab eo habenda. In pane
vino cervisia & pisse emptis, xxiii d. In pane feno & avena
pro equis emptis, xvi d.

Item lib. pro dicto brevi, xii d.

Item die Veneris proxima sequente. In vino empto pro supradictis comedentibus apud Holpatryk cum Priore ibidem,
iiii d.

Item uni garcioni eunti post Hugonem Broun narratorem pro
consilio de dicto brevi de se habendo, i d.

Item lib. Willelmo de Drayton, clerico cancellar' ex dono Prioris
pro consilio suo & auxilio pro quodam brevi perquirendo
habendis, iii s. iiii d.

Item lib. clericis cancellar' pro sigillo dicti brevis, iii s. x d.

Item cuidam garcioni eunti apud Le Naas pro dicto brevi de supersedeas petendo, ii d.

Item lib. Ricardo de Deen subescaetori ex certa convencione ne
ecclesiam causa temporalium in absencia magistri sui noce-
ret nec in aliquo aggravaret, xiii s. iiii d.

Preston to receive money from him. In bread, wine, ale, and
fish bought, 23*d*. ; in bread, hay, and oats, bought for horses,
16*d*.

Also paid for said writ, 12*d*.

Also Friday next following. In wine bought for the aforesaid persons
eating at Holmpatrick with the Prior there, 4*d*.

Also to a serving man going after Hugh Broun, pleader, to obtain advice
as to the said writ, 1*d*.

Also given to William de Drayton, clerk of the chancellor (or Chancery)
of the gift of the Prior, to have his counsel and help for procuring a certain writ, 3*s*. 4*d*.

Also given to the clerks of the chancellor (or Chancery), for the seal of
the said writ, 3*s*. 10*d*.

Also to a certain serving man going to the Naas to procure the said writ
of " supersedeas," 2*d*.

Also given to Richard de Deen, sub-escheator by a settled agreement,
that he should not injure the church on account of its temporalities, in the absence of his master, nor incommode it in anything,
13*s*. 4*d*.

Item Ricardo de Cestria clerico suo occasione predicta, iii s. iiii d.

Item in expensis fratris Johannis Comyn equitantis apud Stabanan pro escaetore petendo pro breve de supersedeas sibi deliberando videlicet de temporalibus qui escaetor tunc erat in comitiam Justiciarii versus Ultoniam per iii dies eundo & redeundo & alia vice pro dicto senescallo equitante de Dublin apud Droghda ad consulendum cum Godefrido Folyngham super dictis negociis, pro se, duobus equis & uno garcione, iii s. iii d.

Item in cirotecis emptis ad usum dicti Godefridi ex curialitate, x d.

Item dat. eidem Godefrido precepto domini ex dono eiusdem ex curialitate, vi s. viii d.

Item in expensis supprioris magistri Nicholai de Brankeston cum duobus equis & uno garcione equitancium & euncium apud Balymor ad dominum Archiepiscopum pro negociis de Kylcolyn, xii d.

Item in expensis eorundem magistri Thome de Kylmor simul equitantium apud Kylcolyn cum v equis iii garcionibus coram commissario domini Archiepiscopi contra magistrum

---

Also to Richard de Chester, his clerk, at the same time, 3s. 4d.

Also in expenses of brother John Comyn riding to Stabannan to seek the escheator, to deliver to him the writ of "supersedeas," viz. concerning the temporalities, which escheator was then in the company of the Justiciary (going) against Ulster; for 3 days going and returning; and another time for the said seneschal riding from Dublin to Drogheda to consult with Godfrey Folyngham upon the said matters; for himself, two horses, and a serving man, 3s. 3d.

Also in gloves bought for the use of said Godfrey, as a gratuity, 10d.

Also given to same Godfrey by command of the lord (Prior), of his gift, as a gratuity, 6s. 8d.

Also in expenses of the sub-prior, master Nicholas de Brankeston, with two horses and one serving man, riding and going to Ballymore to the lord Archbishop for the affairs of Kilcullen, 12d.

Also in expenses of the same persons and master Thomas de Kylmor riding together to Kilcullen, with 5 horses 3 serving men, before the commissary of the lord Archbishop against master Thomas

Thomam Giffard presentatum vicarie ecclesie ville ejusdem
& pro magistris Johanne Craddok, Johanne Petyt, & Ada
de Kyngeston & multis aliis ex parte domini Prioris per
talliam contra suppriorem, x s. v d.

Exhennia
missa
domino
Archiepis-
piscopo &
Curialita-
tes familie
eiusdem.

In primis idem computat in pane dominico empto & misso domino
Archiepiscopo Dublin die dominica in Ramis Palmarum,
ii d. ob.

In vino empto & misso eidem eodem die supradicto, x d.

Item in uno carcosio bovino empto & misso eidem ad Pasch'
prox. sequens, ix s.

Item in ii carcasiis multon' emptis & missis eidem, ii s. viii d.

Item in ii caponibus & missis eidem, xix d. & preter hoc colum-
belli & caprioli de stauro.

Item lib. Petro camerario pro diversis oblacionibus familie dicti
domini Archiepiscopi, exhibendis ad Pascham, xxvi s.
viii d.

Item lib. Clementi Sheman pro tonsura panni qui dabatur familie dicti domini Archiepiscopi ut in mutatoriis & caligis, ad
Pascham, xxi d.

Giffard presented to the vicarage of the church of that town, and
for masters John Craddok, John Petyt, and Adam de Kyngeston,
and many others, on behalf of the lord Prior, by tally against the
sub-prior, 10s. 5d.

Presents
sent to the
lord Arch-
bishop, and
gifts to his
household.

In the first place he accounts in paindemaine bought and sent to the lord
Archbishop of Dublin on Palm Sunday, 2½d.

In wine bought and sent to him on the same day aforesaid, 10d.

Also in one carcase of beef bought and sent to him at Easter next following, 9s.

Also in 2 carcases of mutton bought and sent to him, 2s. 8d.

Also in 2 capons (bought) and sent to him, 19d.; and besides, young
pigeons and kids from stock.

Also given to Peter the chamberlain to offer at Easter divers oblations of
the household of the said lord Archbishop, 26s. 8d.

Also given to Clement Sheman (shearman) for the shearing of the cloth
which was given to the household of the said lord Archbishop, as
in changes of garments, and hose, at Easter, 21d.

Item in uno porco empto & misso domino Roberto Poer, ii s. ii d. pro domino Roberto Poer.

Item in ii carcasiis de multon, emptis & missis eidem, ii s. ii d.

Item idem computat in i pare ferri pro scansilibus empto, iiii d. Expense minute & necessarie.

In ii paribus de coreis emptis pro eisdem scansilibus pendendis, x d.

In pergameno empto pro compotis & aliis negociis pluribus domum tangentibus ut in literis diversimode per Priorem, diversis placitis, excepcionibus scribendis & faciendis, ii s. iii d.

Item in i turribulo empto pro Glasnevyn, vii d.

Item lib. Clementi Sheman pro tonsura pannorum quos Prior liberavit diversimode ad Natalem Domini, ii s. iii d.

Item in xii clut' ferreis emptis pro carecta celarii, vii d.

Item in emendacione unius mallioli pro lapidibus frangendis apud Glasnevyn, ii d.

Item in i serura cum clave empta ad hostium camere Prioris, iii d.

Item in conduccione cuiusdam hominis facientis cathedras stramineas sedes & scanna straminea pro camera Prioris apud Dublin pariter & apud Glasnevyn, xvi d.

Also in one hog bought and sent to sir Robert Poer, 2s. 2d. for sir Robert Poer.

Also in 2 carcases of mutton bought and sent to him, 2s. 2d.

Also he accounts in one pair of stirrup-irons bought, 4d. Small and necessary expenses.

In 2 pairs of straps bought for suspending the stirrups, 10d.

In parchment bought for accounts and many other matters concerning the house, as in writing and making letters in various ways on account of the Prior, and pleas and exceptions, 2s. 3d.

Also in a censer bought for Glasnevin, 7d.

Also given to Clement Sherman for the shearing of cloths which the Prior distributed at Christmas, 2s. 3d.

Also in 12 iron clouts bought for the cart of the cellar, 7d.

Also in repair of one small hammer for breaking stones at Glasnevin, 2d.

Also in one lock with key, bought for the door of the Prior's chamber, 3d.

Also in hire of a certain man making straw chairs, seats, and straw stools for the Prior's chamber at Dublin as well as at Glasnevin, 16d.

Item lib. fratri Roberto de sancto Neoto pro clibano in pistrina faciendo & emendando cum conduccione cementariorum, xix d.

Item lib. eidem fratri Roberto pro quodam gurgite inter hostium celarii & portam purgando & faciendo, ut in lapidibus calce zablone, una cum conduccione cementariorum, xvi d.

Item lib. fratri Johanni Dolphyn pro ii fenestris vitreis ad cancellam de Glasnevyn faciendis repagulis clavis & hokes ferreis pro eisdem faciendis, ii s. ii d. ob.

Item lib. fratri Johanni Savage pro xviii imaginibus cindendis & depictandis pro feretro, xvii s.

Item in i coreo equino empto & pro eodem dealbando, xiii d.

Item lib. fratri Johanni Dolphyn pro cementariis precepto Prioris, viii d.

Item lib. Petro Camerario pro fabricacione ferri pro quadam fenestra pro aula de Glasnevyn, xxiii d.

Item in ferro empto pro repagulis ad fenestras de Glasnevyn inde faciendis, ii s. vii d.

Item lib. eidem Petro pro panno emendo, ad usum Laurentii garcionis de camera Prioris, xx d.

Also given to brother Robert de S. Neot for making and repairing the oven in the bake-house, with the hire of masons, 19*d.*

Also given to the same brother Robert for cleaning and making the water-channel between the door of the cellar and the gate, as in stone, lime, sand, with hire of masons, 16*d.*

Also given to brother John Dolphyn for making 2 glass windows for the chancel of Glasnevin, with bars, nails, and hooks of iron, for the same, 2*s.* 2½*d.*

Also given to brother John Savage for carving and ornamenting 18 images for a shrine, 17*s.*

Also in one horse skin bought, and for tanning it, 13*d.*

Also given to brother John Dolphyn for masons, by command of the Prior, 8*d.*

Also given to Peter the chamberlain for fashioning iron for a certain window for the hall of Glasnevin, 23*d.*

Also in iron bought to make bars for the windows of Glasnevin, 2*s.* 7*d.*

Also given to the same Peter to buy cloth for the use of Laurence serving-man of the Prior's chamber, 20*d.*

Item lib. Ymne lotrici, pro lotura pannorum lineorum de camera Prioris de termino Pasche, vi d.

Item in emendacione unius somersadul, ii d.

Item in ollis luteis, ob. pro camera Prioris.

Item in iii petris ferri de spayne emptis pro strakes strakenayl & gropes pro rotis ad carectam de celario faciendis & emend', unacum stipendio fabri, ii s. vii d. ob.

Item idem computat in uno equo empto ad usum senescalli, xix s. viii d. *Empcio Stauri.*

Item computat in salario Johannis coci Prioris a festo sancti Petri Advincula usque festum Purificationis Beate Marie Virginis, iii s. iiii d. *Salaria liberorum servien-cium.*

Item in panno empto ad usum Johannis Rous clerici, vi s. iiii d.

Item idem computat in expensis Ricardi de Deen subescaetoris, & Ricardi de Cestria clerici sui cum ipso venientis absente domino Priore, ad prandium pro negociis ecclesiam tangentibus. In pane dominico, i d., in vino empto, v d., in stokfich, iii d. *Expense supervento-rum & aliquando pro Priore.*

Item lib. Petro Camerario pro uno capone emendo precepto Prioris pro quodam famulo Roberti de Thenewell, ii d.

Also given to Ymna the washerwoman, for the washing of linen cloths of the Prior's chamber for the term of Easter, 6d.

Also in the repair of one sumpter saddle, 2d.

Also in earthenware pots, ½d., for the Prior's chamber.

Also in 3 stones of Spanish iron bought for making and mending tires, nails for the tires, and gropes, for wheels of the cellar cart, with the hire of a smith, 2s. 7½d.

Also he accounts in one horse bought for use of the seneschal, 19s. 8d. *Purchase of stock.*

Also he accounts in the salary of John, the Prior's cook, from the feast of S. Peter ad Vincula (Aug. 1), to the feast of the Purification of the Blessed Virgin Mary (Feb. 2), 3s. 4d. *Salaries of free servants.*

Also in cloth bought for the use of John Rous, clerk, 6s. 8d.

Also he accounts in expenses of Richard de Deen, sub-escheator, and Richard de Chester, his clerk, coming with him, in the absence of the Prior, to dinner, on business touching the church; in pain-demaine, 1d.; wine bought, 5d.; stockfish, 3d. *Expenses for strangers and sometimes for the Prior.*

Also given to Peter the chamberlain to buy a capon, by order of the Prior, for a certain servant of Robert de Thenewell, 2d.

Item lib. eidem Petro pro uno capone emendo ad jantaculum Prioris, versus Glasnevyn, ii d., in pane dominico, ob., in vino, ii d. ob., in sale albo, ob.

Item die Mercurii proxima ante festum Sanctorum Fabiani & Sebastiani. In vino empto pro adventu fratris Thome Carmel, i d. quad.

Item lib. eidem Petro pro iii gallinis emendis, & lib. fratri Johanni Dolphyn, ex dono Prioris, iii d. ob.

Item lib. eidem Petro pro speciebus emendis pro Priore, ii d.

Item in pane dominico pro Johanne Haket jantante ibidem cum Priore & ii filiis dicti Johannis, ob., in vino empto, iii d. ob. quad., in i capone empto, ii d.

Item lib. eidem Petro pro i li. piperis emenda, xx d.

Item lib. Hugoni coco pro i salmon', anguillis & columbellis furniendis contra Pascham, xviii d.

Item lib. Petro supradicto pro pulcinis emendis pro Priore apud Clonken in septimana Pasche, iii d.

Item eidem Petro pro ancerulis emendis, x d. ob.

Item alia vice lib. Hugoni coco, pro salmon' furn', iii d. ob.

Also given to same Peter to buy a capon for the Prior's breakfast (when going) to Glasnevin, 2d.; in paindemaine, ½d.; wine, 2½d.; white salt, ½d.

Also on Wednesday (Jan. 19) next before the feast of Saints Fabian and Sebastian. In wine bought for coming of brother Thomas Carmel, 1¼d.

Also given to the same Peter to buy three fowls given to brother John Dolphyn, of the gift of the Prior, 3½d.

Also given to same Peter to buy spices for the Prior, 2d.

Also in paindemaine for John Haket breakfasting there with the Prior and two sons of said John, ½d.; in wine bought, 3¾d.; in one capon bought, 2d.

Also given to same Peter to buy 1 lb. of pepper, 20d.

Also given to Hugh the cook to provide one salmon, eels, and pigeons for Easter, 18d.

Also given to Peter aforesaid, to buy chickens for the Prior at Clonken in Easter week, 3d.

Also to same Peter to buy goslings, 10½d.

Also another time given to Hugh the cook to provide salmon, 3½d.

Item iu viridi succo empto pro Priore, viii d.

Item in diversis neccessariis pro senescallo ut in caligis crepitis cyrotecis & aliis per tempus compoti, vi s. viii d.

In primis idem computat iu vino empto pro Priore & Conventu in refectorio die Natali Domini, xv d.

In vino empto pro Conventu in refectorio die Circumcisionis Domini, x d.

Item in vino empto pro Priore & Conventu in refectorio die Epiphanie Domini, xv d.

Item in focali empto per diversas vices pro Priore & Conventu in refectorio, xvii d.

Item in vino empto pro Priore & Conventu in refectorio die Purificationis Beate Marie Virginis, xv d.

Item in vino empto pro Conventu in refectorio die Sancti Patricii, x d.

Item in vino empto pro Conventu in refectorio die Dominica in Ramis Palmarum, precepto Prioris, v d.

Item in vino empto pro Conventu in refectorio in vigilia Pasche, v d.

Marginal notes: Expense pro Seneschallo. Expense pro Priore & Conventu in refectorio.

Also in verjuice bought for the Prior, 8*d.*

Also in divers necessaries for the Seneschal, as in hose, sandals, gloves, and other things, during the time of account, 6*s.* 8*d.*

In the first place he accounts in wine bought for the Prior and Convent in the refectory, on Christmas Day, 15*d.*

In wine bought for the convent in the refectory, on the day of the Circumcision of our Lord, 10*d.*

Also in wine bought for the Prior and Convent in the refectory, on the day of the Epiphany of our Lord, 15*d.*

Also in fuel bought on divers occasions for the Prior and Convent in the refectory, 17*d.*

Also in wine bought for the Prior and convent in the refectory, on the day of the Purification of the Blessed Virgin Mary, 15*d.*

Also in wine bought for the Convent in the refectory, on S. Patrick's Day, 10*d.*

Also in wine bought for the Convent in the refectory on Palm Sunday, by order of the Prior, 5*d.*

Also in wine bought for the Convent in the refectory, on Easter Eve, 5*d.*

Marginal notes: Expenses for the Seneschal. Expenses for the Prior and Convent in the Refectory.

Item in vino empto pro Conventu in refectorio die Pasche, xv d.

Item in vino empto pro Conventu die Martis proxima sequente in refectorio, v d.

Item in vino empto pro Conventu in refectorio in octava Pasche, v d.

Item in vino empto pro Conventu in refectorio die Invencionis Sancte Crucis, x d.

Item lib. fratri Willelmo Sterre in Cena Domini, pro elemosina ad mandatum facienda, ii s. vi d.

Item in vino empto pro Priore & Conventu in refectorio die Ascensionis Domini, xv d.

Debita, feoda, pensiones subsidia & procuraciones, solute post festum Natale Domini.

Item idem computat lib. Radulpho de Same pro debito, xxvi s.

Item pro retorno habendo per Escaetorem de super modo & causa ad Cancellariam, xx s.

Item Jacobo Broun pro panno ab eodem empto, vi s. v d.

Item Alicie Raggley pro pane ab eadem empto, in autumpno, xx s.

Item Willelmo de Pannton mercatori pro diversis rebus ab eo emptis ad usum Prioris, x s.

––––––––––

Also in wine bought for the Convent in the refectory, on Easter Day, 15*d*.

Also in wine bought for the Convent on Tuesday next following, in the refectory, 5*d*.

Also in wine bought for the Convent in the refectory, on the octave of Easter, 5*d*.

Also in wine bought for the Convent in the refectory, on the day of the Finding of the Holy Cross, 10*d*.

Also given to brother William Sterre on Holy Thursday to give alms, by command, 2*s*. 6*d*.

Also in wine bought for the Prior and Convent in the refectory, on the day of the Ascension of our Lord, 15*d*.

Debts, fees, pensions, subsidies and proxies paid after Christmas.

Also he accounts as given to Ralph de Same, for a debt, 26*s*.

Also to have a return (to the writ) of " Super modo et causa " by the Escheator to Chancery, 20*s*.

Also to James Broun for cloth bought from him, 6*s*. 5*d*.

Also to Alice Raggley for bread bought from her in harvest time, 20*s*.

Also to William de Pannton, merchant, for divers things bought from him for the use of the Prior, 10*s*.

Item magistro Ricardo Corneyser de debito precepto Prioris, ix s. iii d.

Item Hugoni Louestok pro debito fratris Gilberti Bolyniop, xxvi s. viii d. per literam.

Item lib. Waltero Gybyn pro debito ipsius Gilberti, xxix s. ix d., ut patet per unam literam.

Item lib. Kenewrico Scheman, in partem solucionis vii li. x s. argenti, iiii li.

Item lib. eidem Kenewryco pro panno ab eodem empto ad usum Johannis de Grauntsete ut patet per literam obligatoriam inde cancellatam, xxiiii s. vi d.

Item Crosseby pro debito, iii s. vi d.

Item fratri Thome de Beuley canonico de debito de autumpno ultimo elapso, iiii s.

Item Hugoni Broun narratori pro feodo suo ut patet per literam de termino Omnium Sanctorum, x s.

Item Willelmo Stapenhull narratori pro feodo suo, x s.

Item Johanni Cusak narratori pro auxilio suo inpenso ex dono Prioris, vi s. viii d.

Also to master Richard Corneyser for a debt, by order of the Prior, 9s. 3d.

Also to Hugh Louestok, for a debt of brother Gilbert Bolyniop, 26s. 8d., by letter.

Also given to Walter Gybyn, for a debt of the same Gilbert, 29s. 9d., as appears by a letter.

Also given to Kenewric Sherman, in part payment of £7 10s. of silver, £4.

Also given to same Kenewric for cloth bought from him for the use of John de Grauntsete, as appears by a letter obligatory for it cancelled, 24s. 6d.

Also to Crosseby, for a debt, 3s. 6d.

Also to brother Thomas de Beuley, canon, for a debt from the harvest last past, 4s.

Also to Hugh Broun, pleader, for his fee, as appears by a letter, for the term of All Saints, 10s.

Also to William Stapenhull, pleader, for his fee, 10s.

Also to John Cusak, pleader, for his assistance given, of the gift of the Prior, 6s. 8d.

Item lib. domino Archiepiscopo Ardmachano pro quodam subsidio sibi per Clerum concesso, xiii s. iiii d.

Item Archidiacono Glindel' pro procuracione racione ecclesiarum de Kylcolyn & alibi in archidiaconatu suo in persolucionem omnium procuracionum usque Pascham anno Domini m⁰ ccc^{mo} xliiii^{to}, xiii s. viii d.

Item lib. Johanni de Kynton pro feodo suo de termino spennynges & Omnium Sanctorum, ut patet per literam aquietancie, xx s.

Item lib. pro lapidibus emptis ad fabricam Ecclesie per visum fratris Nicholai de Eseden, xxv s.

Item fratri Gilberto Bolyniop in persolucionem pensionis sue videlicet ii mar. per annum, viii s.

Item lib. fratri Hugoni le Jeune, xxxvi. v d.

Item Willelmo de Burton, xii li.

Item Hugoni Broun, x s. de termino seppnynges.

Expense pro Camera Prioris. — Item idem computat in expensis pro camera Prioris ab in crastino Natalis Domini usque diem Dominicam post festum Apostolorum Petri & Pauli, ut in pane dominico vino cervisia

---

Also given to the lord Archbishop of Armagh, for a certain subsidy granted to him by the clergy, 13s. 4d.

Also to the Archdeacon of Glendalough, for proxies by reason of the churches of Kilcullen and elsewhere in his archdeaconry, in full payment of all proxies to Easter, 1344, 13s. 8d.

Also given to John de Kynton, for his fee of the term of Spennyngs and All Saints, as appears by a letter of acquittance, 20s.

Also given for stone bought for the fabric of the church, with approval of brother Nicholas de Eseden, 25s.

Also to brother Gilbert Bolyniop, in completion of payment of his pension of two marks a year, 8s.

Also given to brother Hugh le Jeune, 36s. 5d.

Also to William de Burton, £12.

Also to Hugh Broun, 10s., for the term of Spennyngs.

Expenses for the Prior's chamber. — Also he accounts in expenses for the Prior's chamber from the morrow of Christmas to the Sunday (July 3) after the feast of the Apostles Peter and Paul, as in paindemaine, wine, ale, flesh, all kinds of

carnibus omnimodis speciebus & hujusmodi emptis ut patet
in quodam rotulo inde confecto de dietis, vi li. xii s. v d.

Item idem computat lib. Hugoni Belynges ballivo de Gorman _{Lib. den.}
pro husbandriis ibidem, ix li. ii s. iii d. ob. unde respon- _{pro hus-
bandria.}
debit.

Item Nicholao Chaumbrelayn ballivo de Glasnevin, vi li. x d. quad.
unde respondebit.

Item Johanni Chambrelein ballivo de Clonken, xxxiii s. v d. ob.
unde respondebit.

---

spices, and the like, bought, as appears in a roll made of them
by daily entries, £6 12s. 5d.

Also he accounts as given to Hugh Belyngs, bailiff of Gorman, for hus- _{Payments}
bandry there, £9 2s. 3½d., whereof he will answer. _{of money
for hus-}

Also to Nicholas Chamburleyn, bailiff of Glasnevin, £6 0s. 10½d., whereof _{bandry.}
he will answer.

Also to John Chamburleyn, bailiff of Clonken, 33s. 5½d., whereof he will
answer.

V.

Compotus fratris Thome de Beuley Senescalli ac Thesaurarii Ecclesie Cathedralis Sancte Trinitatis Dublin de omnibus receptis & expensis in dictis officiis ibidem per ipsum factis, a die Mercurii proxima ante festum Nativitatis beati Johannis Bapthiste, Anno domini millesimo ccc^{mo} xlvi^{to}, usque festum Omnium Sanctorum prox. sequens, videlicet per ————.

In primis idem reddit compotum de lx s. receptis de fratre Simone de Ludegate nuper priore Ecclesie antedicte.

Et de ii s. receptis de Gregorio de Taunton per manus Johannis ballivi de Clonken.

Et de xviii d. receptis de redditu de Coulok de redditu de termino Spennynges.

Et de iiii s. viii d. quad. receptis de Nicholao Chamburleyn ballivo de Glasnevyn, de redditu des les Blakeleyes de eodem termino.

Et de xxiii s. receptis de porcione Johannis Comyn.

Et de xix s. xi d. receptis de domino Philippo capellano de

Account of brother Thomas de Beuley, Seneschal and Treasurer of the Cathedral Church of the Holy Trinity Dublin, of all receipts and expenses incurred by him in said offices there, from Wednesday (June 21) next before the feast of the Nativity of S. John the Baptist, 1346, to the feast of All Saints (Nov. 1) next following, viz. for [19 weeks].

In the first place he renders account of 60s. received from brother Simon de Ludegate late prior of the aforesaid church.

And of 2s. received from Gregory de Taunton by the hands of John, bailiff of Clonken.

And of 18d. received from the rent of Coolock, of the rent of the term of Spennyngs.

And of 4s. 8¼d. received from Nicholas Chamburleyn, bailiff of Glasnevin, of the rent of the Black leas for the same term.

And of 23s. received from the portion of John Comyn.

And of 19s. 11d. received from sir Philip chaplain of Rathtoole, for the

Rathozell pro firma Ecclesie de Balycor de termino sancti Petri quod dicitur Advincula.

Et de ix li. receptis de domino Willelmo Watur capellano in partem solucionis x li. de decimis de Kylcolyn & capellarum de termino —— de anno ——.

Et de x li. receptis de domino archiepiscopo Dublin archiepiscopo, ex mutuo per literam obligatoriam.

Et de ii s. receptis de Alexandro Wellus de redditu de termino Apostolorum Philippi & Jacobi ultimo preterito.

Et de iiii li. xiii s. iiii d. receptis de fratre Johanne Dolphyn, suppriore de decimis de Kyldenhall.

Et de viii d. receptis de Willelmo Paynot de termino supradicto de Gorman, de illo messuagio quod quondam tenuit ibidem quidam Laweles in partem solucionis ii s.

Et de xxvii s. iiii d. receptis ex mutuo, unde i mar. de domino Johanne Dendredeby.

Et de vi li. receptis de Roberto de Hoghton ex mutuo, per literam obligatoriam.

———

farm of the church of Ballycore, for the term of S. Peter called Ad Vincula.

And of £9 received from sir William Watur, chaplain, in part payment of £10, of the tithes of Kilcullen and of its chapels for the term —— of the year ——.

And of £10 received from the lord archbishop of Dublin as a loan, by letter obligatory.

And of 2s. received from Alexander Wellus, of the rent of the term of the Apostles Philip and James last past.

And of £4 13s. 4d. received from brother John Dolphyn, sub-prior, of the tithes of Killenaule.

And of 8d. received from William Paynot, for the aforesaid term, for that messuage at Gorman which a certain Laweles formerly held, in part payment of 2s.

And of 27s. 4d. received on loan, one mark of which was from sir John Dendredeby.

And of £6 received from Robert de Hoghton, as a loan, by letter obligatory.

Et de x s. receptis de Priore de Instyok de termino Sancte Trinitatis anno domini millesimo ccc^mo. xlvi^o.

Summa tocius recept' xxxvii li. v s. iii d. quad.

INDE IN EXPENSIS.

Expense
forinsece.

In primis idem computat lib. Johanni carectario de celario eunti
cum carectis & equis apud le Naas cum h'nes' justiciarii, de
prestito Prioris, vi d.

Item lib. cuidam nuncio eunti versus Momoniam ad Willelmum
de Boseuord pro breve habendo contra magistrum Walterum
de Istlep, xiii d.

Item alia vice eidem nuncio eunti versus Momoniam pro aliis
brevibus adquirendis contra eundem, xx d.

Item cuidam E. E. garcioni sequenti unum equm versus Momoniam in comitiva Thesaurarii, de prestito Prioris, iii d.

Item in expensis Johannis Rous clerici cum uno equo & garcione
equitantis apud Rathouze, Skreen, & le Novaan ad Edmun-
dum de Byrford, Hugonem Broun, Johannem de Kynton &
alios per duos dies & i noctem, causante Waltero de Istlep,
xiii d.

And of 10s. received from the prior of Inistioge, for the term of Holy
Trinity, 1346.

Sum of all Receipts, £37 5s. 3¼d.

IN PAYMENTS FROM THIS :

Extern
expenses.

In the first place he accounts as given to John carter of the cellar going
with carts and horses to the Naas with the harness of the Justiciary,
as an advance by the Prior, 6d.

Also given to a messenger going towards Munster to William de Boseuord,
to obtain a writ against master Walter de Istlep, 13d.

Also another time to the same messenger going towards Munster, to
procure other writs against him, 20d.

Also to a certain E. E. servingman following a horse towards Munster,
in the company of the Treasurer, as an advance by the Prior, 3d.

Also in expenses of John Rous clerk, with one horse and one servingman,
riding to Ratoath, Skreen, and the Navan, to Edmund de Byrford,
Hugh Broun, John de Kynton, and others, for two days and one
night, on account of Walter de Istlep, 13d.

Item lib. clerico vicecomitis pro copia brevis habenda per fratrem Willelmum Sterre vi d. contra dictum Walterum.

Item in expensis fratris Roberti de Sancto Neoto, equitantis apud Kylcolyn ad dominum Willelmum Watur pro argento ab eo petendo cum uno equo & uno garcione per iii dies eundo & redeundo, ix d.

Item lib. Ricardo Taylour eunti apud Droghda ad Hugonem Bron & Johannem de Kynton pro negociis domus, ii d.

Item in una lagena vini albi empta & missa Johanni Haket die Martis in festo sancti Colmani precepto Prioris, vi d.

Item in i lagena vini albi & missi Johanni de Redenesse precepto ejusdem, vi d.

Item cuidam nuncio eunti apud Kylcolyn pro domino Willelmo Watur peteudo, ii d.

Item in expensis fratris Thome de Beuley, clerici sui equorum & aliorum cum ipsis euncium apud Swerd ad dominum Archiepiscopum pro pecunia ab eo habenda de prestito, per iii vices, ix d.

Item cuidam nuncio eunti apud Stabanan, pro Johanne de Kynton petendo pro negociis domus, iii d. die sancti Ruffi.

Also given to the sheriff's clerk, for obtaining a copy of the writ by brother William Sterre against said Walter, 6*d.*

Also in expenses of brother Robert de S. Neot, riding to Kilcullen to sir William Watur, to apply for money from him, with one horse and one servingman. for 3 days going and returning, 9*d.*

Also given to Richard Taylour, going to Drogheda to Hugh Bron and John de Kynton, on business of the house, 2*d.*

Also in one gallon of white wine bought and sent to John Haket, on Tuesday the feast of S. Colman (Sept. 26) by order of the Prior, 6*d.*

Also in one gallon of white wine (bought) and sent to John de Redenesse, by order of the same, 6*d.*

Also to a messenger going to Kilcullen, to seek sir William Watur, 2*d.*

Also in expenses of brother Thomas de Beuley, his clerk, horses and others with them, going to Swords to the lord archbishop, to obtain money from him as an advance, on 3 occasions, 9*d.*

Also to a messenger going to Stabannan, to seek John de Kynton, on business of the house, 3*d.* on S. Rufus's day.

Item eodem die lib. alii nuncio eunti pro Edmundo de Byrford
    & Willelmo Petyt ut venirent apud Dublin contra diem
    inter Priorem & dictum Walterum de Istlep, ii d.

Item lib. fratri Johanni Dolphyn, pro expensis suis versus Kyl-
    denhall & apud Ardagh pro diversis negociis domus, xi s.

Item pro ii brevibus de supersedeas adquirendis, xii d.

Item commissario domini Archiepiscopi Cassell', xii d.

Item ejusdem Archiepiscopi Tabellioni, vi d.

Item cuidam¹ garcioni eunti cum fratre Johanne Dolfyn, xv d.
    versus partes predictas.

Item lib. Willelmo Fallynges eunti ad dominum Rogerum Darcy
    eschaetorem hibernie, cum litera domini Archiepiscopi, ii d.

Item cuidam garcioni eunti apud Kylcolyn, pro fratre Johanne
    de Castro, ii d.

Item computat lib. fratri Johanni Dolfyn suppriori eunti apud
    Dunmowe ad Eschaetorem hibernie cum breve de supersedeas,
    vi d.

Item cuidam nuncio eunti pro Edmundo de Byrford & Willelmo

Also on same day given to another messenger, going for Edmond de
    Byrford and William Petyt, that they might come to Dublin by
    the day (of hearing of the case) between the Prior and said Walter
    de Istlep, 2*d*.

Also given to brother John Dolphyn, for his expenses towards Killenaule,
    and at Ardagh, for divers business of the house, 11*s*.

Also for procuring two writs of "Supersedeas." 12*d*.

Also to the commissary of the lord archbishop of Cashel, 12*d*.

Also to the notary of the same archbishop, 6*d*.

Also to a certain servingman going with brother John Dolfyn towards
    the said parts, 15*d*.

Also given to William Fallynges going to sir Roger Darcy escheator of
    Ireland, with a letter of the lord archbishop, 2*d*.

Also to a servingman going to Kilcullen, for brother John de Castro, 2*d*.

Also he accounts as given to brother John Dolfyn sub-prior going to
    Dunmoe to the Escheator of Ireland with a writ of "Supersedeas,'
    6*d*.

Also to a messenger going for Edmund de Byrford and William Petyt, on

---

¹ *Cuidam* repeated in original.

Petyt, die Martis post festum Exaltacionis sancte Crucis, ii d.

Item lib. fratri Roberto de sancto Neoto equitanti apud Kylcolyn pro argendo petendo de Willelmo Watur, iiii d. videlicet in vigilia sancti Michaelis.

Item lib. domino Rogero Darcy eschaetori pro execucione brevium faciendo, xx s.

Item duobus clericis suis ex curialitate, iiii s.

Item in vino empto & misso Waltero Bayssham precepto Prioris, ii d.

Item duobus cocis in vico cocorum ex dono Prioris, i d.

Item lib. domino Elie de Assheborn & baroni de Castrocnok', ex dono Prioris, iii d.

Item lib. fratri Johanni Dolfyn supradicto pro expensis Prioris & ejus sequele apud Kylkenn' ad parliamentum & pro brevibus &[1] aliis neccessariis expediendis, ut patet in i cedula de parcellis huic rotulo consuta, xxii s. viii d.

Item lib. Willelmo Fallyng eunti ad Holpatrik pro cuniculis habendis, i d.

Tuesday (Sept. 12) after the feast of the Exaltation of the Holy Cross, 2*d.*

Also given to brother Robert de S. Neot, riding to Kilcullen, to apply for money from William Watur, 4*d.*, on the eve of S. Michael (Sept. 28).

Also given to sir Roger Darcy, escheator, for executing the writs, 20*s.*

Also to his two clerks, as a gratuity, 4*s.*

Also in wine bought and sent to Walter Bayssham, by order of the Prior, 2*d.*

Also to two cooks in Cook-street, of the gift of the Prior, 1*d.*

Also given to sir Elias de Assheborn and the baron of Castleknock, of the gift of the Prior, 3*d.*

Also given to brother John Dolfyn aforesaid, for expenses of the Prior and his retinue to Kilkenny for the Parliament, and for writs and arranging other necessary things, as appears in a schedule of particulars sewn to this roll, 22*s.* 8*d.*

Also given to William Fallyng, going to Holmpatrick to get rabbits, 1*d.*

---

[1] & repeated in original.

Item in vino albo empto pro magistro Thoma Kylmor die Lune
   proxima ante festum Omnium Sanctorum post prandium,
   iii d.

Summa lxxi s. xi d.

... domino Item computat in pigmento empto & misso domino Archiepiscopo
Archiepis-
copo Dub-   apud Balymor, xii d.
liu.
Item in pigmento empto & misso eidem alia vice apud Tauelach,
   xii d.

Item in vino empto pro domino Archiepiscopo justiciario hibernie
   & aliis simulconsulentibus in camera Prioris, die Jovis in
   octaba apostolorum Petri & Pauli, xiiii d.

Item in ii lagenis vini emptis & missis eidem domino Archiepiscopo, in septimana proxima sequente, viii d.

Item in pane dominico, vino, & piris emptis pro domino Archiepiscopo veniente ibidem in refectorio, xvii die mensis Augusti
   ad simulconsulendum de debitis & tractandum, viii d.

Item die Mercurii proxima post festum sancti Colmani in ii
   lagenis & i quart. albi vini emptis & missis eidem domino
   Archiepiscopo, xiii d. ob.

Summa v s. vii d. ob.

Also in white wine bought for master Thomas Kylmor, on Monday next
   before the feast of All Saints after dinner, 3*d.*

Total 71*s.* 11*d.*

For the   Also he accounts in piment bought and sent to the lord archbishop, at
lord arch-
bishop of   Ballymore, 12*d.*
Dublin.
Also in piment bought and sent to him another time, at Tallaght, 12*d.*

Also in wine bought for the lord archbishop, the justiciary of Ireland,
   and others consulting together in the Prior's chamber, on Thursday
   (July 6), the octave of the Apostles Peter and Paul, 14*d.*

Also in 2 gallons of wine bought and sent to the same lord archbishop
   in the week following, 8*d.*

Also in paindemaine, wine, and pears, bought for the lord archbishop in
   the refectory, 17th August, coming to consult together and to treat
   about the debts, 8*d.*

Also on Wednesday (Sept. 27) next after the feast of S. Colman, in
   2 gallons 1 quart of white wine bought and sent to the same lord
   archbishop, 13½*d.*

Total 5*s.* 7½*d.*

Item die dominica proxima post festum Apostolorum Petri & . . . . . .
Pauli, in vino empto pro Priore comedente in sacrist' ᴾʳⁱᵒʳ . . .
magistro Johanne Petyt & aliis cum eorum sequela, iiii d.

Item in pane dominico, vino, & cervisia emptis, pro Priore, domino
Ada de Kyngeston magistro Thoma de Kylmor & Johanne
de Evesham, apud Gorman ad simulconsulendum in vigilia
sancti Petri quod dicitur Advincula, viii d. ob.

Item in expensis Edmundi de Byrford venientis apud Dublin
& ejus sequele per i noctem, pro negociis domus, iii s. iiii d.

Item in aqua rosata empta pro Priore infirmo, & in sucre, xiiii d.

Item in pynsonns emptis pro eodem pro ejus sepultura, iii d.

Item in factura unius ciste in qua frater Simon de Ludegate
sepeliebatur, una cum bordis & clavis emptis pro eadem cista,
iiii s.[1]

Item die dominica proxima post festum Nativitatis beate Marie
Virginis in carnibus bovinis & multon' assatis emptis, ad jantaculum Electi & ejus confratrum, v d.

Also on Sunday (July 2) next after the feast of the apostles Peter and For the
Paul, in wineb ought for the Prior, master John Petyt and others Prior.
with their retinue, eating in the sacristy, 4d.

Also in paindemaine, wine, and ale bought for the Prior, sir Adam de
Kyngeston, master Thomas de Kylmor and John de Evesham, at
Gorman to consult together, on the eve (July 31) of S. Peter which
is called Ad Vincula, 8½d.

Also in expenses of Edmund de Byrford and his retinue, coming to
Dublin, for one night, on business of the house, 3s. 4d.

Also in rose water bought for the Prior when sick, and in sugar, 14d.

Also in shoes bought for him, for his burial, 3d.

Also in the making of a coffin, in which brother Simon de Ludegate was
buried, with boards and nails bought for the same coffin, 4s.

Also on Sunday (Sept. 10) next after the feast of the Nativity of the Blessed
Virgin Mary, in roast beef and mutton bought for the breakfast
of the Prior Elect and his fellow canons, 5d.

---

[1] Over this amount, and also in the margin is written, Ca.

1

Item in cervisia empta pro jantaculo Electi die Exaltacionis saucte
    Crucis, iii d.   Item in i auca empta, iii d.

Item die Lune proxima sequente Iu viuo empto pro dicto Electo,
    domino Johanne Dendredeby, & aliis in sacrist', iiii d.

Item eodem die ad cenam in vino pro eisdem, ii d.   In carnibus
    assatis, ii d.

Item in pane dominico viuo & cervisia emptis, pro Decano saucti
    Patricii, magistro Willelmo Notyngham & eorum sequela, ad
    vigiliam dicti fratris Simonis mortui, x d. ob.

Item die Mercurii proxima post festum sancti Colmani in iii quart.
    viui albi emptis pro dicto Electo, magistro Simone Lichefeld,
    & aliis (cenantibus[1]) in sacrist', iiii d. ob.   Item pro i bulchagh
    furn' ob. quad.   In carne assata empta pro servientibus dicti
    Simonis i d. ad prandium.

Item die Martis in festo sancti Colmani, In vino & pulcin' emptis
    pro Electo, & dicto magistro Simone simul cenantibus in
    sacrist', iii d.

Item in vino pro Electo, & magistro Willelmo de Notyngham

Also in ale bought for breakfast of the Prior Elect on the day of the
    Exaltation of the Holy Cross (Sept. 14), 3*d*.   Also in one goose
    bought, 3*d*.

Also on Monday next following (Sept. 18), in wine bought for the said
    Prior Elect, sir John Dendredeby, and others, in the sacristy, 4*d*.

Also on same day, at supper, in wine for same, 2*d*., in roast meat, 2*d*.

Also in paindemaine, wine, and ale, bought for the dean of Saint
    Patrick's, master William Notyngham, and their retinue, at the
    wake of the said brother Simon, deceased, 10½*d*.

Also on Wednesday (Sept. 27) next after the feast of S. Colman, in 3 quarts
    of white wine bought for the said Prior Elect, master Simon
    Lichefield, and others in the sacristy, 4½*d*. : also for a bulchagh
    cooked ¾*d*.   In roast meat bought for the servants of the said
    Simon for dinner, 1*d*.

Also on Tuesday the feast of S. Colman (Sept. 26), in wine and chickens
    bought for the Prior Elect and said master Simon, supping
    together in the sacristy, 3*d*.

Also in wine for the Prior Elect and master William de Notyngham, for

---

[1] The word *cenantibus* is marked in original as to be omitted.

ad adventum fratris Johannis Dolfyn de Kyldenhall & Ardagh, ix d.

Item die Martis proxima post festum Exaltacionis sancte Crucis, ad prandium & cenam pro Priore, quo die erat installatus, in ii aucis, vi d. In carnibus assatis, ii d. In vino & cervisia, iiii d. Post Installacionem.

Item die Jovis in festo sancti Math' Apostoli, pro Johanne Haket veniente ibidem post prandium. In vino, ii d.

Item in vino & cervisia eodem die pro Willelmo Haket & i armigero venientibus ibidem, ii d.

Item in vino empto eodem die pro Thoma de Bolton Willelmo de Barton clerico in camera fratris Hugonis de Sutton, ii d.

Die dominica proxima sequente. In vino empto pro Priore, uno monako de Malverne simuljantantibus in sacrist', i d. In i dimidia auca, i d. ob.

Item eodem die ad prandium, pro Priore, Johanne Haket & Johanne Passelewe & aliis comedentibus in sacrist'. In vino, iiii d. In i auca, iii d.

---

the coming of brother John Dolfyn from Killenaule and Ardagh, 9d.

Also on Tuesday (Sept 19) next after the feast of Exaltation of the Holy Cross, at dinner and supper for the Prior, on which day he was installed, in two geese 6d., roast meat 2d., wine and ale 4d. After the Installation.

Also on Thursday, the feast of S. Matthew the apostle (Sept. 21), for John Haket coming there after dinner, in wine, 2d.

Also in wine and ale on the same day for William Haket and one esquire coming there, 2d.

Also in wine bought on the same day for Thomas de Bolton, William de Barton clerk, in the chamber of brother Hugh de Sutton, 2d.

On Sunday next following, in wine bought for the Prior, and a monk of Malvern, breakfasting together in the sacristy, 1d.; in half a goose, 1½d.

Also on same day, at dinner for the Prior, John Haket, and John Passelewe, and others, eating in the sacristy, in wine 4d., a goose 3d.

Item in vino empto eodem die post prandium pro dicto monaco de Malverne & i armigero, ii d.

Item in vino empto, pro Priore, fratre Thoma de Beuley, & aliis cenantibus in sacrist', die dominica proxima ante festum sancti Michaelis, i d.

Item in vino empto, die sancti Michaelis pro Johanne Haket precepto Prioris, i d. ob.   In cervisia, i d.

Item post prandium eodem die in vino albo & rubro empto pro Priore Roberto de Hoghton, Roberto de Moenes seniore & Roberto de Moenes juniore, ii d. ob. quad.

Item in vino empto, pro Priore & Willelmo de Barton clerico die Sabbati in crastino sancti Michaelis, iii d.   In cervisia, i d.

Item in vino empto Archidiacono Dublin, Rogero de Preston, Nicholao de Suyterby & eorum sequela die dominica proxima post festum sancti Michaelis post prandium, vi d. ob.

Item die Martis proxima sequente in vino empto pro Priore dominis Johanne Dendredeby, Johanne atte Gate in camera Prioris, ii. d. ob.

Also in wine bought on same day after dinner, for the said monk of Malvern and one esquire, 2*d.*

Also in wine bought for the Prior, brother Thomas de Beuley and others, supping in the sacristy, on Sunday (Sept 24) next before the feast of S. Michael, 1*d.*

Also in wine bought on S. Michael's day, for John Haket, by order of the Prior, 1½*d.*, in ale 1*d.*

Also after dinner on same day, in white and red wine bought for the Prior, Robert de Hoghton, Robert de Moenes senior, and Robert de Moenes junior, 2¾*d.*

Also in wine bought for the Prior and William de Barton, clerk, on Saturday the morrow of S. Michael, 3*d* ; in ale 1*d.*

Also in wine bought for the archdeacon of Dublin, Roger de Preston, Nicholas de Suyterby, and their retinue, on Sunday (Oct. 1) next after the feast of S. Michael, after dinner, 6½*d.*

Also on Tuesday next following, in wine bought for the Prior, sir John Dendredeby, and sir John atte Gate, in the Prior's chamber, 2½*d.*

Item in vino empto pro Priore apud Gorman per, i noctem, die Jovis proxima post festum sancti Michaelis, iii d. In cervisia, i d. ob. In alaudis emptis, ii d.

Item in cervisia empta, pro Priore, Priore de sancto Wlstano simulcomedentibus in camera coquine, iii d.

Item in vino empto pro Priore domino Johanne Dendredeby & domino Johanne atte Gate alia vice, iii d.

Die Sabbati proxima ante festum sancti Dyonisii, in cervisia pro Priore, fratre Thoma de Beuley & Johanne Rous & aliis in Sacrista venientibus de domino Archiepiscopo de Fynglas, ii. d.

Die dominica proxima sequente, in vino empto pro eodem Priore, fratribus Thoma Beuley & Willelmo Sterre, ad compotum dicti fratris Willelmi reddendum, ii d. In cervisia, i d. ob. quad.

Die Lune proxima sequente. In pane dominico pro Priore, Johanne Haket, magistro Thoma de Kylmor, Thoma Pypard & aliis ad jantaculum in sacrist', i d. In i auca assata i cuniculo furn' & columbellis furn', vi d. In vino empto, v. d.

Also in wine bought for the Prior at Gorman, for one night, on Thursday next after the feast of S. Michael, 3*d.* ; in ale 1½*d.*, larks bought 2*d.*

Also in ale bought for the Prior, and the prior of S. Wolstan's, eating together in the chamber of the kitchen, 3*d.*

Also in wine bought for the Prior, sir John Dendredeby, and sir John atte Gate, another time, 3*d.*

On Saturday (Oct. 7.) next before the feast of S. Denis, in ale for the Prior, brother Thomas de Beuley, and John Rous, and others, in the sacristy, coming from the lord archbishop at Finglas, 2*d.*

On Sunday next following, in wine bought for same Prior, brothers Thomas Beuley and William Sterre, at the rendering of the account of said brother William, 2*d.* ; in ale, 1¾*d.*

On Monday next following, in paindemaine for the Prior, John Haket, master Thomas de Kylmor, Thomas Pypard, and others, at breakfast in the sacristy, 1*d.* ; in one roast goose, a rabbit cooked, and pigeons cooked, 6*d.* ; in wine bought, 5*d.*

Item eodem die ad noctem in cervisia empta pro Priore ad Gorman, i d. ob.

Item die Mercurii proxima ante festum apostolorum Simonis & Jude. In vino empto pro Priore redeunte de Kylkenn' de Parliamento, & Willelmo GoodDrych subserviente, iii d. In dimidia auca, i d. ob.

Die Jovis proxima sequente. In vino empto pro Priore, magistro Thoma de Kylmor, Johanne Haket & aliis, iii d. In i gallina pista, ii d.

Summa xxi s. iii d. quad.

Pro Celario. Frumentum. Item idem computat in ii cran. frumenti emptis die sancti Pantaleonis pro celario, xxi s. iiii d.: precium p⁶, xvi d.

Item in ii cran. frumenti emptis, iii° die mensis Augusti, xxi s. iiii d.: precium p⁶, ut supra.

Item in iii cran. frumenti ultimo emptis, xxvi. s.: precium p⁶, xiii d.

Panis. Item in pane empto pro Refectorio, die Veneris proxima ante festum sancti Petri quod dicitur Advincula, xiii d.

Item in pane empto pro conventu, in vigilia Assumpcionis beate Marie Virginis, xv d.

Also on same day at night, in ale bought for the Prior at Gorman, 1½d.

Also on Wednesday (Oct. 25) next before the feast of the apostles Simon and Jude, in wine bought for the Prior returning from Kilkenny from the Parliament, and William Goodrych under-serjeant, 3d.; in half a goose 1½d.

Thursday next following, in wine bought for the Prior, master Thomas de Kylmor, John Haket and others, 3d., in one baked fowl, 2d.

Total 21s. 3¼d.

For the Cellar. Wheat. Also he accounts in 2 crannocs of wheat bought on the day of S. Pantaleo, for the cellar, 21s. 4d.: price 16d. a peck.

Also in 2 crannocs of wheat bought on 3rd August, 21s. 4d.: price as above.

Also in 3 crannocs of wheat last bought, 26s.: price 13d. a peck.

Bread. Also in bread bought for the refectory on Friday (July 28) next before the feast of S. Peter called Ad Vincula, 13d.

Also in bread bought for the convent on the eve (Aug. 14) of the Assumption of the Blessed Virgin Mary, 15d.

Item in pane empto pro conventu in Refectorio die Assumpcionis
    beate Marie Virginis, xvi d.

Item in pane empto pro Conventu in Refectorio, die Jovis in festo
    sancti Addaui, xviii d. quad.

Item in vino empto pro conventu in Refectorio die Exaltacionis Vinum.
    sanote Crucis, v d.

Item in cervisia empta pro collatione in refectorio, die Jovis in
    vigilia sancti Michaelis Archangeli, iiii d.

Item die sancti Michaelis Archangeli in cervisia empta pro toto Cervisia.
    die ob deffectum celarii, in Refectorio, xvi d. & alibi.

Item in cervisia pro conventu in refectorio in crastino sancti
    Michaelis ad prandium, vi d. ob.

Summa lxxvi s. v d. ob. quad.

Item in pergameno empto per totum tempus compoti pro rentali- Expense
    bus faciendis, curiis, compotis, literis, & aliis neccessariis neccessarie.
    soribendis, xv d.

Item in emendacione selle Prioris, vii d.

Item in acubus & phillo emptis pro sacois & ventilabris suendis,
    i d. ob.

Also in bread bought for the convent in the refectory, on the day of the
    Assumption of the Blessed Virgin Mary, 16*d.*

Also in bread bought for the convent in the refectory, on Thursday the
    feast of S. Addan, 18¼*d.*

Also in wine bought for the convent in the refectory, on the day of the Wine.
    Exaltation of the Holy Cross (Sept. 14), 5*d.*

Also in ale bought for a collation in the refectory, on Thursday Ale.
    (Sept. 28) the eve of S. Michael the archangel, 4*d.*

Also on the day of S. Michael the archangel, in ale bought for the whole
    day on account of default of the cellarer, in the refectory and
    elsewhere, 16*d.*

Also in ale for the convent in the refectory, on the morrow of S. Michael,
    for dinner, 6½*d.*

Total 76*s.* 5¾*d.*

Also in parchment bought during the whole time of the account for Necessary
    making rentals, courts, accounts, letters, and other things neces- expenses.
    sary to be written, 15*d.*

Also in repair of the Prior's saddle, 7*d.*

Also in needles and thread bought for sewing bags and banners, 1½*d.*

Item in twistes & hokes unacum emendacione serure toralis apud
Gorman, iii d.

Item in i warrok empto pro harnesio Prioris, i d.

Item in i brace emendo pro coffero domini, iii d.

In iiii°ʳ capistris de canabo emptis, ii d.

Item pro decimis de Glasnevyn, cariandis de cimiterio ibidem,
infra manerium per ii vices, In pane & cervisia, xii d.

Item in sale pro salmone salsando, v d.

Summa iiii s. i d. ob.

Expense
Senescalli. Item in cervisia & pulcinis emptis pro fratre Thoma de Beuley,
clerico suo, & aliis apud Glasnevyn, pro uno rentali de novo
faciendo, iiii d.

Item in expensis eorundem quando venerunt de Clonken & fece-
runt unum rentale ibidem, & tenuerunt curiam, ii d. quad.

Item in expensis dicti fratris Thome diversimode perhendinantis
apud Gorman, Clonken, & alibi per dies pariter & noctes, a
festo sancti Michaelis usque festum Omnium Sanctorum,
xviii d.

Summa ii s. quad.

Also in twists and hooks, with the repair of the lock of the malt kiln at
Gorman, 3*d.*

Also in one warrok bought for the Prior's harness, 1*d.*

Also in one brace bought for the Prior's coffer, 3*d.*

Also in 4 halters of hemp bought, 2*d.*

Also for carrying the tithes of Glasnevin, from the cemetery there, into
the manor, on two occasions, in bread and ale, 12*d.*

Also in salt for salting salmon, 5*d.*

Total 4*s.* 1½*d.*

Expenses
of the
Seneschal. Also in ale & chickens bought for brother Thomas de Beuley, his clerk,
and others, at Glasnevin for making a rental anew, 4*d.*

Also in expenses of the same, when they came from Clonken and made a
rental there, and held court, 2¼*d.*

Also in expenses of said brother Thomas occasionally stopping at Gorman,
Clonken, and elsewhere, by days as well as by nights, from the
feast of S. Michael (Sept. 29) to the feast of All Saints (Nov. 1), 18*d.*

Total 2*s.* 0¼*d.*

Item in i pare calciamenti empto pro Priore, v d. In tibialibus emptis pro dicto fratre Thoma senescallo, per tempus compoti, ii s.

Necessaria Prioris & Seneścalli.

Summa ii s. v d.

Item computat lib. ix famulis de Gorman, in partem solucionis salariorum eorum de termino sanctorum Philippi & Jacobi,[1] iiii s., cuilibet eorum ix, iiii d. ballivo vi d. & servienti vi d.

Stipendia famulorum.

Item carectario de celario pro eodem, iiii d.

Item Henrico Wyhtbon, in partem solucionis salarii sui de eodem termino, i d.

Item Johanni Calfhurd, ii d.

Item lib. Johanni Rous clerico pro pane emendo apud Glasn' pro metentibus, die Lune proxima ante festum Exaltacionis sancte Crucis, xv d.

Custus Autumpnales.

Item lib. Johanni Notyngham apud Clonken pro calciamento suo, xii d.

Item Thome Haket pro calciamento suo ibidem, iii d. ob.

Also in one pair of shoes bought for the Prior, 5*d*. In leggings bought for said brother Thomas, the seneschal, during the time of the account, 2*s*.

Necessaries of the Prior and Seneschal.

Total 2*s*. 5*d*.

Also he accounts as given to 9 servants of Gorman in part payment of their wages for the term of SS. Philip & James, 4*s*. : to each of the nine, 4*d*., to the bailiff, 6*d*., and to the serjeant, 6*d*.

Wages of servants.

Also to the carter of the cellar, for same, 4*d*.

Also to Henry Wyhtbon, in part payment of his wages for the same term, 1*d*.

Also to John Calfhurd, 2*d*.

Also given to John Rous clerk, for buying bread at Glasnevin for the reapers, on Monday (Sept. 11) next before the feast of the Exaltation of the Holy Cross, 15*d*.

Harvest expenses.

Also given to John Notyngham at Clonken, for his shoes, 12*d*.

Also to Thomas Haket, for his shoes there, 3½*d*.

---

[1] Written over *Omnium Sanctorum*, struck out.

Item cuidam Andree custodienti decimas de Karrykbrenan, pro
calciamento, viii d.

Item Stephano filio ballivi apud Clonken, pro sotularibus, iii d.

Item Ricardo de Derby existenti ibidem, pro carectis piohandis, &
alia neccessaria faciendis, x d.

Item lib. Johanni Rous existenti apud Glasn' pro bladis intrandis
viii d.

Item Ricardo Comyn existenti ibidem & laboranti, xviii d.

Item lib. Johanni Bathy clerico existenti apud Gorman, iiii d. pro
sotularibus.

Item Ricardo Palefridario & E. E. garcioni senescalli, viii d.

Summa xii s. viii d. ob.

Staurum. Item in iii porcellis pro stauro habendo apud Gorman, viii d. ob.

In vi anatibus emptis, vii d.

In xviii pulcinis emptis xi d.

Item in ii aucis mariol' emptis, vi d. pro stauro habendo.

Summa ii s. viii d. ob.

Lib. Den. Item computat lib. fratri Roberto de sancto Neoto, per unam
Respond.' talliam contra eundem, xi li. vi s. viii d. unde respondebit.

Also to one Andrew guarding the tithes of Carrickbrennan, for shoes, 8*d.*

Also to Stephen, son of the bailiff at Clonken, for shoes, 3*d.*

Also to Richard de Derby, being there for pitching carts and doing other
things necessary, 10*d.*

Also given to John Rous being at Glasnevin for the incoming of the corn,
8*d.*

Also to Richard Comyn, being there and working, 18*d.*

Also given to John Bathy clerk, being at Gorman, 4*d.* for shoes.

Also to Richard the palfreykeeper & E. E. the seneschal's servingman.
8*d.*

Total 12*s.* 8½*d.*

Stock. Also in 3 young pigs to keep as stock at Gorman, 8½*d.*

In 6 ducks bought, 7*d.*

In 18 chickens bought, 11*d.*

Also in 2 mariol geese bought, 6*d.* to keep as stock.

Total 2*s.* 8½*d.*

Payments
of money
to be ac-
counted
for.   Also he accounts as given to brother Robert de S. Neot, by one tally
against him, £11 6*s.* 8*d.*, whereof he shall answer.

Item Johanni Chamburleyn, ballivo de Clonken, per i talliam
  contra eundem, lxx s. iiii d. unde respondebit.

Item Hugoni Belynges ballivo de Gorman, per i talliam contra
  eundem, lii s. vii d. ob. unde respondebit.

Item Nicholao Chamburleyn ballivo de Glasnevyn, per i talliam
  contra eundem, viii s. i d. ob. unde respondebit.

Item lib. Petro Camerario per ii vices per i talliam contra eundem,
  iii s. x d. unde respondebit.

Item computat lib. Nicholao Latonner per manus Petri Arnold de Soluciones Debito-rum.
  sancto Mauro in partem solucionis debiti antiqui, de tempore
  fratris S. Ludegate, xx s.

Item magistro Roberto de Cestria per manus dicti Petri, de
  antiquo debito de tempore ejusdem, x s.

Item Waltero Gybyn per manus dicti Petri, de antiquo debito de
  tempore ejusdem, xi s. viii d.

Item Andree Taylour per manus dicti Petri, de debito, vii s iiii d.

Item Edmundo de Byrford, de antiquo debito de tempore ejusdem
  fratris S., vi s. viii d.

Item Johanni Taylour civi Dublin in partem solucionis x li. de

---

Also to John Chamburleyn bailiff of Clonken, by one tally against him
  70*s.* 4*d.*, whereof he shall answer.

Also to Hugh Belynges bailiff of Gorman, by one tally against him
  52*s.* 7½*d.*, whereof he shall answer.

Also to Nicholas Chamburleyn bailiff of Glasnevin, by one tally against
  him, 8*s.* 1½*d.*, whereof he shall answer.

Also given to Peter the chamberlain on two occasions, by one tally
  against him, 3*s.* 10*d.* whereof he shall answer.

Also he accounts as given to Nicholas Latonner, by the hands of Peter Payments of debts.
  Arnold de S. Maur, in part payment of an old debt of the time of
  brother Simon Ludegate, 20*s.*

Also to master Robert de Chester, by the hands of said Peter, for an old
  debt of the time of the same, 10*s.*

Also to Walter Gybyn, by the hands of said Peter, for an old debt of the
  time of the same, 11*s.* 8*d.*

Also to Andrew Taylour, by the hands of said Peter, for a debt, 7*s.* 4*d.*

Also to Edmund de Byrford, for an old debt of the time of same brother
  Simon, 6*s.* 8*d.*

Also to John Taylour citizen of Dublin, in part payment of £10 of a debito ejusdem fratris S. per i aquietanciam, die dominica proxima post festum sancti Michaelis Archangeli, c s.

Item Thome de Bolton de debito de promisso dicti fratris S., vi s. viii d.

pro cu- quina. Item Ricardo le Rede piscatori de Oxemanton, pro debito coquine, viii s. ix d.

Item Ricardo Glover pro debito ejusdem coquine per literam aquietancie xii s. ix d.

Item Johanni Nachs, pro debito ejusdem, & in parte pro husbon- deria, per talliam, xiii s. viii d.

Respond.' Item fratri Willelmo Sterre coquinario pro officio suo adjuvando, vi s. viii d. unde respondebit.

> Summa xxviii li. v s. ix d.

> Summa Omnium Misarum & Expensarum xxxviii li. iiii s. xi d. ob. quad.

> Et sic expendit in superplusagio xix s. viii d. ob. unde debentur pro ii bendis ferri viii s. vi d., pro ii vome-

---

debt of same brother Simon, by one acquittance, on Sunday (Oct. 1) next after the feast of S. Michael the archangel, 100*s.*

Also to Thomas de Bolton, for a debt on a promise of said brother Simon, 6*s.* 8*d.*

For the kitchen. Also to Richard le Rede fisherman of Oxmantown, for a debt of the kitchen, 8*s.* 9*d.*

Also to Richard Glover, for a debt of the same kitchen, by letter of acquittance, 12*s.* 9*d.*

Also to John Nachs, for a debt of the same, and in part for husbandry, by a tally, 13*s.* 8*d.*

To be ac- counted for. Also to brother William Sterre kitchener, to help in the expenses of his office, 6*s.* 8*d.* for which he shall answer.

> Total £28 5*s.* 9*d.*

> Total of all payments and expenses £38 4*s.* 11¾*d.*   And so he expended in excess 19*s.* 8½*d.*, whereof there are owed for 2 bends of iron, 8*s.* 6*d.*, for 2 ploughshares, 12*d.*   Also

ribus xii d. Item pro xii lezerlegges ii s.   Item pro
vi paribus tractuum de canabo xii d.   Item pro sale
vi d.   Item pro ii aucis mariolis vi d.

    Summa debitorum xiii s. iiii d.

    Et sic in supplusagio vi s. ii d. ob.

---

for 12 lezerlegges, 2*s.*   Also for 6 pairs of hemp traces,
12*d.*   Also for salt, 6*d.*   Also for 2 mariol geese, 6*d.*
    Total of debts, 13*s.* 4*d.*
    And so in excess, 6*s.* 2½*d.*

[*The following lines, in a hand somewhat later than the* ACCOUNTS,
are found on the back of Account No. IV. above]:—

    "   Jay en vous tout ma fyaunce
        Ma bele dame par ma foy
        Et de autry ne ay souenaunce
    "   Qar forsque vous nat pussaunce
        De reioer le ceor de moy
    "   Et prengne cy grant plesaunce
        A toutz le foyth quant ieo vous voy
        Que parenplie[1] su de sofysaunce.

---

  [1] proenplic in original.

[_The following_ POEM _is written upon the unused parts of the back of Account No. II. above, in hands of the middle of the fifteenth century. As it is without title I have suggested the name,_ THE PRIDE OF LIFE.]

Pees & horkynt hal ifer
[ric] & por yong & hold
men & wemen ʒat bet her
bot lerit & leut stout & bold   (4)

lordinge & ladiis þat beth hende
herkenith al with mylde mode;
. . . . . ke gam schal gyn & ende
lorde us wel spede þat sched his blode (8)

Nou stondit stil & beth hende
. . . . yith al for þe weder
[&] ʒe schal or ʒe hennis wende
be glad þat ʒe come hidir   (12)

her ʒe schullin here spelle
of mirth & eke of kare
herkenith & i wol ʒou telle
. . . . schal ffare   (16)

. . . . lif i wol ʒou telle
. . . . first bi ffore
. . . . of fflessch & ffel
. . . . bore   (20)

. . . . . stronge to stonde
. . . . . by comin of kinge
. . . . lawis in eche a londe
. . dradd of no thinge   (24)

. . pride & likinge his lif he ledith
lordlich he lokit with eye;
. . . ce & dukes he seith him dredith
. . . dredith no deth ffor to deye (28)

. . hath a lady louelich al at likinge
ne may he of no mirth mene ne misse
he seit in swetnisse he wol set his likinge
& bringe his bale boun in to blisse   (32)

kyntis ȝe hat cumlic
in bred & in leiut
not i neuir non suc
of stocey ne off strynt   (36)

wat helpit¹ to yilp mucil of his mit
or bost to mucil of his blys
. . . sorou may sit onis sit
. . . ryt . . . . ay ȝe not miss   (40)

. . . . ladi of lond
. . . . . . st a lord sort to led
. . . . may ȝe be fort to stond
. . . . hold yat blisful bled   (44)

. . ladi is lettrit in lor
as cumli becomit for a quen
tun mit hir mac euirmor
as a dar for dred him to ten   (48)

ho bid him bewar or ȝe suirt
. . or in his lond det wol alond
. . ho leuit him gostlic in hert
. . it him bewar of his hend   (52)

. . begynit to charp of char
. es wordis wyt out lesing
det dot not spar
kyntis cayser ne kyng   (56)

nou lord leu yi likynd
wyt bringit ȝe soul gret bal²
yis answer ho had of ȝe kyng
ȝe yis a womanis tal   (60)

---

¹ lelpit in original.   ² bas in original.

ӡe kyng hit ne toke not to hert
for hit was a woman is spec
. . et hit mad him to smert
. . an him mit help no lec (64)

. . quen ӡit can hir undirstond
wat help ӡar mit be
& sent aftir ӡe bicop of ӡe lond
for he chont mor ӡan ӡe (68)

ӡe cham & precit al ӡat ӡe couþe
& warnit him hal of his hind
. it saurit not in ӡe kyng is mout
bot hom ӡe bad him wynd (72)

wand ӡe bicop is ӡam wend
fram ӡat . . . . stryf
. . . . ssenger ӡan send
. . . . . . ӡe kyng of lif (76)

. . . . him wold do undirston
. . . ӡe may del & dit
. . wold cum into his ouin lond
on him to kyt his mit (80)

Deth comit & dremit a dredfful dreme
welle aӡte al carye;
& slow ffader & moder & þen heme
he ne wold none sparye. (84)

sone affter hit be fel þat deth & life
beth to geder i take;
& ginnith & striuith a sterne strife
king of life to wrake. (88)

with him driuith a doun to grounde
he dredit no thing his kniӡtis;
& delith him depe deþis wounde
& kith on him his miӡtis. (92)

Qwhen þe body is doun i broӡt
þe soule sorow a wakith;
þe bodyis pride is dere a boӡt
þe soule þe ffendis takith. (96)

& throgh priere of oure lady mylde
al godenisse scho wol qwyte;
scho wol prey her son so mylde
þe soule & body schul dispyte. (100)

þe cors þat nere knowe of care
No more þen stone in weye;
schal . . of sorow & sore care
. . . . . . be twene ham tweye. (104)

þe soule þer on schal be weye
þat þe ffendes haue i kaȝte;
& oure lady schal þer for preye
so þat with her he schal be lafte. (108)

Nou beit in pes & beit hende
& distourbit noȝt oure place
ffor þis oure game schal gin & ende
throgh ihesus crist is swete grace. (112)

Rex viuus incipiet sic dicendum.

Pes now ȝe princes of powere so prowde
ȝe kinges ȝe kempes ȝe kniȝtes i korne
ȝe barons bolde þat beit me o bowte
. . schal ȝu my sawe swaynis i worne. (116)

sqwieris stoute stondit now stille
& lestenit to my hestes i hote ȝu now her
Or [I] schal wirch ȝu wo with werkes of wil
& doun schal ȝe drive be ȝe neuer so dere. (120)

king ic am kinde of kinges i korre
Al þe worlde wide to welde at my wil
Nas þer neuer no man of woman i borre
O ȝein me with stonde þat i nold him spille. (124)

lordis of lond beit at my ledinge
Al men schal a bow in hal & in bowr; (126)

* * * * * * * *

baldli þou art mi bot
tristili & ful treu
of al mi rast þou art rot
I nil chong fer no new (130)

Rex.

al in wel ic am bi went
may ne grisful þing me grou
likyng is wyt me bi . . .
alyng is it mi behou (134)

strent & hel kyntis kete
det rift in ded
lak y for ne ying ȝe let
smartli to me sped (138)

bringit wyt þou brit brondis
helmis brit & schend
for ic am lord ofir al londis
& yat is now i sen (142)

Primus miles fortitudo.

lord in truþe þou mit trist
feyfuli to stond
þou mit liu as ȝe list
for wonschild is þu fond. (146)

Ic am strent stif & strong
ne uar is suc non
in al yis world brod & long
Imad of blod & bon. (150)

Hau no dout of no ying
yat euir may befal
ic am strenyt yi derling
flour of knitis al. (154)

SECUNDUS MILES SANITAS.

King of lif þat berist þe croun
As hit is skil and riȝte;
I am hele i com to toun
þi kinde curteyse kniȝte.   (158)

þou art lord of lim & life
& king with outen ende;
stif & strong & sterne in strif
in londe qwher þou wende.   (162)

þou nast no nede to sike sore
ffor no thing on lyue;
þou schal lyue euer more
Qwho dar with þe striue.   (166)

REX.

Striue nay to me qwho is so gode
hit were bot ffolye;
þer is no man þat me dur bode
any vileynye.   (170)

Qwher of schuld i drede
Qwhen i am king of life;
fful evil schuld he spede
to me þat worth striue.   (174)

I schal lyue ever mo
& croun ber as kinge;
I ne may neuer wit of wo
I lyue at my likinge.   (178)

REGINA.

Sire þou saist as þe liste
þou liuist at þi wille;
bot somthing þou miste
& þer ffor hold þe stille.   (182)

K 2

thinke þou haddist beginninge
Qwhen þou were i bore;
& bot þou mak god endinge
þi sowle is ffor lore.   (186)

loue god & holy chirche
& haue of him som eye;
ffonde his werkes for to wirch
& thinke þat þou schal deye.   (190)

Rex.

douce dam qwhi seistou so
þou spekis noȝt as þe sleye
I schal lyue euer mo
ffor boþe two þin eye.   (194)

woldistou þat i were dede
þat þou miȝt haue a new
hore þe deuil gird of þi hede
bot þat worde schal þe rewe.   (198)

Regina.

dede sire nay god wote my wil
þat ne kepte i noȝte;
hit wolde like me fful ille
were hit þare to broȝte.   (202)

. . þogh þou be kinge
Nede schalt haue ende;
deth oure comith al thinge
hen so euer we wende.   (206)

Rex.

ȝe dam þou hast wordis fale
hit comith þe of kinde;
þis nis bot women tale
& þat i wol þe ffinde.   (210)

I ne schal neuer deye
ffor I am king of life;
deth is vndir myne eye
& þer ffor leue þi strife. (214)

þou dost bot mak myn hert sore
ffor hit nel noȝt helpe;
I prey þe spek of him no more
qwhat wolte of him ȝelpe. (218)

Regina.

ȝilpe sire nay so mot i the
I sigge hit noȝt qwher ffore
bot kinde techit boþe þe & me
ffirst qwhen we were bore (222)

ffor dowte of deth is maistri
to wepe & make sorowe;
holy writ & prophecye
þer of i take to borowe. (226)

þer ffor qwhile ȝe have miȝte
& þe worlde at wille;
I rede ȝe serue god almiȝte
boþe loude & stille. (230)

þis world is bot ffantasye
& fful of trechurye;
gode sire for ȝoure curteysye
take þis for no ffolye. (234)

ffor god wel þe soþe
I ne sey hit for no fabil
deth wol smyte to þe
in ffeith loke þou be stabil. (238)

Rex.

Qwhat prechistou of dethis miȝt
& of his maistrye
he no durst onis wit me fiȝt
ffor his boþe eye. (242)

streinth & hele qwhat say ȝe
my kinde kornin kniȝtes
schal deth be lord ouer me
& reue me of miȝtes.   (246)

I MILES.

Mi lord so brouke I my bronde
God þat me ffor bede;
þat deth schold do þe wronge
qwhile i am in þi ȝede.   (250)

I wol with stonde him with strife
& make his sidis blede;
& tel him at þou art king of life
& lorde of londe & lede.   (254)

II MILES.

May I him onis mete
with þis longe launce;
in ffelde oþer in strete
I wol him ȝiue mischaunce.   (258)

REX.

ȝe þes be kniȝtes of curteisye
& doghti men of dede;
Of deth ne of his maistrie
Ne have i no drede.   (262)

Qwher is mirth my messager
swifte so lefe on lynde;
he is a nobil bachelere
þat rennis bi þe wynde.   (266)

Mirth & solas he can make
& ren so þe ro;
liȝtly lepe oure þe lake
Qwher so euer he go.   (270)

Com & her my talente
A none & by þe blyue;
Qwher any man as þou has wente
dorst with me to striue.   (274)

Nuncius.

King of lif & lord of londe
as þou sittis on þi so;
& florresschist with þi briȝt bronde
to þe i sit on kne.   (278)

I am mirth wel þou wost
þi mery messagere
þat wostou wel with oute bost
þer nas neuer my pere;   (282)

doȝtely to done a dede
þat ȝe haue ffor to done;
hen to berewik o pon twede
& com o ȝein fful sone;   (286)

þer is no thing þe i liche
in al þis worlde wide;
Of gold & siluer & robis riche
& hei hors on to ryde.   (290)

I haue ben boþe fer & nere
in bataile & in strife;
Ocke þer was neuer þy pere
ffor þou art king of life   (294)

Rex.

A ha solas now þou seist so
þou miriest me in my mode
þou schal boy ar þou hennis go
be auaunsyd bi þe rode   (298)

þou schal haue for þi gode wil
to þin auauncemente;
þe castel of gailispire on þe hil
And þe erldom of kente.   (302)

Draw þe cord sire streynth
Rest I wol now take;
On erth i*n* brede ne leynth
Ne was ner*e* ȝet my make.   (306)

¹ Et tu*n*c clauso tentorio dic*et* Regi*n*a secrete
    nu*n*cio.

¹ REGINA.

Messag*er* i pray þe nowe
ffor þi curteysye.
Go to þe bisschop for þi prowe
& byd hi*m* hydir to hye.   (310)

bid hi*m* be war*e* be ffore
sey hi*m* þ*at* he most pr*e*che;
My lord þe ki*n*g is ney lore
bot he wol be hi*s* leche.   (314)

sey hi*m* þ*at* he wol leue noȝt
þat eu*er* he schal deye;
he is i*n* siche erro*ur* broȝte
Of god stont hi*m* no*n* eye.   (318)

NUNCIUS.

Ma da*m* i make no tariyng
W*ith* softe wordis mo;
ffor I a*m* solas i most si*n*ge
Ouer al qwh*er* i go. *et* cant*at*   (322)

sir*e* bisschop þ*ou* sittist o*n* þi se
w*ith* þi mitir on þi heuede
My lady þe qwe*n* pr*e*yith þe
hi*t* schold noȝt be bi leuyd   (326)
*   *   *   *   *   *   *

[Eᴘɪsᴄᴏᴘᴜs.]

ʒe world is nou so wo lo wo
in suc bal i bound
yat dred of god is al ago
& treut is go to ground   (330)

med is mad a demisman
streyint bet it ʒe lau
gocyl is mad a cepman
& truyt is don of dau   (334)

Wyt is nou al trecri
oyis fals & gret
play is nou uileni
& corteysi is let   (338)

lou is nou al lecuri
cildrin bet onlerit
halliday is glotuni
yis lan is bot irerit   (342)

slot men blet bleyud
& lokit al amis
he bicomit onkynd
& yat is reut i uis   (346)

frend may no man find
of fremit ne of sib
ʒe ded bet out of mind
gret soru it is to lib   (350)

yes ricmen bet reuþyles
ʒe por got to ground
& fals men bet schanles
þe sot ic hau i found   (354)

ʒe ric kynyit it is wrong
al yat ʒe por dot
far yat is sen day & nit
wo sa wol sig sot   (358)

paraventur men halt me a fol
to sig yat fot tal
yai farit as ficis in a pol
ȝe gret eteit ȝe smal   (362)

ric men spart for noying
to do ȝe por wrong[1]
yai yingit not on hen ending
ne on det yat is so strong   (366)

noyir yai louit god ne dredit
noyir him no his lauis
touart hel fast him draut
ayeins har ending daus   (370)

bot god of his godnis
ȝif ham gras to amend
Into ȝe delful derkyns
þe got wyt out hend   (374)

yer is dred & sorow
& wo wytoutin wel
no man may oyir borou
be ȝer neuir so fel   (378)

yer ne fallit ne maynpris
ne supersidias
þaȝt þe be kyng or iustis
ȝe passit not ȝe pas   (382)

lord yat for his manhed
& also for his god
þat for lou & not for dred
deit oppon ȝe rod   (386)

ȝif ou gras or lif to led
yat be ȝour soulis to bot
god of heuin for his godhed
leu yat hit so mot. Amen   (390)

---

[1] worng in original.

Tunc dicet regi.

schir kyng þing oppon þin end
& hou yat þou schalt dey
wat uey yat þou schalt wend
bot þou be bisey   (394)

þeke yat þou art lenust man
& haddist begyning
& euirmor han þout opon
þi dredful ending   (398)

þou schalt þing þanne
& mac ʒe euir þyar
yat det is not ʒe man
for no ying ʒe nil spar   (402)

þou schalt do dedis of charite
& lernd crist is lor
& lib in heuin lit
to sauy yi soul fre sor   (406)

Rex.

wat bissop byssop babler
schold y of det hau dred
þou art bot a chagler
go hom yi wey i red   (410)

wat com þou yerfor hidir
wet deþt me to afer
þit þou & he wer bot togidir
into ʒe se irot uer   (414)

go hom god yif ʒe sorow
þou wreist me in mi mod
war woltou prec tomorou
þou nost uer bi ʒe rod   (418)

troust þou I nold be ded
In mi þyng lif
þou lisst screu bolhed
euil met þou triwe. (422)

wat schold i do at churg wat
schir bisop wostoner
nay churc nis no wyl cot
hit wol abid yer. (426)

I wool let car away
& go on mi petying
to hontyng & to oir play
for al yi long prechyng (430)

I am þyng as þou mit se
& hau no ned to char
þe wyld ȝe quen & . . me
about me bet yar. (434)

Episcopus.

thynk schir kyng one oyir trist
yat tyng misst son
þot þou leu nou as ȝe list
det wol cum rit son. (438)

& ȝiue þe deth is wounde
ffor þin outrage ;
with in a litil stounde
þen artou but a page. (442)

Qwhen þou art grauen on grene
þat mete is ffeyt & moide ;
þen helpith litil I wene
þi gay croun of golde. (446)

sire kyng haue goday
Crist i ȝou be teche.

Rex.

ffare wel bisschop þi way
& lerne bet to preche.   hic adde   (450)

Nou maifay hit schal be sene
I trow ʒit to daye;
Qwher deth me durst tene
& mete in þe waye.   (454)

Qwher artou my messagere
solas bi þi name;
loke þat þou go ffer & nere
as þou wolt haue no blame   (458)

My banis ffor to crye
by dayis & bi niʒte;
& loke þat þou aspye
ʒe bi al þi miʒte.   (462)

Of deth & of his maistrye
Qwher he durst com in siʒte;
O ʒeynis me & my meyne
with fforce & armis to ffiʒte.   (466)

loke þat þou go both est & west
& com o ʒeyne on one;

Nuncius.

lorde to wende I am prest
lo now I am gone.   & eat pla . . . (470)

Pes & listenith to my sawe
boþe ʒonge & olde;
as ʒe wol noʒt ben a slawe
be ʒe neuer so bolde.   (474)

I am a messager i sente
ffrom þe king of life;
þat ʒe schal ffulfil his . . . ente
on peyne of lym & lif.   (478)

his hestes to hold & his lawe
vche a man on honde ;
lest ʒe be henge & to draw
Or kast in hard bonde.   (482)

ʒe wittin wel þat he is king
& lord of al londis ;
kepere & maister of al thing
with in se & sondis.   (486)

I am sente ffor to enquer
o boute ferre & nere ;
ʒif any man dar werre a rere
a ʒein suche a bachelere.   (490)

to wroþer hele he was i bore
þat wold with him stryue ;
be him sikir he is i lore
As here in þis lyne   (494)

þegh hit wer þe king of deth
& he so hardy were ;
bot he ne hath miʒt ne meth
þe king of lif to a ffere   (498)

be he so hardy or so wode
in his londe to a ryue
he wol se his herte blode
And he with him stryue   (502)

*   *   *   *   *   *

NOTES.

―

Account of Thomas de Beuley.—This account, as extant, is but a fragment of a much longer document. There now remain one complete membrane, 22½ inches by 9½ ; and a ragged fragment about 7 by 8½ inches. The fragment, so far as it has been deciphered, is printed on pages 1 to 4, and 16 to 20. Its ending, as well as illegible and defective parts, are indicated by dots. . . . . Of Thomas de Beuley nothing is known beyond the notices to be found in these accounts.

The *Translation* is slightly shortened by the omission of a few words where unnecessarily repeated.

Seneschal.—The Seneschal was the land agent and judge of the manor courts of the possessions of the Priory. A treatise on the office of Seneschal, attributed to about the time of Edw. I., is included in a volume recently published by the Royal Historical Society ("Walter de Henley's Husbandry," &c.). This treatise thus describes the duties of a Seneschal:—"He ought to know the law of the realm, to protect his lord's business, and to instruct and give assurance to the bailiffs who are beneath him, in their difficulties. He ought two or three times a-year to make his rounds, and visit the manors of his stewardship ; and then he ought to inquire about the rents, services, and customs hidden or withdrawn, and about franchises of courts, lands, woods, meadows, pastures, waters, mills, and other things which belong to the manor ; and if he be able, let him amend these things in the right way without doing wrong to any ; and if he be not, let him show it to his lord, that he may deal with it if he wish to maintain it." In the larger monasteries the Seneschal was frequently a layman, often a lawyer. In our Priory the office was undertaken by one of the canons, who also acted as treasurer.

Maurice Howel was among the most prominent men of the southern part of Co. Dublin. In the Memorandum Roll of 5 & 6 Edw. III. he is found accounting for the King's lands at Bray. Among other lands which he rented, he was brought into direct contact with the Priory, by holding from it the lands of Carrickmines and Brennanstown. He had frequently been one of the leaders of the county levies against the O'Byrnes.

John Aket.—This is no doubt the John Haket mentioned frequently afterwards. Other instances of the uncertain use of the aspirate about this period are not infrequent.

Wine, 3d.—The price of wine was probably, as at a later time it is stated to be (p. 109), 6*d.* a gallon. The maximum price was regulated by proclamation. A few years previously wine had thus been forbidden to be sold at any higher price than 5*d.* a gallon on pain of forfeiture (*Mem. Rot.*, 5 & 6 Edw. III.). Before this the price had been fixed at 4*d.*, and a few years still earlier at 3*d.* A prosecution against a seller of wine, when the price was fixed by proclamation at 3*d.*, is printed in Hist. & Mun. Doc., ed. Gilbert, p. 530.

Prior.—At this time Gilbert de Bolyniop, who had very recently been raised to the office in the room of Roger de Goioun, deprived in the preceding July. In 1343 (*see* p. 27) he found himself obliged to resign, and is afterwards chiefly remembered by the debts which remained from his time of rule. He was after his retirement allowed a pension of two marks a-year (p. 104).

Holmpatrick.—An early religious foundation of Augustinian canons, originally seated on S. Patrick's Island, but subsequently removed to the adjoining mainland, at or near the present town of Skerries, Co. Dublin, where the house at this time stood.

John de Novo Castro, or **Newcastle,** was about this time appointed gauger of wines for Ireland. He had before (in 1317) been employed as acting keeper of the temporal property of the See of Dublin when in the King's hands during vacancy (*Christ Church Deeds*, No. 548); and had acted as paymaster of the forces sent from Ireland to Scotland in the King's service in the campaign of 1333 (*Mem. Rot.*, 7 Edw. III.). He is to be distinguished from John de Castro afterwards mentioned.

Robert de Houton, or **Hoghton,** was a citizen of Dublin; at this time one of the bailiffs of the city. He appears afterwards making small loans to the Priory.

Balscaddan is a village and parish in the extreme north of the Co. Dublin, about three miles inland from Balbriggan. It was granted to the Priory in 1250 by Henry III., in lieu of the manor of Oconogh and its castle previously granted to them by King John. It was then valued at 30 librates of land, and the issues were to be shared with the dean and chapter of S. Patrick's (*Sweetman Cal.* I., p. 462). At this time the entire parish belonged to the Priory, forming one of the most valuable manors among its possessions. *See Rental in Appendix.*

William de Asheburne was probably at this time one of the Prior's esquires. Twelve years previously he had been the Prior's attorney in a *Quare impedit* suit (*Mem. Rot.*, 18 Edw. II.). He perhaps afterwards became a professed member of the Convent; from page 42 onward he is always mentioned as " brother." Twenty years previously there had been an abbot of S. Mary's, Dublin, of this name.

PAGE 2.

Bread for Horses.—Panis equinus, or horse bread, is a not infrequent item in English household accounts down to the 16th century. It has usually been explained as being a mash made from meal; but must certainly have been baked loaves. In the London Liber Albus (vol. III., p. 426, *Rolls Series*) a baker is convicted of being found " cum tribus panibus equinis," each of which was light in weight. In the glossary to same volume " Payn pur chivalx " is described as : " Horse bread. This was, made of beans as well as peas. It was also made into loaves, the weight and quality of which were regulated by assize." That the material for horse bread in Dublin was similar may be seen from an entry on p. 81.

Dromsalon.—Drumshallon, Co. Louth, six miles due north of Drogheda. This was another of the manors belonging to the Priory. It appears from a memorandum preserved in the Black Book of Archbishop Alan (p. 28, Marsh's Lib. copy), that it had been granted to the Priory a little before 1258 by Philip de Nugent. The Priory was to erect a cell here, where three of the canons were to remain in residence, serving the church of S. Mary at Drumshallon, as well as the church of Philipston Nugent (Philipstown parish, near Dundalk), with its chapels of Drumorcher and Hesmachlenyne, with which, as well as two carucates of land, the cell was endowed. The canons in the cell of Drumshallon soon incurred the displeasure of the Archbishop of Armagh, in whose diocese they were placed. The Archbishop, on the ground that the cell had not sufficient goods, and was too far distant from the mother church for a healthy religious life, suppressed the cell, and with the sanction of Geoffrey de Nugent, son of the founder,

L.

permitted the endowments to pass to the Priory. This act was in 1359 confirmed by John de Kinton, who seems to have succeeded the Nugents in the property.

John Passeleu was one of the tenants of the Priory at Balscaddan, visited a few days before. His obit is entered in the Mortilogium of the house at the 21st Dec. The family of Passelewe was intimately connected with this manor. In the grant from Henry III., in 1250, Robert and Andrew Passelewe are named as tenants there (*Sweetman Cal.* II., p. 79). Notwithstanding the Norman form of the name, the family may have been Irish. In 1282 there was a grant to one Simon Passelewe, "born of an English mother, though of an Irish father," that he and his heirs may for ever use English law and custom (*Sweetman Cal.* II., p. 423). The name is afterwards met among the Dublin citizens, passing into the form Paslow.

In the Rental in the Appendix this name is found at Balscaddan in immediate juxtaposition with the similar name Passavaunt. The latter name is quite Norman. The first of this name is stated to have been sent to Ireland in 1222, as one of the King's balisters on foot—artillery officers (*Sweetman Cal.* I., p. 165). Later, John Passavaunt the balister was employed to fortify the castles of Roscommon and Randon. Members of the family became leading citizens of Dublin in the 14th and 15th centuries. Passavant was the war-cry of the Counts of Champagne (*Dict. de l'Acad. Franc. Complément*).

Page 3.

Swords lies on the road to Drogheda and the other places mentioned during the preceding days, and was now passed on the homeward journey from them.

Hugh de Saltu, the Marshal of the Archbishop.—These may be the same or two different persons. The term marshal, originally a groom, was still, with decreasing frequency, connected with horses in the senses of a veterinary surgeon and a farrier; its more general use at this time was, however, that of the controller of the household or master of the ceremonies in the hall of a great noble. If De Saltu was the marshal, he may, too, in that capacity, have led the Archbishop's contingent to the hosting against the O'Byrnes (p. 157), for an entry on the memorandum roll of 12 & 13 Edw. III. records an order to pay him 100s. for two horses lost in the company of master John Rees, treasurer, going against the Obrynnes and other Irish enemies in the parts of Leinster. Hugh's full name was De Saltu Salmonum, *i.e.*,

Salmon Leap or Leixlip. Cotton says he was born at that place. Several entries on the rolls testify to his connexion in some form with that manor. He was a canon of S. Patrick's, a position which he obtained by Papal provision (*Regesta Pontificum*, vol. iv., p. 517, *London Record Office*). In 1347 he became bishop of Ferns.

Infirmary.—Properly the apartments devoted to invalided members of the confraternity. From the way the term is frequently used in these accounts (p. 7, &c.) it seems probable that it also included here the hospitium or guest house of the Prior .

Page 4.

Default of the Cellarer.—The home brewing and baking appear to have been under the direction of this officer, whose duty it was also to provide the corn required for these purposes. See Cellarer's account in Appendix.

Master Thomas de Kylmor was a citizen of Dublin. He had probably received some minor orders, as at p. 44 he is described as a clerk. He married Susanna, daughter of William Beydyn of Dublin, clerk, with whom he received a house in Nicholas-street. The original conveyance is preserved (*Ch. Ch. Deeds*, p. 619). His will is preserved in Archbishop Alan's Black Book (p. 470, Marsh's Lib. copy), dated 27th July, 1354. He possessed a tenement in Dublin (probably that in Nicholas-street), which he inhabited; another called the Newhall, with the little hall next the pillory; and a farm; and left all to his wife Susanna.

Summa iii. s. . . . . . Probata.—Here ends one side of the fragment referred to on p. 142. The rest of this membrane, comprising ntries for six weeks, has decayed away. The extant complete membrane commences with the entry "Die dominica proxima sequente. Omnia de stauro, &c."

Page 5.

Sacrista.—Properly Sacristeria or Sacristia. The form Sacrista, however, seems alone to have been known to the clerks who wrote these accounts, as in the only instances where the termination of this word is written fully it is in the form *sacrista*. The apartment referred to was probably the chamber of the sacristan, the convent officer in whose charge were the building and furniture of the church.

John de Grancet or Grauntsete was a judge of the King's Bench. He was son of Ralph de Grauntsete. He was appointed one of the barons of the Exchequer, 19 Edw. II., and second justice of the King's Bench 1 Edw. III. Soon after he fell into great disgrace for allowing a case before him to be removed to the jurisdiction of the Ecclesiastical Court. For having thus failed to uphold the royal prerogative, he was removed from office, imprisoned, and fined 500 marks. In consideration, however, of his good services, and on representation from members of the King's Council, he was soon pardoned and restored to office (*Mem. Rot.*, 3 Edw. III.). He was afterwards repeatedly employed in responsible services, notably as one of the arbitrators sent to Kilkenny to arrange the disputes between the Earls of Ulster and Desmond (*Ib.* 5 & 6 Edw. III.). He then visited England, and a writ of Liberate testifies to his services to the King in various parts of England as well as in Ireland (*Ib.* 7 Edw. III.).

He married Alice, a daughter of Geoffrey de Morton, who had been Mayor of Dublin 32 Edw. I., and by her, as well as otherwise, acquired much property in and about the city. Relative to some of this property a curious agreement between De Grauntsete and the city authorities may be found in Mr. Gilbert's Hist. & Mun. Doc., p. 281. De Morton had built some houses against the city wall at the end of the bridge in Bridge-street. These impeding the access to the wall for defence, were in part pulled down by royal command. On condition of leaving a well fortified passage along the wall 3½ feet broad, De Grauntsete and wife were permitted to rebuild the houses, with windows, latrines, and other necessary belongings; the latrine to be made through the middle of the wall opening into the river Liffey.

A document still preserved (*Ch. Ch. Deeds*, No. 225) attests in a remarkable way De Grauntsete's piety and the extent of his benefactions to the Priory. The following is a somewhat shortened translation :—

To all sons of holy mother Church who shall look upon this page, Brother Roger Goioun, Prior of the Church of the Holy Trinity, Dublin, and the convent of the same place, health everlasting in God . . . . Whereas, our very dear John de Grauntsete lifting his mind to heavenly desires, and aspiring to extend the office of divine worship, and for the devout increase of divine service, has lovingly offered and obtained for our house many and divers goods for perpetual memory, and to maintain the rights of the said church divers times has laboured much, and has many times performed things pleasing and useful to us and our church in past times. We grant . . . . to the same John in life and in death, and to Alice, formerly his wife, and all for whom they are bound as well living as dead, participation as full as to the founder of our said church in all masses, matins, preces, prayers, fasts, alms, suffrages, vigils, disciplines, and in all other good deeds which by the help of God may be done, within our said church and priory as long as the world shall last. . . . . We will also and by our unanimous consent ordain, and we and all our successors effectively bind our-selves to find two canons priests in our said church serving the Most High under regular observance on every day to celebrate for ever divine offices, and the same celebration solemnly to begin on the day of the completion of these presents, especially for the welfare of the same John while he lives, and that all his works begun to the praise of God may be happily completed, also for the souls of the said Alice, their ancestors, heirs, benefactors, and all those for whom the same John and Alice are in any way bound, and of all the faithful departed. And when the same John shall have passed from this life, the same canons shall daily celebrate specially for the soul of the same John and for the souls of the same Alice and of all aforesaid. Of which two canons one shall celebrate daily the Mass of the Blessed Virgin Mary, as is the custom, and this specially for the said John and for the soul of the said Alice and for all aforesaid. And in each Mass for the said John and others aforesaid so celebrated, while John is living, he shall say spe-cially this collect daily for the same John, " Pretende Domine famulo tuo dexteram celestis auxilii, ut te toto corde perquirat et que digne postulat assequatur." And for the souls of the said Alice and of all the aforesaid he shall say another collect, " Omnipotens sempiterne Deus qui vivorum dominaris simul et mortuorum omniumque misereris quos tuos fide et opere futuros esse prenostis; te supplices exoramus, ut pro quibus effundere preces decrevimus," &c. And when the said John shall have entered upon the way of all flesh, the said canon in every Mass shall say specially for the soul of the same John, this collect, " Quesimus Domine pro tua pietate miserere anime famuli tui et a contagiis mortalitatis exutam in eterne sal-vacionis partem restitue"; with the other collect, " Omnipotens, sempiterne Deus," aforesaid, for the soul of the same Alice and the others aforesaid. Also the other canon shall celebrate daily at the altar before the Holy Cross in our said church, specially for the said John and for the soul of the said Alice, and for the others aforesaid ; and shall say the aforesaid collects in the aforesaid form. Which canons having put on their sacred vestments before the introit of each Mass, privately or openly, shall say, " Pater noster" and " Ave Maria" for the said John and Alice, and for the souls of all faithful departed. And beside this, the anniversaries of the said John and Alice in our priory, we and all our successors as long as the world shall endure will celebrate, with such solemnity as the anniversary of our first and principal founder, and as solemnly as in any time past it was accustomed to be celebrated, to wit, the anniversary of the same John on the day of the Assumption of the Blessed Virgin Mary, and the anniversary of said Alice on the 6 June, and every day on which the commemoration of the dead shall be read through in our chapter or in the choir, the souls of the same John and Alice shall there be absolved by name. And as often as any of the said two canons on account of sickness or other lawful cause shall be prevented from celebrating, then another canon of our house shall faithfully supply his turn, and every Saturday and other days when the table of services of our choir shall be ordered, written, and read, by the hebdomadarius and other ministers of our said church, we will and grant unanimously for us and our successors, that the aforesaid two canons so to celebrate according to the said form for the said John and Alice and others above named, shall be faithfully ordered and written in our said table, and of them by the ministers of our church in the reading of our said table, let there be express mention by name. . . . . And likewise every Prior in our Priory newly created, in his entry into our chapter after his creation, in the presence of the convent, and all and every the novices before they shall be admitted to profession in our said Priory, in our full chapter, shall be bound with the bond of an oath that they will faithfully observe the said ordinance and chantry in every article, and to their ability for ever will maintain it. . . . . We will also and grant for us and our successors that in every missal of the said house in the margin by the secretum of the Mass, there shall be written for perpetual memory of it, " Orate pro Johanne de Grauntsete et Alicia uxore ejus ac pro omnibus quibus tenentur," and so, unremoved for all time, let the writing remain. And lest forgetfulness destroy what loving gratitude has instituted, twice in every year, on All Souls Day and Quinquagesima Sunday, this present ordinance shall be read through in our chapter in the presence of all the brethren; and let this whole agreement and ordinance, word for word, be entered and copied in our Mortilogium for the better record of it. Moreover, we will and grant for us and our successors that the ring of gold with the precious stone and with the silver chain, offered by the said John de Grauntsete in honour of the Holy Trinity in our said church to the Holy Cross there, may from the same Holy Cross, with the said chain, firmly hang for the sick, that those whom Almighty God, by the virtue of the precious stone, shall have restored to health, may pray for the same John and Alice to the Almighty, and that the keepers of the said holy cross and also those who administer the said ring to such sick persons shall openly enjoin and charge the said sick persons to pray specially for the said John and Alice and for those for whom they are bound. Moreover, we will and grant for us and our successors, that that ring remain there for ever and hang from the said holy cross, and under pain of anathema laid by us upon this, that no man should ever remove it from this cross for any cause. . . . . Dated at Dublin in our chapter house 9 July, 1335.

(*Legend on seal*) S. JOHIS FILII RADVLPHI DE GRAVNTSETE.

Notwithstanding the particularity of the concluding provisions, the document is not copied into the Martyrology as preserved to us, nor is there any commemoration of De Grauntsete on the feast of the Assumption. Alice is, however, commemorated on the 6th June, the day of her obit ; and John, under the somewhat obscured form of John de Grameet, is grouped with several other benefactors to be remembered on Whit Sunday.

Another document in the Christ Church Collection (No. 236) is a further evidence of the piety of De Grauntsete. It recites that in 1341 Brother Gilbert (de Bolyniop), with consent of the Chapter of the Priory, had granted to John de Grauntsete, for ten years, all the offerings made before the image, "Beate Marie Virginis Gloriose," upon the bridge of Dublin, in consideration of certain meritorious works to be carried out by him before the same image on the bridge. Brother Robert de Hereforde, Prior, and the Convent, in 1347, consent that instead of the intended works on the bridge, the offerings may be expended on the erection of a certain chapel in honour of the Holy Trinity within the cemetery of their church of St. Michan in Oustemantoun, on the north side of that church (S. Michan's Church in Church-street, Dublin).

Sir Thomas Wogan seems to have been the son and heir of Sir John Wogan, the vigorous Viceroy of Ireland under Edward I. He had only recently been appointed escheator in succession to Edward Morteyn, and in the execution of this office had probably already been brought into conflict with the Priory. He was made by the King Seneschal of Kildare, while the possessions were in the Crown during minority of the earl ; and was afterwards Seneschal of the Lordship of Meath. The annalist Clyn, under the year 1346, tells that about the feast of S. Clement, thirty men of the O'Dempseys were slain by two, Thomas Wogan and Walter Lenfaut, at Ardscull.

Elias de Assheburne was a justice of the King's Bench. He appears to have been a member of a family already, for some time, seated in Dublin. His father Roger de Ashbourne had been Mayor of Dublin about the end of the 13th century; William was Abbot of S. Mary's Abbey somewhat later; and others of the name are met with. Elias sought advancement in England and was taken into the service of John bishop of Ely, Treasurer of England (*Cal. Pat. Rot.*, p. 25). He first came into prominence on the fall of the Archbishop de Bykenor and Walter de Istelep, in 1326. He appears to have been sent specially to Ireland to superintend the seizure, on behalf of the King, of the goods of these two delinquents (*Mem. Rot.*, 19 Edw. II.). To carry out this purpose he was appointed constable of the Castle of Swords, and Seneschal of the Archbishop's Manor of S. Sepulchre (*Ibid.*). He obtained a grant of lands which had been held by Walter de Istelep. These were situated near Tallaght, along the foot of the Dublin mountains, about Bohernabreena (*Lib. Nig. Alani*, p. 55, Marsh's Lib. copy). He had already acquired considerable property as a middleman; and in the extent of the Archbishop's lands taken on their seizure, his name appears as tenant of six different holdings in the manor of Swords. He led during many years an active public life. He is mentioned on the rolls as leader of the county levies; as constable of the Castle of Arklow; commander at Newcastle; fighting when necessary, treating when possible, with the O'Byrnes and other Irish of the mountains. In 1342 he was appointed chief justice. He had two sons, Robert and Sir Thomas. A daughter Elizabeth, married William Marward, and from her the descent of the barons of Screen for several generations is traced in Archbishop Alan's Black Book (p. 55, Marsh's Lib. copy). An inquisition taken on his death, 30 Edw. III., is preserved in the same work (p. 672, T. C. D. copy).

Justices Itinerant.—The Justices in Eyre or circuit judges. They were, perhaps, entertained officially before setting out on their circuit. See an entry on p. 19, which probably relates to the same visit.

Page 7.

John Haket was one of the most frequent visitors to the Prior. He was probably at this time the tenant of Stillorgan, and was the owner of a mill near Clonken (pp. 83 and 87), perhaps on one of two streams which flow by Stillorgan. He held also some position for which he received a fee from the Priory of 20s. (p. 44). He was a principal man in the district; had been a leader of the counties levies against O'Byrne; and was appointed one of four keepers of the peace appointed by the viceroy and council to assess the men of the county for service in the field (*Mem. Rot.*, 7 Edw. III.). Three other members of the family, William, Oliver, and Thomas Haket are mentioned in these accounts, chiefly as helping in a neighbourly way at the manor of Clonken. The name is still preserved in the district, in the townland of Hacketsland, lying to the south of Killiney.

Gilbert de Moenes held the lands now known as Rathmines. For a notice of him and of the family of De Meones, see the *Journal* of the Society for 1889, p. 36.

John de Balygodman was also, apparently, a neighbour of the manor of Clonken (p. 69). He had a few years previously been chosen Sheriff of Co. Dublin, but being engaged in military service with the Justiciary was excused from acting.

PAGE 8.

Sheriff.—William Comyn was, this year, sheriff of the county of Dublin. He was proprietor of Kinsaley, Co. Dublin, for which he paid a head rent to the Priory.

PAGE 9.

Kilcullen, Co. Kildare.—The rectory of this parish was a valuable property of the Priory. It appears to have been usual for one of the canons to reside here. See a curious instance of this quoted below under the head of John Comyn.

Mackyngan, Newcastle, Co. Wicklow.—Now a small village, it was then a place of some consequence. It possessed a royal castle of which the remains still stand. Its burgesses were governed by a provost, and paid an annual rent to the Crown of £20. (*Pipe Roll*, 5 & 6 Edw. III.). In 1303 the town received a grant of customs to be devoted to enclosing the town, implying, by the variety of articles on which duties were specified, an extensive trade (*Chartae Rec. Com.*, p. 41). A little later an assize court was held here (*Mem. Rot.*, 33 Edw. I.). But its position was much exposed to attack. In a petition in 1344, the burgesses urge that, "the manor was in the Marches, and divers times by the Irish felons and rebels was burned and devastated " (*Ib.*, 16 & 17 Edw. III.). And they were soon after permitted to retain a portion of their rent, to be expended in clearing and repair of the fosses round the town (*Ib.* 18 & 19 Edw. III.).

To Ward.—That is to take part in the garrisoning of Newcastle. W. de Asshebourne probably commanded the men levied on the manors of the Priory for this service. Entries on p. 18 relate to the defensive armour furnished for those going on this service. The *Mem. Rot. Exch.*, 13 Edw. III., contains an order for John Aunger, clerk, who was assigned to pay the wages of the men-at-arms, hobelars, and footmen, placed at Newcastle M·Kynegan, for the custody of the castle, and of the faithful people of those parts against the hostile attacks of Irish enemies and rebels. From two to five men-at-arms, and eight or ten hobelars, the former at 1*s.* the latter at 6*d.* a-day, were then retained. See also p. 18.

Master John de Pylattenhale is described as official of the archdeacon of Dublin (*Mem. Rot.*, 3 Ed. II.). He returned an account to the Exchequer of goods which came to his hands from Sampson de Shaftesbury, clerk of the works of Dublin Castle, and vicar of S. Kevin's, Dublin. (*Mem. Rot.*, 5 & 6 Edw. III.). See another entry referring to him on p. 16.

PAGE 10.

Friars Preachers of Arklow.—A Dominican friary was founded at Arklow, in the present county of Wicklow, by Theobald Fitz Walter, in the thirteenth century. Scarcely anything is known of its history.

PAGE 11.

Prior of S. Wolstan's, two of the canons.—The Priory de Scala Coeli, of canons of the congregation of S. Victor, at S. Wolstan's, on the Liffey, near Celbridge, Co. Kildare. This visit must have been connected with the following incident :—" It was commanded to the Sheriff [of Co. Kild.] to take the Prior of the house of S. Wolstan, brother Gilbert Broun and brother Philip the Olde, fellow canons of said Prior, and put them in safe custody in prison, so that he have their bodies here to make fine with the King for a certain trespass made against John Norreys, *valettus* of Simon Fitz Richard, chief justice of the Bench." The Sheriff returned that they were not to be found, and was commanded to arrest them by the following term. (*Plea Roll* No. 183, *m.* **18** *f. Easter*, 12 Edw. III.).

John de Moenes was Mayor of Dublin for the third time in this or the preceding year.

PAGE 12.

Robert de Clifford held land of the King at Any, Co. Limerick.

Robert Tanner became Mayor of Dublin this year, in succession to John de Moenes. He, too, had twice before held the office.

Laetare Jerusalem.—The fourth Sunday in Lent, or Mid-Lent, is called Laetare Sunday, from the opening word of the antiphon of the introit—"Rejoice O Jerusalem, and gather together all ye who love her," &c.—*Catholic Dict.*, Addis and Arnold.

PAGE 13.

Mustrison.—The assembly and inspection of the military levy. The form used here, an old French one—Mustreson = Monstraison, action de montrer, de faire voir.—*Godefroy Dict.* A corresponding Latin form—mustrizona—is found on the Patent Rolls.

Gregory Taunton was tenant of lands of the Priory at Cornelscourt in the manor of Clonken. He held other lands in the neighbourhood.

PAGE 14.

John Callan, a citizen of Dublin. He became one of the bailiffs of the city in this year.

Peter Howel was tenant of the lands of Ballymorthan, or Ballymolwhan, now represented by Murphystown.

PAGE 15.

Parasceve.—Παρασκευη, the Preparation. The term is usually applied to Good Friday, but here is referred to the preceding day.

Holy Oil at Kildare.—The holy oil is consecrated by the Bishop on Holy Thursday, and received from him by the priests who have charge of parishes. In the absence of the Archbishop from Dublin,

Kildare would be the nearest place where a bishop had his seat.   See
again, p. 92.

Robert Hony was a citizen and merchant of Dublin.   He had been
bailiff of the city in 1335.   He became surety for the merchants of
Aquitaine for the payment of certain customs on leather, for which
they were liable.   (*Mem. Rot.*, 13 and 14 Edw. III.).

Page 16.

William Mareschall was a prominent citizen of Dublin.   He had
been Mayor in 1327.   A chaplain of the same name also is mentioned
on the Patent Roll of 11 Edw. III.

Summa x d. Probata.—With this entry ends the extant complete
membrane of this account.   The succeeding entries to p. 20 are upon
the reverse of the fragment noted at p. 143.

John de Castro.—He seems to have been one of the canons, and
his other employments show him to have been specially trusted.

To Trim.—The Escheator was at this time Thomas Wogan, who
among other offices held the position of seneschal of the lordship of
Trim.

Escheator of Ireland.—For some years past an intermittent
struggle had been carried on with the Escheators as representing the
interests of the Crown, as to the Crown's right to hold the property of
the Priory during the vacancy of the office of Prior, as in the case of
bishoprics and other tenants in chief.   It appears that the claim had
never been put forward until 1326, when on the resignation of the
Prior, Hugh le Joevene, the possessions were formally seized by the
Escheator Walter de la Pulle; and, though an Inquisition found that
he had no right to do so, he only withdrew on receiving substantial
personal security that the issues would be made good, if afterwards
found to be legally belonging to the King.   On the death of Prior
Robert de Gloucester, a few years later, the possessions were seized by
the then Escheator John Moris, but were restored by writ from the
deputy 20th April, 1331.   Again, on the deposition of Prior Roger Goioun
July, 1337, they were seized by Edmund Morteyn, and then by his
successor Thomas Wogan, Escheators; but no effective attempt was
made to take the profits.   A letter in French from the prior and convent to the Justiciary and council at this time, asking for relief, is

preserved. A commission was issued for an inquiry, which proved entirely favourable to the Priory. But no definite concession was made, and the claim continued as a source of vexation and expense to the convent, and without any profit to the Crown. Numerous references will be met in these accounts to expedients for staying the hands of the Escheators on the occurrence of the two vacancies which arose during the period covered by the accounts. The claim was not finally relinquished until 1348, when a royal writ directed the restoration of the temporalities of the Priory, and that they should not be taken on occasion of any future vacancy. (*Ch. Ch. Deeds*, Nos. 220, 224, 229-31, 237.) A number of documents in this case may be found collected on the Memorandum Roll, 12 Edw. III. (*m.* 15).

Poynteston.—Probably Punchestown, Co. Kildare.

Pro subsidio spiritualium.—Probably in payment of the subsidy of one-tenth granted by the clergy in Parliament of 11 Edw. III. in aid of the wars of the land (*Mem. Rot.*, 13 & 14 Ed. III.).

PAGE 17.

Treasurer of Ireland was master John Rees, a Welshman, who in 1337 came to Ireland in that capacity, in the company of sir John Cherleton, then appointed Justiciary. Camden's Annals say that with sir John and his brother Thomas Cherleton, bishop of Hereford, came "master John Rees, Treasurer of Ireland, and Doctor in the Decretals, bringing with them many Welshmen, to the number of two hundred, and arrived in the haven of Dublin." He soon afterwards became justice of the Bench.

Hobelarii.—Light armed horsemen. The pay of hobelars engaged at this time was 6*d.* a-day (*see* p. 154). The small payment in the text must therefore have been only a gratuity.

Going with the Treasurer upon the Obrynnes.—No account is given of this expedition in the Annalists. Some entries on the Memorandum Rolls, however, seem to refer to it. Fynok Otothil (O'Toole) was paid 66*s.* 8*d.* for wages of 10 hobelars and 12 footmen who took part in an attack against the O'Byrnes and others of Leinster (*Mem. Rot.*, 12 Edw. III.). Hugh de Saltu's horses, mentioned above (p. 146), were evidently lost in this expedition.

N. de Barton.—Nicholas de Barton had 20 years previously acted as proctor of the Prior and Convent in a suit with reference to Kilcullen (*Ch. Ch. Deeds*, No. 198). He was a canon, and is afterwards described as cellarer.

John de Evesham was a canon of S. Patrick's, who had been employed on several fiscal posts. Thus he is found acting as paymaster of the men employed by the Justiciary against the Leinster rebels (*Cal. Pat. Rot.*, p. 20).

Subsidy . . . towards . . . Scotland.—By letters of 8th May, 9 Edw. III. (1335), printed in Rymer, the King directed the Government of Ireland to obtain aid in men and money for war against Scotland.

In obedience to the first part of this order, the Justiciary went over in person with a force of men.

It does not appear that any parliament was assembled to raise the money aid. The next parliament held here was in the 11th year, and the subsidy voted there was for the wars of the land, that is in Ireland. Money was raised for the Scotch wars nevertheless; probably by direct appeals to the different towns and districts. The city of Dublin granted a subsidy of £100 for the Scotch wars (*Mem. Rot.*, 9 Edw. III.). The bishop and clergy of Cork granted the 20th penny, and the county of Dublin 12*d.*, a carucate from the temporalities of the clergy, and 2*s.* a carucate of lay fee (*Pipe Roll*, No. 60, 9 Edw. III.). The sum now paid was no doubt in discharge of this grant.

PAGE 18.

Clerk of the Markets.—The transaction referred to in this entry was not an isolated case. On the 20th Feb., 1367, it was represented to the King by the prelates, magnates, and people that many persons had been excessively and unduly amerced by, and great abuses had taken place in the office of Clerk of the Market, who made journeys through the country, and charged exorbitant fees even where they did not examine the weights and measures. The King directed that no fees should be charged or enforced but those payable in England and which should be moderate. (*Betham, Hist. of the Constitution,* p. 302.)

The following standard measures were in care of this officer, and seven or eight years later were lodged in the Exchequer by a successor, John fitzSimon of Clondalkin, "custos mercati Regis" in Ireland (*Mem. Rot.*, 19 & 20 Edw. III.) :—

> 1 bushel bound with iron.
> 1 brass gallon.
> 1 brass quart.
> 1 iron ell.
> 3 iron seals for sealing weights and measures.
> 1 lead weight of the weight of a stone.
> 1 brass ,, ,, 1 lb.
> 1 lead ,, ,, lb.
> 1 ,, ,, ,, $\frac{1}{4}$ lb.
> 1 brass ,, ,, $\frac{1}{8}$ lb.

Chancellor.—The Chancellor referred to was most probably Thomas de Cherlton, Bishop of Hereford, who had but a few months before come over to take up this office, under his brother, Sir John de Cherlton, whom he soon after succeeded in the government of the island.

John Passelewe, was a tenant of the manor of Balscadden. See p. 146. The entry when complete may have meant that Passelewe having entertained the Seneschal when he went to Balscadden to hold the usual manor court, was unwilling to receive payment for such service, and that the Seneschal had instead given money as a present to Passelewe's children. See a reference to this court on p. 24.

Rolegh.—Maurice Rolegh was about this time and afterwards Sheriff of the county Kildare. The transaction was no doubt connected with the Escheator's claim to the temporalities of the Priory consequent on their technical seizure after the deprivation of Prior Goioun in July, 1337.

PAGE 19.

Henry Whyte.—A Henry Whyte was archdeacon of Emly in 1355. (*Cotton.*)

Trumpeters of the Justices in the Refectory.—This entry refers no doubt to the formal reception of the justices itinerant by the convent, mentioned on p. 5.

Waferer, a maker or seller of wafer cakes, a confectioner. In the household ordinances of Edward II. the waferer was a member of the household, and had allowance of eggs and sugar, apparently for use in his work. The editor of Bishop Swinfield's Household Book states that waferarius had also the meaning of a minstrel who performed tricks of sleight-of-hand.

PAGE 20.

John de Castro going to the Court of the King.—The business of the house was no doubt connected with the attempted seizure by the Escheator mentioned at p. 156. There are extant among the *Ch. Ch. Deeds* (No. 230), two petitions by the Prior and Convent about this time upon this subject. They are in French, the language of the Court, and are practically, though not verbally, the same. One, however is addressed "A vous sire gardein et conseil nostre seigneur le Roi en Irland." The other "Au counseail nostre seignur le Roi." The latter is probably a draft or copy of the actual letter carried by De Castro to the Court. That some such communication was made is probable from the existence of a writ from England to the Irish Exchequer, demanding a certificate of all proceedings in the matter (*Mem. Rot.*, 12 Edw. III.). But no further result followed from the mission.

Fynnok Otozill, perhaps rather Otoȝill, *i.e.* O'Tothill or O'Tuathaill, the Fynnok O'Tooll mentioned at p. 157. I do not find this name in the O'Toole pedigree. But the clan war-cry is said to have been Fianac abo, which in the Book of Howth (p. 135) takes the from of Fenock abo. Fynnok as a name may be connected with this.

With this entry ends the fragment described on p. 142. The following entries are on the reverse of the principal membrane of the account.

Robert de Moenes was Mayor of the city in 1351. He appears again as a creditor at pp. 21 and 28. His obit was commemorated in the house on the 5th Sept. as "Robertus de Meonis frater nostre congregacionis." (*Martyrology*, p. 40.)

The Seneschal went to Munster.—This was a business visit to the property of the Priory there. The most important part of their property there was Killenaule, mentioned in the next entry. The sum here was cash to meet current expenses, which in the absence of the Seneschal the Prior took under his own care.

Killenaule is situated in the barony of Slieveardagh, Co. Tipperary, ten miles E.N.E. of Cashel. The church here with lands was granted to the Priory early in the 13th century, by Adam de Stanton, with the intention that a cell should be founded here and occupied by canons from the Priory. The deed conveys "two carucates of land, of my land of Kilbrenin, except twelve acres, and on the other side I give them twelve acres which John Bedellus held, and the church of Kildenal with all chapels belonging to it, and the mill of Kilbrenin, and the tithe of all expense of my house of Kildenal, in bread and ale, and flesh and fish, in pure and perpetual alms, freely and fully, peacefully and honourably, with all liberties and free customs belonging to the lands; under this condition that the said canons (of the Church of the Holy Trinity, Dublin) build a cell on the said land, and have canons resident there serving God." (*Ch. Ch. Deeds*, No. 31). The last condition seems never to have been fully carried out, and perhaps did not meet with the approval of the Archbishop of Cashel, whose confirmation in 1315 only requires the Prior to provide a proper vicar. There are, however, several references in the accounts to visits made by canons of the Priory to Killenaule.

apud . . . officiali.—The word *Kildenale* was written here, but has been erased.

Nicholas de Esenden.—His obit was commemorated on the 7th September, as "Nicholaus Esyden sacerdos et canonicus noster."

Kitchener was a canon to whom was committed the duty of providing the food for the Refectory, except bread, which seems to have belonged to the cellarer's province.

PAGE 21.

Kenewrek.—Kenewrik Sherman, or the shearman, mentioned below.

R. Goioun. Roger Goioun, late Prior. He had been deprived, July 1337. In the absence of any extant reference to the cause of his deprivation in the records of Christ Church, or in the Roman transcripts in the London Record Office, which I have examined for this purpose, it seems not improbable that the debts here and elsewhere mentioned as incurred by him, which, though individually small, must have been collectively a serious addition to the monetary difficulties of the house, may have rendered pressing the necessity for his removal.

Hugh Louestok, an aged Dublin merchant. A few years later he is described as "so broken down by age and infirmity, that he cannot conduct his own business." He accordingly gave a power of attorney to Adam Louestok and Thos. Lof. (*Cal. Pat. Rot.*, p. 49, 19 & 20 Edw. III.)

M

William Sterre, Kitchener.—He was one of the canons, and afterwards became cellarer. The shops mentioned in this entry may have been part of the special fund for maintenance of the kitchen, and improperly conveyed by the Prior to Desewell. The payment to the Kitchener would then be for the purpose of recouping his fund for what was thus lost to it.

Page 22.

Gorman.—Still known as Grangegorman in the north-west suburbs of Dublin. The ancient manor house and farm buildings seem to have stood off Grangegorman-lane, near the Richmond Asylum. Grangegorman was the home farm of the Priory, and its lands extended over the ground now occupied by the Richmond Asylum and Penitentiary, the workhouse, and adjoining land. It appears from these accounts that the Prior had apartments here which he frequently occupied. The Seneschals of Christ Church held their courts here until the present century.

Gloves for Harvest.—Throughout the accounts gloves are a frequent form of ceremonial present. Those here referred to may have been presented to persons whose servants helped, or they may have been for the men actually employed in the work. A fac-simile illustration of about this period in Dr. S. R. Gardiner's History of England represents many of the workmen wearing gloves.

John Callan was about this time bailiff of the city.

Page 24.

William de Burthon, or **Burton**, was one of the Remembrancers of the Exchequer. He had been appointed to direct the commissariat for the war against Scotland, 9 Edw. III. Among other confidential employments, he was commissioned in 1345 to arrest the Earl of Kildare. Camden, in narrating the stratagem by which he effected this, calls him a knight; but he is not so described in the commission (*Mem. Rot.*, 18 & 19 Ed. III.). A Wm. de Burton knight in 48° Edw. III. was, with doctor John de Wicliff and others, one of the king's ambassadors to the Pope (*Cal. Rot. Pat. Ang.*, p. 190). I have met no explanation of the large payments made to him here, and in each of the following Seneschal's accounts, beyond the statement here that they were for debts of the house.

Court of Balscaddan.—Balscaddan, Co. Dublin, was one of the manors of the Priory. The manor court was held occasionally by the

Seneschal as part of his duty, and the fines imposed in it should be accounted for by him, or by the bailiff of the manor.

An Irishman of the town of Dermodstown for having entry in 40 acres.—Dermodstown is a townland in the manor and parish of Balscaddan. In the Rental, in the Appendix, the principal tenant there was Raymond Colyn, who held 40 acres at a rent of 33s. 4d. The person here mentioned was probably Raymond's heir, whose succession was thus formally recognized.

PAGE 26.

Brother John Comyn.—The family of Comyn had long been connected with the Priory. As early as the beginning of the 13th century, Kinsaley, a valuable possession of the Priory, had passed into the hands of Elias Cumin, who was almost certainly a relation of John Comyn, then Archbishop of Dublin. A few years later the Priory buildings were enlarged on land which belonged to Gilbert Comin. Later, in the same century, the Convent again granted the lands of Kinsaley to John Cumin (*Ch. Ch. Deeds*, No. 19, 30, 90). A pedigree of the family, not easily understood, is contained in the Black Book of Christ Church (p. 225). Of John Comyn, the canon, with whom we are now interested, there is a curious account among the Christ Church Deeds. It is undated, but must have been before 1354, as Thomas de Kilmore (*see* p. 147) is prominently concerned. Comyn, apparently as part of his duty as a canon, went into residence at Kilcullen, taking with him two brothers—sir Nicholas a chaplain, and Elias, and a kinswoman named Milsanda. They evidently made themselves obnoxious to the clergy of the chapels in the parish, and to the labourers on the lands. Complaints led to a formal inquiry, the report of which is thus preserved (*Ch. Ch. Deeds*, No. 72). This Inquisition was taken at Kilcullen on Friday, the Feast of S. Matthias, in what year is not stated, before Master Thomas Kylmore. The jury included three chaplains, two other clerks, and four laymen. They found that Comyn had entertained his two brothers and his kinswoman for eight weeks from eight days before Christmas to S. Valentine's Day, at a cost of 10s. to the Convent. His brother Nicholas was suspected of impropriety with the housemaid, who wasted the goods of the Prior to the extent of 2s. to allay suspicion. John Comyn sold two crannocs of oats for 6s., which it is implied that he did not account for. He also took away linen thread to the value of 5s., and half a stone of wool worth 10d. Nicholas gave six fleeces of wool for a supper. John and Nicholas,

M 2

by bullying the servingmen, and stopping their food, interrupted the cultivation of the land to the loss of 4s. A farm horse died, valued at 5s. He lent a cart to Henry Tallon to carry a mill-stone, and gave him a piece of iron worth 2d. On the day of the Purification of the Blessed Virgin, John refused to celebrate his office in the church, which led to a loss of 2 lb. of wax worth 16d. Also he took away articles of Brother Nicholas (probably another canon) found there, and other things to the value of 12d.

The charges against John Comyn personally seem to be generally of a trivial character. There is no means of learning what action was taken in the matter.

His obit was commemorated in the *Martyrology*, at 4 Nov., as " Johannes Comyne sacerdos et canonicus noster."

Rent of Gorman.—For notes of names of places, and further details of the rents, see the Rental in the Appendix.

Robert Poer was chamberlain and treasurer, and afterwards chief baron of the Exchequer. He does not appear to have retained the last office, but was appointed one of the barons of the court (*Mem. Rot.*, 9 Edw. III.). On the Memorandum Roll of the Exch., 9 Edw. III., is an acknowledgment by the Prior and Convent that they were bound to Robert Poer in the sum of £25.

Kynturk is the old form of the name now preserved as Clonturk, the parish name of Drumcondra, near Dublin. Kenturk always belonged to the Priory of All Saints. Some lands here must for a time at least have belonged to this Priory, as an extant deed (*Ch. Ch. Deeds*, No. 172) in 1302 surrenders to the Prior land in Kenturk held under grant from him.

Killester and the following two small rents are not noticed in the Rental. Killester had been granted by the Priory soon after the Norman Invasion, to the family of Brun, rendering yearly half-an-ounce of gold on the altar of the church of Holy Trinity (*Ch. Ch. Deeds*, No. 468).

PAGE 27.

Archbishop of Dublin.—Alexander de Bykenor, a learned and vigorous prelate, who had held civil offices of Escheator, Treasurer, Chancellor, and Justiciary of Ireland. He had been employed by the King for some years in diplomatic missions on the Continent ; and was the founder of the university of Dublin, to which in 1320 he gave statutes, printed in Harris's Ware (*Ant.*, p. 243). In his diocese he was a determined enemy of idleness, and even in old age an active opponent of the mountain Irish, to whose incursions into the plains his see lands were much exposed. The two occasions in these accounts when the Prior had to send to Kildare on Holy Thursday to procure the episcopally consecrated Holy Oil imply that his episcopal functions sat lightly on the Archbishop. See accounts of him in Ware's Bishops (ed. Harris, pp. 330-2) and Dalton's Archbishops (pp. 123-134).

De prestito.—Properly, money paid as an advance. Hence it comes frequently to mean simply a loan.

Thomas de Beuley.—The present Seneschal's predecessor. Money probably paid on account of his balance.

Gilbert de Bolyniop had been Prior since 1337 (*see* p. 144). He must have resigned that office about this time.

PAGE 28.

Adam Louestok.—Perhaps the son of Hugh Louestok (*see* p. 161). A citizen of Dublin; was Bailiff of the city 1338, and Mayor 1352. He married Margery, daughter of Henry de Cestria, from whom he got as a marriage portion, a bond for 100 marks. Louestok, however, had to sue his father-in-law for the money, and obtained a judgment for it (*Mem. Rot.*, 5 & 6 Edw. III. m. 22). A few years later he got into trouble again. Two stranger merchants, and the master and mariners of a ship from Tynemouth, were charged before the Court of Exchequer in Dublin. Louestok, fearing that they would not receive justice, and relying on his position as jurat of the city, came into court and demanded justice for them, using abusive language to the Treasurer. For this contempt he was, on petition of the Mayor and citizens, excused, on payment of a fine of one mark (*ib.*, 16 Edw. III.).

Plough.—The plough was made chiefly of timber. There was a long wooden beam, to which in front the oxen were yoked. At its other end, on the under side, there was apparently a shorter timber fixed to it, called a chippe: on this was mounted the share. Some of the ploughs appear to have had wheels (*see* p. 29, where four axletrees are included among articles bought for ploughs). There is no mention of the coulter, unless this, not the share, is intended by the *romer*. (Vomer, culter of a plow.—*Catholicon*, p. 281, n.) If this be so, *ferrum carucale* must mean the share. The *ferrum carucale* is generally made by the hired smith, while the *romer* is almost always purchased. A lighter plough was used in the dry summer fallow lands. This is the *caruca estivalis*, p. 29.

PAGE 30.

Hugh Belynges was bailiff of the manor of Gorman.

Installation.—The installation of Simon de Ludgate, elected Prior on the resignation of Gilbert de Bolyniop. This must have been in the spring or early summer of 1343.

Ad warectandum—Ad rebinandum.—In the most approved farming of the period the arable land was divided into three equal parts, each of which lay fallow every third year. In April, when all the sowing was completed, the section which was to lie fallow that year was ploughed. This ploughing of the fallow land was called warectatio. The same land was, towards the end of June, again lightly gone over with the plough to destroy the weeds. This was called rebinatio. (See Cowel's *Dict.*; also *Walter of Henley*, ed. Miss Lamond, p. 13.)

PAGE 31.

Carts.—The references to the carts in use lead us to infer that they were similar to the very rude and primitive conveyances which Malton's views of Dublin show to have been the only one-horse vehicle for goods carriage in Dublin 100 years ago. It survived in the Wicklow mountains to within living memory. A pair of small solid wheels seem to be fixed to a massive axle; the body of the cart rests in front on the shafts, and behind is supported from the ends of the shafts (which incline greatly owing to the very low wheels) by two uprights about 1½ feet high. Such was the Dublin cart of the last century. That of the account was no doubt similar. Its probably solid wheels were bound with iron strakes or tires, fastened to the wheels by strake-nails. Iron plates or clouts were nailed on where necessary, to reduce friction; while it was often necessary to bind the cart together with iron clamps or ropes. The clouts were thought very necessary. Tusser, in his directions for June, says:—

> " Let cart be well searched without and within,
> Well clouted and greased, ere hay-time begin."

Smaller iron articles called lezerlegs and gropes were used possibly for attachment of the wheels to the axle and shafts.

Besides the carecta or cart, wains and cars are sometimes mentioned. The latter must have been merely sledges without wheels.

PAGE 32.

Apud Kylcolyn.—The senior or more trusted brethren of the house are frequently found in residence at Kilcullen and Killenaule, in charge of those possessions, at a distance from the Priory. For a notice of John de Castro, see p. 160. See also pp. 42, 46.

PAGE 34.

Messor.—The messer, a farm officer, or ganger, who had oversight of the men and crops. " This word soundeth a mower, but his office was to oversee the workmen, and to kepe the cornefieldes from harme." Lambarde quoted in Introduction to *Walter of Henley*, p. xxxvi.

Ploughmen.—The regular wages of a ploughman, besides allowances, was 5*s.* a-year (p. 62). The sums mentioned here may, therefore, have been additional gratuities.

Robert Dryvere.—This is a description as much as a name, representing one who was a driver of a plough team. In the Rental he appears among the Gorman tenants as Robert le Dryver. On next page *fugantes carucas* is the corresponding Latin term.

PAGE 35.

Woman drying malt.—The malting and brewing were usually carried on by women. The phrase drying malt seems to be used for the whole process of malting, just as malt kiln seems to be used for the house in which all the process was carried on and the malt was stored.

PAGE 36.

Wicklow boards.—Frequent licences are to be met with permitting the carriage by sea of timber, fire-wood, &c., from the town of Wicklow to Dublin.

Earth to raise the floor of the barn.—In Henry Best's Farming Book, 1641 (*Surtees Soc.*, p. 107), are minute instructions for the making and repair of earthen barn floors.

Drawing straw.—In the process of drawing, straw is prepared by the hand into suitable state for thatching.

Roofer planing, and fitting roof couples.—The word *coopertorii* here is probably a mistake of the writer of the account for *carpentarii*. See p. 60 where the same work is to be done by a *carpentarius*.

Digging mud and serving a roofer.—A description of thatching carried out in this manner, in the North of England in 1641, may be found in Best's Farming Book (*Surtees Soc.*, p. 145). The thatcher was assisted as here by two men, one of whom drew the straw and got it ready for use, while the other made and tempered mud, which he carried up in a scuttle, apparently to fix the straw in position.

Long Stack of Peas.—Peas and beans in the farming of this period were not pulled green. They were considered a species of corn and allowed to remain in the field till ripe. They were then harvested, and subsequently threshed like corn. A minute description of this treatment is to be found in a 17th-century treatise on farming. The peas harvest began in September, as soon as the barley reaping was ended. Wet weather was thought the most favourable, so that the stalks might come up easily by the root. The peas-pullers were provided with sharpened peas-hooks; striking with their hooks near the root, the stalk is either cut, or pulled up by the roots. As they strike they roll the mass forward until a bundle is formed not so large as to be unwieldy. These heaps were left on the land for about a week; then carted into the haggard, stacked, and carefully thatched. (Best's *Farming Book*, Surtees Soc., pp. 56-60, and 93.)

Coopertorii facientis speres.—Here also coopertorii is, perhaps, a mistake in the original for carpentarii.

Kiln,—That is the malt kiln. Probably used generally for the houses in which the malting processes were carried on. The drying being the part of the work which was looked on as most important, the maltster's work is repeatedly referred to as "siccans brasium." "Maulte in the kylne" is used as corresponding to "Corne in ye barne." (Best's *Farming Book*, p. 172.)

PAGE 41.

Vangis nudis. — Spades entirely of wood. The Glossary to "Finchal Priory" (*Surtees Soc.*) says that vanga was a wooden shovel used in winnowing corn. On the other hand, in every early use of the word I have met, it is placed among the instruments for field work. See, for example, the 15th-century *Pictorial Vocabulary*, in Wright's *Vocabularies* (ed. 1884, p. 809), where it is translated "spade," and is grouped with dyker, mattock, shovel, and barrow. An illustration there exactly resembles a modern garden spade.

PAGE 42.

Sir Philip. — His surname was Walsh. See note, p. 181. Balycor is now Ballycore, on the borders of Cos. Wicklow and Kildare, the tithes of which belonged to the Priory.

Kilgowan and Castlemartin were two chapels in the parish of Kilcullen. They had been granted to the Priory early in the 13th century (*Ch. Ch. Deeds*, No. 16), but continued to be served by a separate chaplain.

William de Bosworth was keeper of the writs of the King's Bench.

Walter de Istelep, ex-treasurer of Ireland. He came to Ireland probably in the train of Richard de Ferings, Archbishop of Dublin, from whom he received a power of attorney in 1300 (*Sweetman's Cal.*). He is afterwards described as treasurer and proctor of the same archbishop (*Mem. Rot.*, 1 Edw. II.). On that prelate's death the custody of the temporalities of the see was committed to De Istelep, while in the King's hands. In the following year, 1307, he was made a baron of the Exchequer, soon after he became escheator, and in 1314 treasurer of Ireland. In 1326, when his predecessor, Archbishop de Bykenor, fell into disgrace, charged with irregularities in his accounts, De Istelep was accused of complicity, and all his property seized. He was soon after pardoned for a fine of 500 marks; and apparently restored to office, but only to fall before new charges of irregularity. This time there were no personal goods forthcoming, and for several years writs were being issued for the seizure of his property, his total indebtedness being stated at £1330; and not until 1346 were the claims of the Crown finally satisfied (*Mem. Rot.*, 19 & 20 Edw. III.).

De Istelep in the days of prosperity succeeded in securing a very large share of church revenue. Beside the golden prebend of Swords, he obtained the specially valuable rectory of Trim, the rectory of Athboy, the precentorship of Ferns, and the prebend of Blackrath in the diocese of Ossory. Not satisfied with these, he extorted from our Priory a pension of 20 marks a-year, 5 marks from that of All Saints, and 6 marks from the abbey of St. Thomas, Dublin.

So great was the wealth he had amassed, that on the seizure of his goods in 1326 one box which nearly escaped detection was found to contain several hundred pounds worth of silver and jewels (*Mem. Rot.*, 19 Edw. II.). Portion of his wealth (including the pension from our poor Priory) he had expended in the purchase of a corrody from the Prior of the hospital of St. John of Jerusalem at Kilmainham. A very full abstract of the deed conveying this corrody is given in Archdall's *Monasticon* (p. 283), from which the following is abstracted :—

The Prior granted to Master Walter, for life, entertainment for himself, two armigers, a chamberlain and another servant, five garciones (inferior retainers), and five horses. Walter was to sit at the Prior's table on his right hand, the chaplain at the table of the brethren, and the retainers with those of the Prior of the same rank ; his horses were to have forage with the Prior's. At Christmas he was to have a gown and four garments of good cloth, the same as the Prior's, or 5 marks. The chaplain should be clothed as the brethren, and the retainers as those of the Prior, a suit at Christmas every second year ; or the Prior should pay 20s. for the chaplain, 40s. for 2 armigers, 2 marks for 2 servants, and 50s. for the 5 garciones. Walter should have the whole house and chapel formerly built by the Prior Walter de Aqua. If he pleased, Walter, his chaplain, armigers, and upper servants, might have their meals in this house. Walter to have three white loaves equal to those served to the Prior ; the chaplain and the others 7 loaves the same as those served to the brethren ; and 10 gallons of the best ale, and from the kitchen meat raw or cooked as he desired ; the five garciones always to dine in the hall with those of the Prior. Walter might erect a kitchen for himself ; should have free passage through the Priory gates ; might erect a stable for his horses outside the wall of the castle near the great gate ; and have part of the garden for his use. He should be allowed for use after dinner three gallons of the best ale ; and in the season of Lent and other times of fasting, he should be served with meat as usual, unless he chose to abstain.

Among the goods of De Istelep seized in 1326 was his library, consisting of three books : 1 bublia, 1 liber de la rose, et unus liber de seint graal (*Mem. Rot.*, 19 Edw. II., transcript, p. 64). The two latter were well known French mediæval romances.

John Rous, clerk, was probably the Prior's chaplain (*see* p. 99). He is previously described as vicar of Clonshillow, dio. Kildare (*Pipe Roll*, No. 60).

John de Kinton, pleader.—The narrator was a counsel or barrister. John de Kinton, as was very commonly the case, seems to have been a gentleman of property. In the entry in the *Black Book* of Archbishop Alan, mentioned above, p. 145, he is described as lord of the knights' fee in which Drumshallon was, and as such he in 1359 confirmed the grant of that manor and rectory to the Priory.

Uriel.—Oirghialla, a territory comprising the present counties of Armagh, Monaghan, and Louth. In English documents it is frequently used as an equivalent for the county of Louth.

Page 44.

Master Hervey Bagot was archdeacon of Glendalough, and in that capacity received the proxies of Kilcullen parish in his arch-deaconry.

Writ of Supersedeas of the temporalities. Supersedeas is a writ, and signifies a command to stay or forbear the doing of that which ought not to be done, or something which might legally be done, but for the special reason for which the writ is granted (Cowel's *Law Dict.*). In this case it must have forbidden the Escheator to proceed to the seizure of the temporal possessions of the house, on the vacancy caused by the resignation of Prior Gilbert de Bolyniop.

Page 45.

Stephen de Gascoyne.—This is the only instance of the purchase of wine in large quantity. Judging from the merchant's name, the wine was probably a claret.

William Petit, pleader, was now King's serjeant. His obit was commemorated on the 24th Dec. as "Willelmus Petytt qui dedit operibus ecclesie vi s. viii d. (*Martyrology*, p. 55).

Hugh de Sutton, also known as le Joevene, was a former prior who had resigned in 1326. This payment must have been a pension. He was also permitted to have a separate chamber (see p. 115). The following entry is also a pension to a retired prior, Gilbert de Bolyniop. The position of these retired priors may have been similar to that of a retired vicar in 1396, who was provided with a chamber, a pension, cloth for clothing, food in the refectory, which on account of illness, cold, or hospitality might be served in his own chamber, when he was to have three loaves of the best convent bread of the weight of 2 marks each, two loaves of second bread, one gallon of second ale, with service from the kitchen on flesh days as the refectory was served, both at dinner and supper; he might also have a servant who was likewise to be maintained. (*Ch. Ch. Deeds*, No. 784. The original is much obliterated, and most of the details cannot now be read.)

John Gernoun.—This lawyer retained by the convent became in this year chief justice of the Bench.

PAGE 46.

Hugh Brown was at this time King's serjeant-at-law.

William Sterre.—Brother William Sterre was a former kitchener.

PAGE 47.

John Whyte, of Tipperstown.—The original lease to this tenant is preserved (*Ch. Ch. Deeds*, No. 554). It is dated the feast of SS. Philip and James (May 1), 1320; from brother Hugh prior of the cathedral church of the Holy Trinity and the convent of the same, to John le Wyte son of Walter le Wyte. It demises to him all their land in Ballytiper which Letitia le Wyte, mother of said John, formerly held of the Prior and Convent. To hold for 20 years. Rent first year 16s., second year 2 marks, third year 3 marks, and thereafter 3½ marks a-year. Lessee to make suit to the Prior's court of Clonken, and perform all other accustomed services. (*Ch. Ch. Deeds*, No. 554.)

The services claimed from the tenant of these lands are set out minutely in a subsequent lease of the same land.

This lease is dated 6 Nov., 1352; and is made to Robert Haketh. The term granted is 16 years; rent during first 8 years 30s., and during remainder of term 40s. The tenant was bound to plough with his plough for one day at winter seed time, and for one day at Lent seed time, upon the land of the demesnes of the priory at Clonken; to reap with one man for one day the corn there in harvest; to carry with his cart the corn for one day, or with a car for two days or with two cars for one day; to give two gallons of ale as often as he brewed; to render suit to the manor court as often as he is summoned. He was to forfeit the lease if the rent was a fortnight in arrear, though continuing liable for the arrears. He should not give or let the land except to a kinsman without consent of the Convent. The Convent should have a heriot or half a mark on the death of the tenant. Also the tenant should with his whole force come when summoned for the assistance of the Convent anywhere within the county of Dublin. (*Ch. Ch. Deeds*, No. 646. The text is printed in the Appendix.)

Page 48.

Stephen Olyn, was a tenant in Clonken, where he held lands at a total rent of 51s. See Rental in Appendix.

Page 49.

Exitus Hagardi.—The entries from this to page 54 are written on the back of the preceding account.

Hugh de Calce was the deputy in Ireland of master Raymond Pelegrini, special nuncio of the supreme pontiff in England and Ireland (*Mem. Rot.*, 21 Edw. III.), and was made Chancellor of S. Patrick's. A document in the Regesta Pontificum (*Roman Transcripts*, P. R. O., Lond., vol. 5, p. 246) describes him as a priest of the dioc. Caturcensis (Quercy in France) and testifies that he had reverently served the Apostolic See in Ireland and elsewhere for 17 years (in 1344). He was murdered in 1347. He had while living received the King's letters patent of protection, and his murder was specially excepted in the royal pardons after his death.

Page 50.

Cellarer.—It was a principal part of the cellarer's duty to manage the supply of corn for baking and brewing for the Convent. A specimen of a cellarer's account will be found in the Appendix. Brother Stephen was probably Stephen Derby mentioned on p. 53. He was afterwards Prior.

Heaped measure.—In measuring corn the bushel or peck was either heaped up as high as the grain could stand, when it was called heaped measure; or its surface was with a stick made level with the sides of the measure, when it was called stricken, rased or level measure. As is shown by an entry on this page, a peck rased was to a peck heaped as $6\frac{1}{4}$: 8. This proportion, however, depended on the breadth of the bushel measure used; and this uncertainty gave rise to frequent abuses. (*See Walter of Henley*, p. 17.)

PAGE 55.

Bailiff.—The bailiff of a manor occupied a very responsible position. He was steward and sub-agent of the manor over which he was placed. The accuracy and minuteness of the accounts required from him can be judged from the following pages. A full account of the duties of such a bailiff may be found in the tract called *Seneschaucie* (printed with *Walter of Henley*, ed. Miss Lamond, pp. 89–97).

Clonken.—The demesne lands of this manor lay round Kill-of-the-Grange, near Kingstown. The tenants who owed service to it stretched from Murphystown to Killiney inclusive.

Profits of Court.—The court intended is the manor court, which would have been held in the manor before the Seneschal of the Priory. The profits would arise from fees paid by litigants and amercements imposed by the court.

Small tithes consisted of the tithes of lambs, calves, wool, and others, varying somewhat according to local custom ; here they seem to include turf.

The great tithes—those of corn—are accounted for below in the haggard account.

Clay for making earthenware. Coarse pottery and tile making is an industry still carried on at Kill-of-the-Grange. On an old map of these lands made in 1684, among the *Ch. Ch. Records* in P. R. O., there is a place marked as " Pollaughs, a common to Kill." A comparison of this map with the Ordnance Survey shows that Pollaughs exactly corresponds with the site of the present tile works. Now Pollagh means in Irish " a place of holes," a very apt description of ground used for excavating potter's clay. We may therefore infer that before 1684, and while Irish was still the spoken language of the district, not improbably therefore as long ago as these accounts, the site of the present tile works was used as now for pottery.

PAGE 58.

Custom ploughs.—The tenants of lands were bound to aid the work on the demesne lands by supplying ploughs and workmen for a given number of days. Particulars of these duties will be found in the Rental in Appendix. See also p. 172.

PAGE 61.

Draghtbord.—Boards apparently of very large size, perhaps such as were too large to be placed on a cart, and which had to be drawn. In the Society's Journal for 1891, p. 569, occurs the term "a great draughte tre to cast pypes of leade."

Glenwhery, probably Glencree, in the previous century a royal forest, from which timber was often obtained.

PAGE 62.

Wages.—In addition to these small money wages these workmen received the large allowances of corn set out on pp. 84–5.

PAGE 64.

Abbatiam.—The priory house. The term abbey is frequently applied to religious houses which were not technically abbeys.

PAGE 66.

Half a day, at full wages. Rather "at wages in full discharge of their service"; that is without food which they would be entitled to for a full day's work.

PAGE 70.

Men of Gregory Taunton.—He was tenant of the manor, of lands at Cornelscourt, but does not appear to have been bound by his tenure to render customary service to the manor farm. The payment was therefore probably for help given voluntarily.

John Punchard was now employed as baker and brewer for the harvest labourers (p. 69). The harvest over, he s found in charge of the threshing (p. 78). He occupied a cottage in the adjoining village, with half an acre of land for which he paid in money and service 8½d. a-year.

Ale brewed.—The brewing as well as baking here was done generally once a week. "Ale shulde not be dronk under v dayes olde. Newe Ale is vnholsome for all men. And sowre ale, and dead ale, and ale the whiche doth stand a tylte is good for no man." (*Borde's Regiment*, quoted by Furnivall in *Manners and Meals in the Olden Time*, p. 208.)

Little Stephen was probably the bailiff's son. See p. 122.

PAGE 74.

John Kendal.—Was tenant of the lands of the priory in Dalkey. A John de Kendale in 1376 received license to import 400 quarters of wheat from Ireland to Kendal in England (*Cal. Pat. Rot. Ang.* 192*b*).

PAGE 76.

Sheriff.—Michael Montgomery. See p. 83.

Prior went away.—The bailiff's table account stops here, because he seems to be authorized to maintain a table out of the manor funds only during harvest, or when specially authorized by his lord.

PAGE 77.

Hoeing by custom.—This work was done by the cottagers in the village as part of their tenure. See also p. 79.

Exitus Hagardi.—The entries from this to p. 87 are written on the back of the preceding account.

PAGE 79.

Carragh olyn.—The edge of the skin is torn close to the ' o ' of olyn, so that this may be the end only of the name. The name Olyn, however, occurs on p. 48, and in the Rental.

PAGE 82.

Wulfran de Berneuall was the then head of the family afterwards known as Barnewall, and was seated at Drimnagh, near Dublin. He married Nichola daughter of Robert de Clahull (*Mem. Rot.*, 3 Edw. III.). He was repeatedly sheriff, and was also escheator of the county Dublin. In 1333–4 he with three others was made *custos pacis* of the county Dublin. As such his duty was to assess the inhabitants of the county for horses and arms, and the maintenance of horsemen and footmen, according to ancient ordinance and to the Statute of Wynton ; so that they should be prepared to set out in the service of the King, when called upon by the Justiciary of Ireland (*Mem. Rot.*, 7 Edw. III. m. 10 d) He seems still to have held this office ; and the *pluribus de exercitu* must refer to the men of this county levy.

Page 84.

S. Dunstan.—This seems to be a mistake. From the morrow of S. Dunstan to S. Peter ad Vincula is only about 10 weeks. Moreover, it is obvious that this allowance should be for the period outside that for which the bailiff has already accounted in the maintenance of the general table during the progress of harvest and the work consequent upon it, from 1st Aug., 1344, to Friday, the 8th Oct. (pp. 70–6). From 10th Oct. to 31st Aug., 1345, would be 42 weeks as stated. As the 10th Oct. is the morrow of S. Denis, Dunstan is probably an error for Denis.

Page 88.

Pellura.—A fur skin prepared for use. Every man of the better classes had his outer garments lined or trimmed with fur.

Capa.—A kind of loose gown reaching to the ankles, worn over other clothes by laymen and women as well as by the clergy. It is to be distinguished from capa choralis, the church cope. (*Du Cange.*)

Capucium.—A furred hood was usually a portion of the dress of a person of any position.

Amice.—This was the canonical vestment lined with fur to cover the head and shoulders. It was perfectly distinct from the sacerdotal vestment of fine linen also called amice. (*Prompt. Parv.* p. 11 n.). By an order of the archbishop in 1420, the prior and canons of Christ Church were on state occasions, and apparently also at other times, to wear amices of skins of gray fur without and minever within, as the canons of other cathedral churches in England and Ireland do in solemn processions and all other times. This order recites that in solemn processions the archbishop was followed by the prior of Holy Trinity and dean of S. Patrick's side by side, after them the sub-prior and the precentor of S. Patrick's, and so the other canons of the two cathedrals two and two; and shows that the dress then worn by the canons of Christ Church was unlike that worn by the other canons, and unfitted for such occasions (*Ch. Ch. Deeds.* No. 277).

Tunica.—Always translated 'cote' in Wright's *Old English Vocabularies.* It was a short vest worn under the Capa, Supertunica or other outer garment.

N

PAGE 89.

William Broun was at this time summonister of the Exchequer He afterwards became escheator of Ireland. He was probably the person whose obit is entered in the *Mortilogium* at xii Kal. Aug. as " Willelmus Brune frater noster ad succurrendum."

Saucers were vessels intended for serving the sauces at table.

PAGE 90.

Tholsel court.—The city court held before the mayor and bailiffs.

PAGE 91.

Gerald Obryn.—The Four Masters record the death of a chief of the O'Byrnes of this Christian name in 1399.

John Barby was vicar of Maynooth, and held some official position in the court of the liberty of Kildare (*Mem. Rot.*, 5 & 6 Edw. III.).

Writ of Prohibition.—A writ which lieth for one that is impleaded in the Court Christian, for a cause belonging to the temporal jurisdiction, whereby the party as well as the Judge are forbidden to proceed any further in the cause. (Cowel, *Law Dict.*) In this case it was probably to prevent action in the archbishop's court in reference to the disputed presentation to Kilcullen. See p. 96.

PAGE 92.

For oblations.—The meaning probably is that these presents to the officers of the mayor, and of the Tholsel court, professed to be to enable them to make the customary Christmas offerings in the Church. See also p. 96. About 1300 the oblations in Christ Church were valued at £10 yearly (*Ch. Ch. Deeds*, No. 164).

Kilcullen.—The parish church and advowson had been granted to the priory soon after the Norman invasion of Ireland (*Ch. Ch. Deeds*, Nos. 7, 12-15) ; and the right of presentation had been exercised by the Prior (*ib.* 82). Shortly before the end of the 13th century this right was contested (*ib.* 160-1); and the contest was repeatedly renewed (*ib.* 181, &c.). In 1326 the earl of Kildare claimed the presentation as appendant to his manor of Kildare (*Mem. Rot.*, 18 Edw. II.). He seems to have obtained judgment which was afterwards set aside (*Ch. Ch. Deeds*, 574, 222). But the claim was soon renewed by the Crown during the minority of the Earl (*Mem. Rot.*, 6 Edw. III.). The result of the present suit was probably favourable to the Prior as a few years later the Earl of Kildare relinquished his claim to the Priory. (*Ch. Ch. Deeds*, No. 241-2.)

Master Thomas Giffard was already chancellor of Kildare, and in 1353 became bishop of that see.

Kildare.—A visit to Kildare for the same purpose on Holy Thursday, 1338, is referred to on page 15.

The Assize.—No doubt for the hearing of an action as to the right of presentation to Kilcullen.

Page 93.

Super modo et causa.—This writ was addressed to the escheator (*see* p. 102) to require him to state the ground for a seizure made by him. The writ ran, " Quia volumus certiorari super modo et causa capcionis," &c.

Page 94.

Supersedeas.—See as to this writ on p. 171. In this case it was addressed to the Escheator, as shown by the entry of its service on p. 95. The Escheator's claim to the temporal possessions of the Priory, arising out of Prior Gilbert de Bolyniop's resignation in the previous year, had evidently not yet been satisfied.

Page 95.

Justiciary going against Ulster.—The expedition of Ralph de Ufford, the Justiciary (whose wife was countess of Ulster), is placed by Clyn in Lent, 1344. It would appear from this entry to have really been in 1345.

Page 96.

Paindemaine.—Fine white bread or cakes made of specially fine flour, with eggs, &c. (see note in *Prompt. Parv.*, p. 378). The Glossary to the *Lib. Alb.*, Lond., says that it was so called from the figure of our Saviour impressed upon it. The *Promptorium*, however, translates paynmayne as *panis vigoris*, which seems to connect it with *demaine* in the sense of *pouvoir* (see *Godefroie*).

Two capons, 19d.—There must be a mistake in the number here. The usual price for a capon is 2*d.*

PAGE 97.

Sir Robert Poer was one of the barons of the Exchequer.

Straw chairs.—Chairs, mats, and stools of straw, made like the old straw beehives, were in common use in Dublin until some years ago.

PAGE 98.

Feretrum.—A shrine for relics. Feretrum ubi sunt nunc reliquiæ Sanctorum, honestissimo decore composuit. Feretra reliquias Sanctorum continentia ad corrogandas eleemosynas in reædificationem Ecclesiarum aut in alias necessitates cum processionibus circumlata. *De Cange, s. v.* This was probably one of the many shrines and chests in which the jewels and relics of the Church were preserved, which were broken by the fall of the east window of the church in 1461 (*Martyrology*, p. xix.).

Laurence, garcio of the Prior's chamber. Perhaps the same as Laurence the Prior's kinsman mentioned on pp. 88–9.

PAGE 101.

Verjuice.—The juice of unripe grapes, crab apples, &c. It was a favourite ingredient of the sauces, so important a branch of mediæval cookery. For this purpose John Russell recommended—

" Verdius to boyled capoun, veel, chiken, or bakon " (*Babees Book*, p. 152).

Expense pro Senescallo.—The entry thus distinguished is in a different hand, perhaps that of the Seneschal himself. The whole of head Ferura and the entry preceding it (p. 90), and the last three entries in the head Debita, &c. (p. 104), are also in this added hand.

PAGE 102.

Ralph de Same.—A Ralph de Saham appears on the Memorandum Roll of 5 & 6 Edw. III. (m. 9) as a person to whom Fromund le Brun owed £40.

PAGE 103.

Kenewrik Sherman, or le Shearman, was mayor of Dublin, 1339-41. His death in 1351 is thus noticed :—" Kenwrick Sherman sometime maior of the citie of Dublin died, and was buried under the Belfray of the Preaching Friers of the same city : which Belfray and Steeple himselfe erected, and glazed a window at the head of the Quire, and caused the roof of the Church to be made, with many more good deeds. In the same Convent he departed, the sixth day of March ; and at his end he made his will or testament, amounting to the value of three thousand marks ; and he bequeathed many good legacies unto the Priests of the Church, both religious and secular, that were within twenty miles about the city."—(*Camden's Annals*, ed. 1637.)

PAGE 104.

Hugh le Jeune, also known as Hugh de Sutton, a former Prior who had resigned. See p. 171.

PAGE 105.

The account which ends here is apparently imperfect, the parchment being cut away close to the last entry.

PAGE 106.

Philip, chaplain of Rathozell, or rather Rathoʒell, now Rathtooll, a small parish in Co. Wicklow on the borders of Co. Kildare, consisting o but two townlands, Rathtooll and Ballycore. The tithes of the latter belonged to the Priory, and seem to have been farmed by Philip Walsh, the vicar of Rathtooll. Soon after this time the Bishop of Leighlin granted the church of Rathtooll also to the Prior and Canons of Holy Trinity (*White Book of Christ Church*, cap. xix.). They thereupon entered into an agreement with the vicar, dated on the Nativity of S. John Baptist, 1347, which is still preserved. By it the Prior and Convent granted to sir Philip Welsshe, chaplain, all the tithes of corn and hay, and the oblations and small tithes belonging to their church of Rathothul, for five years ; Philip paying them four marks yearly and supporting all other charges. He was within a year and a-half to repair properly the gable of the chancel, and roof the chancel efficiently with double boards, making it stiff and stanch ; to put in order the chancel below and the altar fittingly, and to bind and repair all the books in the church ; and to celebrate service in the church. (*Ch. Ch. Deeds*, No. 635.) The text is printed in the Appendix.

Kilcullen tithes.—Archbishop Luke in 1253 had ordained that the vicars of Kilcullen presented by the Prior and Convent of Holy Trinity should pay to them 40 marks yearly, the remainder of the fruits and obventions of the church to be taken by the vicar (*Ch. Ch. Deeds*, No. 82).

John Dolphyn.—His obit is commemorated in the *Martyrology* on 9th Nov., " Johannes Dolfyn sacerdos et canonicus noster.".

Laweles.—The Rental in Appendix, of a somewhat earlier period, shows two tenants of this name, master John Laweles, and master Roger Lawles, each paying 4*s.* a-year, or 2*s.* a term, rent.

Sir John Dendredeby.—Cotton mentions a John de Endredeby as a canon of S. Patrick's about this time.

Justiciary going to Naas.—Sir Walter de Bermingham, the recently-appointed Justiciary, with the aid of the Earl of Kildare, attacked and defeated in November of this year O'More and his allies, who earlier in the year had taken the castle of Ley and other places.

Edmund de Byrford was a lawyer who afterwards became King's serjeant.

Rathouze, or rather Rathouȝe.—Hugh Brown mentioned here was found by inquisition to have held 7 burgages and land in Rathtouthe (*Cal. Pat. Rot.*, p. 77).

John de Redenesse became chief justice in 1356.

Notary.—A papal rescript obtained by Hugh de Calce about this time recites that there were in Ireland few or no notaries under apostolic authority. It enjoins the archbishop of Dublin to give this office to two clerks to be named by Hugh. (*Roman Transcripts, Reg. Pont.* v. 5, p. 246).

Sir Roger Darcy.—A son of sir John Darcy, several times Justiciary of Ireland, an office which Roger had himself held for a few months, earlier in the present year.

PAGE 111.

Argendo.—Written so in original. For argento.

Baron of Castleknock.—Hugh Tyrell was at this time lord of the manor of Castleknock. Though the title baron was not applied to him in legal documents, it seems to have been commonly used of the lords of this manor.

Parliament at Kilkenny.—This Parliament was held a fortnight after Michaelmas in the 20th year of Edward III. Its only recorded action was to grant the King a subsidy of two shillings on every carucate, to carry on the war against Irish enemies. (Betham, *Hist. of Constitution*, p. 292).

PAGE 112.

Piment.—*Nectar* as well as *pigmentum* is given in the *Catholicon* as Latin for piment. A very full prescription for the making of nectar is printed by Mr. Gilbert from the *Red Book of Ossory* in the Hist. MSS. Comn. Report, 10, part v., p. 256. It consisted of wine, with a large proportion of honey, and ginger, cloves, and other spices.

Ballymore, now Ballymore-Eustace, Co. Kildare, was one of the archbishop's chief manors. He had a castle containing a hall (in ruins in 1326), a chamber for the archbishop, a chapel, a little chamber for clerks, a kitchen, roofed with shingles, a stable and a grange thatched. (*Lib. Nig. Alani*, Marsh's Lib. copy, p. 286.)

Tallaght.—Another of the archbishop's chief manors. The castle here is said with much probability to have been built by the present archbishop De Bykenor.

Justiciary.—Sir Walter Bermingham had arrived in Ireland as Justiciary about a fortnight before (*Clyn Annals*).

PAGE 113.

Pynsonns seem to have been low shoes of leather. See an exhaustive note on the word in the *Catholicon*, p. 280.

Prior Elect.—Robert de Hereford was elected on the death of Simon de Ludgate. He lived only two years afterwards.

PAGE 114.

William Notyngham was preeentor of S. Patrick's.

Monk of Malvern.—The priory of Little Malvern in Worcester-shire owned half the tithes of Castleknock, near Dublin. Members of the convent appear to have come over occasionally on business connected with this property, as several references to monks of Malvern occur on the rolls.

PAGE 116.

Roger de Preston was second justice of the Common Bench, in which office he was about this time succeeded by Nicholas de Suyterby with whom he is here mentioned.

John atte Gate.—John de Gate was treasurer of S. Patrick's about this time (Cotton). John at Gate was attorney of the archbishop (*Mem. Rot.*, 16 & 17 Edw. III.).

PAGE 117.

Finglas was also one of the archbishop's manors. Archbishop Fulk de Sandford is said to have died at this manor in 1271.

PAGE 119.

Collatio, a late Supper.—Apud Monachos præsertim, dicitur Sacrorum librorum lectio, quæ statis horis, maxime post cœnam, coram eis fiebat. A collationibus Monasticis, quibus finitis, ad bibitionem ibatur, scrotinæ cœnæ collationum appellationem sortitæ sunt.—*Du Cange.*

PAGE 122.

Carrickbrennan.—Now known as Monkstown, Co. Dublin. The land belonged to S. Mary's Abbey, Dublin, but the tithes to our Priory.

PAGE 123.

John Taylour was bailiff of the city 1342–6, and mayor in 1358. He was commemorated in the *Martyrology* on 11th July, " Ob. Johannes Taylwr et Alicia Celi uxor ejus pro quibus fiunt ix lecciones."

PAGE 125.

Total of debts 13*s.* 4*d.*   recte 13*s.* 6*d.*

PAGE 126.

The poem is written on those portions of the reverse of Account No. II., which had been left unoccupied in its original state. It is written in four rather crowded columns. The first being near the edge of the skin has been a good deal discoloured, so that in some places all trace of the writing has disappeared. The defects are indicated here by dots (. . . .).

Besides being divided into four columns the poem is separated into two sections by the writing already upon the roll. When originally copied, another skin must have been attached which has now entirely disappeared, leaving the poem in the incomplete state in which we now find it. The way in which the gaps in the poem occur may be understood from the following table showing the lines contained in the respective columns of the MS. :—

Lines 1 to 36	Lines 127 to 160	Lines 161 to 196	Lines 197 to 234
39 to 126 . . . . continuation lost.	235 to 326 . . . continuation lost.	327 to 416	415 to 502 . . . continuation lost (lines 415 and 416 are repeated).

The copy has been made by the hands of two distinct scribes. One is a clerkly set hand, rather infirm or out of practice, perhaps.

The other is a very irregular current hand. This latter copyist was evidently quite unaccustomed to writing English; hence there is constant confusion between þ and y, and ʒ is used in the most uncertain manner; indeed the spelling generally is often very puzzling.

The following lines are written in this current hand: 1-4, 33-82, 127-154, 327-438.

These in the set hand: 5-32, 83-126, 155-326, 439-502.

Letters printed in italic are, in the original, represented only by contractions.

LINE 1.—horkynt, imp. pl. of herknen, to hearken. In line 6 the same word is written herkenith by the other copyist.

PAGE 127.

LINE 33.—Kyntis. Here and elsewhere for knytis = knights. ʒe is repeatedly written for he.

LINE 44.—bled, Miss Toulmin Smith explains this as "timid one." Blead, timid.—*Stratmann Dictionary* (Clarendon Press edition.)

PAGE 128.

LINES 62, 64.—spec, lec, = speech, leech.

LINE 80.—Kyt. From cydan, to make known.

PAGE 129.

LINE 114.—i korne = icoren, chosen.

LINE 121.—kinde. Dr. Murray suggests that this should be rea without the n. kid = renowned.

PAGE 130.

LINE 146.—wonschild. Miss Toulmin Smith explains this "child of joy." Wunne, joy, pleasure.—*Stratmann.*

PAGE 132.

LINE 188.—eye = awe, fear.

PAGE 133.

LINES 223, 224.—Mr. James Gairdner suggests that these lines should be read with the preceding lines. Thus the sense would be, "But kind (nature) teacheth both thee and me when we were born to weep and make sorrow for fear of the conquest of death."

Page 135.

Line 302.—Mr. Gairdner has pointed out that the earldom of Kent became extinct in 1407, and remained at the disposal of the Crown until 1462.

Page 137.

Line 327.—wo lo wo. Wa la wa, or wo la wo = alas.—*Stratmann*.

Line 335.—This line rhymes with line 339 instead of 337; while line 337 rhymes with 341.

Line 358.—Who so will say sooth (*Dr. Murray*).

Page 138.

Line 365.—y is used here for þ in the MS.—They think. This mistake occurs repeatedly.

Line 379.—No expedient of the lawyers could release from that prison. Mainprise, bail. Supersedeas, a writ to stay proceedings in a court.

Page 139.

Line 415-6.—These two lines ending the third column of second section are repeated with some differences of spelling at the beginning of next column.

Page 140.

Line 431.—þyng apparently for kyng. The words, as þou mit se, are repeated in the same hand immediately below.

APPENDIX.

RENTAL AND CUSTOMAL OF THE LANDS OF THE PRIORY, *Circa* 1326.

Translated from the Latin Original, No. 570, Christ Church Collection, now preserved in the Public Record Office of Ireland.

RENTAL OF THE RENT OF THE PRIOR OF THE CATHE-
DRAL CHURCH OF THE HOLY TRINITY, DUBLIN, to be
paid at different terms of the Year, videlicet : All Saints, Nativity
[of our Lord] . . . . . . for his different Manors and
Granges, to wit :

JOHN COMYN, of Kynsaley[1], holds . . . . and pays 100s. a-year, at
the terms of SS. Philip and James, and All Saints.

WILLIAM LE WHYTE, of Mabil[2] . . . . . and pays 66s. 8d. a-year.
. . . . terms of the year.

THOMAS SMOTH holds[3] . . . . and pays £6 13s. a-year,
at the feasts of Nativity of S. John . . . . . . And
he renders suit to the court of Glasnevin or at Gorman twice
. . . . two days in summer time and two days
with . . . . .

[GLASNEVIN.[4]]

JOHN DE BARRY holds 1 cottage and other tenements, and pays 27s.
a-year, at the feasts of SS. Philip and James and All Saints,
. . . . and suit as above . . . . .

---

[1] Kinsaley, near Portmarnock, co. Dublin.

[2] Mabilstown, now Mabestown, in the parish of Kinsaley.

[3] Thomas Smoth had lands at Donnybrook, co. Dublin, to which were given the name Smothscourt, now known as Simmonscourt ; but it does not appear what lands he held of the priory.

[4] There is in the original no trace of any place name here, but from some of the tenants' names, and from the amount of rent compared with receipts in the Accounts, it is evident that from this point down to John Serjant, at the beginning of the Gorman tenants, the names are those of the tenants at Glasnevin, near Dublin.

and he shall plough at winter seed with his plough . . .
. . . two days, and if he has not a whole plough, he shall
do according as he is able, at the cost of the lord in food and
in drink, and it is worth, beyond drawbacks, 4*d.* a day. Also,
he shall plough at Lent seed time with his plough, if it be
a whole one, for two days, which is worth . . . . . .
and less, if it should be less.[1] And he shall hoe *(cerclabit)* the
lord's corn for two days with one man, and that is worth for
a-day ½*d.* And he shall gather and make up the lord's hay
(collig . . . & lecabit fenum) when there may be need, and
that work is worth ½*d.* And he shall reap in harvest for
two days with one man, and that work is worth, by the
day, 1*d.* And he shall carry the lord's corn, at expense of
the lord in food and in drink, in harvest for two days, and
that work is worth, beyond drawbacks, 4*d.* And he shall
give, at the feast of the Nativity of our Lord, one hen, or 1*d.*

WILLIAM BODENHAM holds 1 messuage and 2 crofts and 23 acres
1 stang, and pays, by the year, at said feasts, 25*s.* 4*d.*

HUGH FABER *(the Smith)* holds 1 messuage and 1 croft and 16 acres
½ stang, and pays, by the year, at said feasts, 18*s.*

NICHOLAS CHAUMBERLEYN holds 1 messuage 1 croft and 21 acres, less
½ stang, and pays, by the year, at said feasts, 22*s.* 9*d.*

ROBERT RICHARD holds 1 messuage and 19 acres ½ stang, and pays, by
the year, at said feasts, 22*s.* 1½*d.*

SALAMON JUXTA AQUAM *(by the water)*, holds 1 messuage and 9½ acres
1½ stang, and pays by the year, at said feasts, 10*s.* 10½*d.*

NICHOLAS KETYNG holds 1 messuage and 3 crofts and 13½ acres
1½ stang, and pays, by the year, at said feasts, 18*s.*

WILLIAM UESTHAM holds one messuage, and pays by the year, at said
feasts, 8*s.*

JOHN MICHEL holds 1 messuage and 1 croft containing 1 acre, and 5 acres
of land, and pays by the year, at said feasts, 7*s.* 11*d.*

JOHN ROWE holds 1 messuage, and pays, by the year, at said feasts,
6*s.* 7*d.*

And the aforesaid William Bodenham, and the other farmers
following, shall do in all things, and by all ways, in the
aforesaid works, as John de Barry shall do, as is aforesaid,
together with a hen at the feast of the Nativity of our
Lord, each of them, as is aforesaid.

---

[1] That is, if he possesses only a share in a plough, not a plough and full plough
team of his own.

GEOFFREY FYNCHE holds[1] 2 crofts, each of them 2*s.*, and 32 acres of land, and pays, by the year, at the aforesaid terms, 40*s.* And he shall reap ..... in harvest with one man, and that work is worth 4*d.* for same time. And he shall give, at the feast of the Nativity of Our Lord, three hens, or 3*d.* And shall plough, hoe, and make up hay, as the aforesaid John de Barry shall do in all things and by all ways.

JOHN FOX holds 1 messuage and 1 croft, and pays, by the year, 16*d.* And he shall work as a cottager.

THOMAS the chamberlain of the lord, holds 2 crofts, 1 at 2*s.*, and the other at 22*d.*, and pays, by the year, at the feasts of SS. Philip and James and All Saints, 4*s.*

JOHN CROBOK holds 1 cottage and 1 croft, and pays, by the year, at said terms, 2*s.* And he shall reap in harvest, and hoe and make up hay, as said John de Barry. And he shall give, at the feast of the Nativity of Our Lord, one hen, or 1*d.*

THOMAS CAMAN holds 1 cottage and 1 croft, and pays, by the year, at said terms, 2*s.* 9*d.* And he shall do, and give, as the aforesaid John.

THOMAS LANG holds 1 cottage and 1 croft, and pays, by the year, at said terms, 21*d.*

MATILDA KYNGHAM holds 1 cottage and 1 croft, and pays, by the year, at said terms, 2*s.*

RICHARD[2] BRACEATOR (*the brewer*) holds 1 cottage and 1 croft, and pays, by the year, at said terms, 2*s.*

CECILIA KNYHT holds 1 cottage and 1 croft, and pays, by the year, at said terms, 2*s.*

MARIOTA SALMAN holds 1 cottage and 1 croft, and pays, by the year, at said terms, 15*d.*

YVOR VERTATOR (*the turner ?*), holds 1 cottage and 1 croft, and pays, by the year, at said terms, 22*d.*

MAURICE DRYVER holds 1 cottage and 1 croft, and pays, by the year, at said terms, 22*d.*

MARGERY KAKHKEK holds 1 cottage, and pays, by the year, at said terms, 6*d.*

ADAM MOYN holds 1 cottage, and pays, by the year, at said terms, 12*d.*

ANNOTA ATTEHILL holds 1 cottage, and pays, by the year, at said terms, 6*d.*

ALICE LOMBE holds 1 cottage and 1 croft, and pays, by the year, at said terms, 18*d.*

---

[1] 1 messuage and 1 croft, 8*s.*, is written above.
[2] Ric. is written over Hugo, struck out.

John Baret holds 1 cottage and 1 croft, and 2 acres of land, less one stang, and pays, by the year, at said terms, 3s. 9d., and for another croft newly taken, 14d.

Eva the widow, holds 1 cottage and 1 croft, and pays, by the year, at said terms. 12d.

Thomas Michel holds a holding there, and pays, by the year, at said terms, 10s. 2d.

Alice Othyre holds a holding there, and pays. by the year, at said terms, 6s. 8d.

John Lombe holds 1 cottage there, and pays, by the year, at said terms, 12d.

Alice Salman holds 1 cottage there, and pays, by the year, at said terms, 12d.

Sir David the chaplain, holds 1 cottage there, and pays. by the year, at said terms, 6d.

Nicholas the clerk, holds 1 cottage and 1 croft. and pays, by the year, at said terms, 18d.

> And all those aforenamed, above written, shall perform works in all things, and by all ways, in all times, as John Crobok shall do.

Simon Fynche holds 1 cottage and 8 acres of land, and pays, by the year, 3s., for all services.

Thomas Callagh holds 1 cottage, and pays, by the year, 8s. 8d.

Robert Olay holds 1 cottage and 1 croft, and pays, by the year, at the terms aforesaid. 22d.

[1]Nicholas le Grete, holds 1 acre of land, and pays, by the year, 12d.

GORMAN.[2]

[3]John Serjant pays, by the year, for land which he holds in the field of the Prior, 43s. 6d. Also the same John pays, by the year, for one messuage, next the cemetery of S. Michan, 8s.

[4]Master John Laweles holds 1 messuage, and pays, by the year, 4s., for all service, at the feasts of the Apostles Philip and James and All Saints, and suit to court twice a-year.

Master Roger Lawles holds 1 messuage, and pays, by the year, 4s. at said feasts, for all service.

---

[1] £8 10d., is written here in the margin.
[2] Grangegorman, adjoining Dublin, now to a great extent absorbed into the city.
[3] *Serjeant* is written in margin.
[4] *Farmers* is written in margin.

ALEXANDER ATTEWELL holds 1 messuage and 18 acres of land, and pays, by the year, at said feasts, 24s. 8d., and suit, &c.

GRANGE GORMAN.

[1]ADAM BOURK holds 1 cottage, and pays, by the year, 2s., at the terms of the Apostles Philip and James and All Saints.

[1]GREGORY LE HOLDER[2] holds 1 cottage, and pays, by the year, at said terms, 2s.

[1]JOHN LE HOLDER holds 1 cottage, and pays, by the year, at said terms, 2s.

[1]CHRISTIANA the widow, holds 1 cottage, and pays, by the year, at said terms, 2s.

[1]WILLIAM LE HOLDER holds 1 cottage, and pays, by the year, at said terms, 2s.

JOHN CATT holds 1 messuage and certain holdings, and pays, by the year, at said terms, 35s. And he shall plough, at winter seed time, and Lent, for four days, or shall give 16d. And he shall carry, in harvest, with his cart, the corn of the lord, for two days. And the said works are worth 6d. a-year. And he shall give, at the feast of the Nativity of Our Lord, one hen, or 1d.

ROBERT LE DRYVER[2] holds 1 cottage, and pays, by the year, 12d., at the said terms. And he shall hoe for two days with one man. And he shall reap for two days with one man. And the said services are worth 4d. a-year. And he shall give, at the feast of the Nativity of Our Lord, one hen, or 1d.

ROGER DEKENT holds 1 cottage, and pays, by the year, at said terms 12d. And he shall do in works, in all and singular things, as the said Robert le Dryver.

ADAM COLBY holds 1 cottage, and pays, and shall do in works by the year, at said terms, as said Robert.

WILLIAM FEROUR holds 1 cottage, and pays, and does in works by the year, at said terms, as said Robert.

WALTER LYMBERNER[3] holds 1 cottage, and pays, and does in works by the year, at said terms, as said Robert.

HENRY CERNEY holds 1 cottage, and pays, and does in works by the year, at said terms, as said Robert.

---

[1] *Cotters* is written in margin.

[2] Le Holder. That is, a man who held a plough, a ploughman. Le Dryver means the driver of a plough team.

[3] The lime-burner.

PETER LE HOLDER holds 1 cottage, and pays. and does in works by the
year, at said terms, as said Robert.

WILLIAM CARECTARIUS (*the carter*) holds 1 cottage, and pays, and does
in works by the year, at said terms, as said Robert.

MICHAEL CARRIK holds 1 cottage, and pays, and does in works by the
year, at said terms, as said Robert.

JORDAN CARECTARIUS (*the carter*) holds 1 cottage, and pays, and does in
works by the year, at said terms, as said Robert.

JOSEP TRITURATOR (*the thresher*) holds 1 cottage, and pays, and does in
works by the year, at said terms, as said Robert.

CLONKEN, WITH ITS MEMBERS.[1]

VILLA CORNER'.[2]

GREGORY TAUNTON holds 1½ acre pence Crowhans by Cornerescourt for
18*d.*, by the year. Also for Cornerescourt, by the year, of
head rent, at the feasts of the Nativity of Our Lord and
of St. John, 4*s.* by the year; and he pays, by the year, at
said feasts, 5*s.* 6*d.* by equal portions.

BALYMORTHAN.[3]

PETER HOWEL holds; and pays, by the year, at said feasts, £4.

FERNECOSTEN.[4]

ROBERT, son of STEPHEN, holds, } and pay, by the year, at said feasts,
GILBERT BEGG } 50*s.*, and the works, by the year, 18*d.*

STALORGAN.[5]

SIR RALPH the chaplain, holds; and pays, by the year, at said feasts,
11*s.* 3*d.*

BALYTYPTR.[6]

JOHN THE WYHTE holds; and pays, by the year, at said feasts, 46*s.* 8*d.*
And he shall do divers works which are worth by the year
8*d.*, or shall give in money 8*d.*

---

[1] Clonken is now represented by Kill-of-the-Grange, Co. Dublin.

[2] Cornerstown, Cornelscourt, near Cabinteely, Co. Dublin.

[3] Ballymorthan. The more usual form of this name is Ballymolghan. Maps
attached to leases in the Christ Church collection show that it is now represented by
Murphystown, Co. Dublin, and Blackthorn lying to the north. The small adjoining
townland of Mulchanstown did not form part of it.

[4] Fernecosten lay S. W. of Leopardstown, Co. Dublin.

[5] Now Stillorgan.

[6] Now Tipperstown, the townland on which Stillorgan Railway Station stands.

CARRICMAYN,[1] BALYBRENAN.[2]

MAURICE HOWELL holds 40 acres for 40s. Also 2 crofts, penes Villam Corner', and pays by the year, 20d. Also he holds Balybrenan or 50s. a year; and pays, by the year, at said feasts, 55s.

SYLLAGH.[3]

DAVID MACNEBURY holds; and pays, by the year, at said feasts, £4.

KILLENY.[4]

JOHN MILIS holds by letter, and pays, by the year, at said feasts, 100s. And there are cotters there. And they shall work in harvest for three days. And each of them shall do divers other works with ploughs and carts or cars (*carcetis vel carrys*), which are worth by the year 3s.

DALKEY.[5]

JOHN KENDALE holds; and pays, by the year, at said feasts, 3s., and suit of court, and tolbol as often as he shall brew.

TOWN OF THE CHURCH.[6]

DOWNALD OHELYLL holds; and pays, by the year, at the said feasts, 28s. And he shall work in harvest for three days, and shall do divers other works with ploughs, carts, or cars, which are worth by the year 3s.

PHILIP son of DAVID, holds; and pays, by the year, at said feasts, 24s. And he shall do works which are worth, by the year, 8d.

Also same PHILIP holds a cottage with a croft, and pays, by the year, 12d.

MILO PASSEMOUNT[7] holds; and pays, by the year, at said feasts, 7s. And he shall plough for two days; and shall hoe for two days, and shall reap; and shall give one hen at the feast of the Nativity of Our Lord.

---

[1] Now Carrickmines.　　　　　　　　　　　　[2] Brennanstown.

[3] Properly Tyllagh, now Tully, adjoining the preceding lands.

[4] Now Killiney.

[5] The property of the Priory in Dalkey was small, the greater part belonged to the Archbishop.

[6] Villa Ecclesie and Villa Grangie appear to have been two hamlets on the manor of Clonken. The present Kill-of-the-Grange combines the two names, but nothing remains to distinguish their several sites.

[7] This name was written Passauant, but corrected to Passemount.

Henr. Othenan holds; and pays, by the year, at said feasts, 6s. 6d. And he shall do works and shall give one hen as the said Milo.

Nicholas OKenan holds; and pays, by the year, at the abovesaid feasts, 6s. And he shall do and give as the said Milo.

Laur. OKenan holds; and pays, by the year, at the said feasts, 3s. 6d. And he shall do and give as said Milo.

Maur. Laueragh holds (Mariota, his wife, for him); and pays, by the year, at the said feasts, 3s. And he shall do and give as said Milo.

Philip, son of David,[1] holds; and pays, by the year, at the said feasts, 12d. And he shall do and give as said Milo.

[2]Stephen OKenan holds 1 cottage, and pays, by the year, at said feasts, 2d., without other works. And he shall give 1 hen.

[2]John de Lyndesey holds 1 cottage, and pays, by the year, at said feasts, 2d., without other works. And he shall give 1 hen.

[2]Hugh Clericus (*the clerk*) holds 1 cottage, and pays, by the year, at said feasts, 2d., without other works. And he shall give 1 hen.

Town of the Grange.[3]

Nicholas Obrode holds; and pays, by the year, at said feasts, 4s.

Eva the widow, holds; and pays, by the year, at said feasts, 18d. (15d., but it is not known whether more or less[4]). And she shall work 4 days, or shall give 4d.

Thomas Faber (*the smith*) holds; and pays, by the year, at said feasts, 14s. And he shall work or give 8d.

Hugh le White holds; and pays, by the year, at said feasts, 11s. 9d. And he shall work or give 5½d.

Stephen Olyng holds; and pays, by the year, at said feasts, 51s. And he shall work for eight days, or shall give 8d.

John the White holds (Rob. Whyte for him); and pays, by the year, at said feasts, 11s. 3d. And he shall work for four days, or give 4d.

John Baillif holds; and pays, by the year, at said feasts, 11s. 6d. And he shall work, and the work is worth 4d.

Johanna Textrix (*the weaver*) holds; and pays, by the year, at said feasts, 15d. And shall work, or give 4d.

---

[1] In margin, q' superius.

[2] *Cottagers* written in margin.

[3] Villa Ecclesie and Villa Grangie appear to have been two hamlets on the manor of Clonken. The present Kill of the Grange combines the two names, but nothing remains to distinguish their several sites.

[4] Interlined in another hand.

CECILIA FRANKAN holds (Peter Theggs for her); and pays, by the year, at said feasts, 3*d.* And shall work, or give 4*d.*

ADAM DROMSALAN, or GIBBE, holds; and pays, by the year, at said feasts, 3*d.* And shall work, or give 4*d.*

ROGER BELLEYNGS holds; and pays, by the year, at said feasts, 3*s.* And shall work, or give 4*d.*

RALPH KENEDY holds (Hugh Rodypakke for him); and pays, by the year, at said feasts, 9*d.* And shall work, or give 4*d.*

WALTER[1] FADD holds; and pays, by the year, at said feasts, 9*d.* And shall work, or give 4*d.*

RICHARD CATHTLAN holds (Henry Bossard for him); and pays, by the year, at said feasts, 6*d.* And shall work, or give 4*d.*

JOHN MANEHAN holds; and pays, by the year, at said feasts, 9*d.* And shall work, or give 4*d.*

WALTER KYLHEEL holds; and pays, by the year, at said feasts, 6*d.* And shall work, or give 4*d.*

JOHN ERCEDEKNE holds (Richard Cathelan for him); and pays, by the year, at said feasts, 7*d.* And shall work, or give 4*d.*

THOMAS SLYMAGE holds; and pays, by the year, at said feasts, 3*d.* And shall work, or give 4*d.*

PÉTER CAMERARIUS (*the chamberlain*) holds; and pays by the year, at said feasts, 6*s.* 9*d.* And shall work, or give 4½*d.*

MARIOTA sister of the smith holds; and pays, by the year, at said feasts, 3*d.* And shall work, or give 4*d.*

ROBERT STAFFORD holds (William Masonn for him); and pays, by the year, at said feasts, 9*d.* And shall work, or give 4*d.*

JOHN PUNCHART holds *1 cottage and half an acre of land*,[2] and pays, by the year, at said feasts, 4½*d.* And shall work, or give 4*d.*

GILBERT LOMBE holds; and pays, by the year, at said feasts, 9*d.* And shall work, or give 4*d.*

ISABELLA HOWRYN holds; and pays, by the year, at said feasts, 9*d.* And shall work, or give 4*d.*

STEPHEN[3] OBRODE holds; and pays, by the year, at said feasts, 5*s.* 6*d.* And shall work, or give 4½*d.*

PATRICK FABER (*the smith*) holds; and pays, by the year, at said feasts, 18*d.* And shall work, or give 1½*d.*

MARIOTA MORE holds; and pays, by the year, at said feasts, 9*d.* And shall work, or give 4*d.*

---

[1] Walter is written over Adam, struck out.   [2] Added in another hand.
[3] Stephen written over Gilbert, struck out.

Elyas Howryn holds ; and pays, by the year, at said feasts, 5s. 2d. And
    shall work, or give 4d.

John Crispe holds ; and pays, by the year, at said feasts, 21d. And
    shall work, or give 4d.

Thomas Bryht holds } jointly two cottages, and pay, by the year at said
Juliana Chamberleyn } feasts, 12d. And shall work, or give 4d.

Henr. Howryn holds ; and pays, by the year, at said feasts, ...[1]

Ricard Brit holds one cottage, with a curtilage, and pays, by the year,
    3d. And the services which the other cottagers do.

Isabella the widow, relict of Gilkeuyn, holds one cottage, with a cur-
    tilage, and pays, by the year, 3d. And the services which the
    other cottagers do.

Milo Cosyn holds one cottage, with a curtilage, and pays, by the year,
    3d. And the services which the other cottagers do.

RENTS OF BALYSCADAN[2] for the term of the Nativity of Our
    Lord, and of other towns for the Nativity of St. John the Baptist
    and St. Michael.

Tobyrton.[3]

'Philip Edward holds 1 messuage, 25 acres of land. And pays for an
    acre by the year, at the feasts of the Nativity of Our Lord,
    and the Nativity of St. John the Baptist, 8d. And he shall
    give one goose at the feast of St. Michael.

Michael M'Heth holds 1 messuage, 25½ acres of land, and pays, and
    shall do in all things as the said Philip. *xxi* s. *iii* d. : *x* d.
    the acre.[5]

Osbert Edward holds 1 messuage, 12½ acres of land, and pays, by the
    year, 8s. 4d. *x* s. *v* d.

Anabilla the widow, holds 1 messuage, 25½ acres of land, and pays, by
    the year, at said feasts, and shall do as the said Philip.

Ralph del Rath[6] holds 1 messuage, 25½ acres of land, and shall pay
    and do as above.

---

[1] Blank in original.

[2] Now Ballyscaddan, a parish in the barony of Balrothery East, Co. Dublin.

[3] Tobertown, in the parish of Balscaddan.

[4] *Farmers* written in margin.

[5] The amounts in italics are in the original written over the other amounts, in the same (or at least a contemporary) hand, but with a paler ink. They represent apparently a revision of the rents.

[6] Rath is the name of a modern townland immediately adjoining Tobertown.

ELYAS FLEMYNG holds 12½ acres of land, and pays, by the year, at said feasts, 8s. 4d. *x* s. *r* d.

¹MICHAEL HASARD holds 1 cottage, and pays, by the year, 3d.

TOWN OF STOBYLDEKNE.

WILLIAM LE REDE holds 27 acres of land, and pays, by the year, at said feasts, 27s.

TOWN OF BALYGADY.²

ROBERT ROSEL holds 77 acres of land, and pays, by the year, at said feasts, 32s. 2d. : 5d. the acre. *li* s. *iiii* d. : *riii* d. *an acre.*

DERMODESTON.³

REMUND COLYN, holds 40 acres of land, and pays, by the year, at said feasts, 26s. 8d. *xxxiii* s. *iiii* d. : *x* d. *an acre.*

ALICE the widow, holds 20 acres of land, and pays, by the year, at said feasts, 13s. 4d. *xvi* s. *viii* d. : *x* d. *an acre.*

JOHN HASARD holds 10 acres of land, and pays, by the year, at said feasts, 6s. 8d. *viii* s. *iiii* d. : *x* d. *an acre.*

NICHOLAS RERYTH holds 20 acres of land, and pays, by the year, at said feasts, 13s. 4d. *xvi* s. *viii* d. : *x* d. *an acre.*

WALTER HASARD holds 10 acres of land, and pays, by the year, at said feasts, 6s. 8d. *viii* s. *iiii* d. John Asard for him.

SIMON SARYN holds 20 acres of land, and pays, by the year, at said feasts, 13s. 4d. *xvi* s. *viii* d. : *x* d. *an acre.*

TOWN OF NEWETON.⁴

MATILDA LA WHITE holds 66 acres of land, and pays, by the year, at said feasts, 44s. : 8d. an acre. *xlix* s. *vi* d. : *ix* d. *an acre.*

JOHN PASSELEW, junior, holds 66 acres of land, and pays, by the year, at said feasts, 24s. : 8d. an acre. *xliiii* s.

WILLIAM PASSAVANT holds 10 acres of land, and pays, by the year, at said feasts, 6s. 8d. : 8d. an acre. *viii* s. *iiii* d. : *x* d. *an acre.*

---

¹ *Cottager* written in margin. ³ Dermotstown, in parish of Balscaddan.
² Now Balgaddy, in the parish of Balscaddan. ⁴ Newtown, in same parish.

BALLYSCADAN.

GEOFFREY M‘HETHE holds 4 acres of land, and pays, by the year, at said feasts, 4*s.*

Town of the GRANGE[1] yields, by the year, at said feasts, £7 3*s.*

Town of TYPYRSOULE[2] yields, by the year, at said feasts, 20*s.*

Town of KYLLOTHTYR[3] yields, by the year, at said feasts, 13*s.* 4*d.*

Town of MILESTON[4] yields, by the year, at said feasts, 13*s.* 4*d.*

For the mill there is rendered, by the year, at said feasts, 36*s.* by indenture for 10 years.

Land next the Church, 30 acres, yields, by the year, at said feasts, 27*s.* 6*d.* : 11*d.* the acre.

––––––

VALUATION OF THE POSSESSIONS OF THE PRIORY IN 1306.

Translated from the Latin Text, printed in Irish Record Commissioners Reports, Vol. I., pp. 311-2, from the Black Book of Christ Church.

TAXATION OF THE GOODS, PROFITS, AND RENTS, OF THE CHURCH OF THE HOLY TRINITY, DUBLIN, for the exaction of the biennial Tenth.

IN THE DEANERY OF DUBLIN.

The Church of S. Michael is worth by the year £6, ... Tenth 12*s.*

The Church of S. John is worth by the year 100*s.*, ... Tenth 10*s.*

The Church of S. Michan is worth, by the year, £4, ... Tenth 8*s.*

Annual rent in the city of Dublin, £16 5*s.* 2*d.*, . Tenth 32*s.* 6¼*d.*

Total, £31 5*s.* 2*d.*, . Tenth 62*s.* 6¼*d.*

––––––

[1] Grange in same parish.
[2] Tobersool in same parish.
[3] Killougher in same parish.
[4] Milestown in same parish.

In the Deanery of Tranche.[1]

In the Grange of Gorman are 4 carucates of
    land which are valued by the year at £24,   .   Tenth 48s.

Also the tithes of the same carucates of land
    are valued at £8 a-year,   .   .   .   Tenth 16s.

In the manor of Glasnevyn are three carucates
    of land which are valued with the tithe
    arising from them by the year at £24,   .   Tenth 48s.

            Total, £56,   .   Tenth 112s.

In the Deanery of Bree.[2]

In the manor of Clonken are 7 carucates of
    land, of which two carucates are let to farm
    with a mill for £14 13s. 4d.,   .   .   Tenth 29s. 4d.

Also one carucate of land let to farm for £4
    10s., ...   Tenth 9s.

Also one carucate of land at Tyllagh, let to
    farm for £6, ...   Tenth 12s.

Also three carucates of land which remain in
    the manor are worth, by the year, £18,   .   Tenth 36s.

The Church of Clonken, with the chapel attached,
    worth, by the year, £18 3s. 4d.,   .   .   Tenth 36s. 4d.

        Total, £61 6s. 8d.   .   Tenth £6 2s. 8d.

In the Deanery of Swerde.

The Church of Balyskadan worth, by the year,
    £10, ...   Tenth 20s.

Yearly rent there, £28,   .   .   .   Tenth 56s.

         Total, £38,   Tenth 76s.

In the Deanery of . . . .

The Church of Kylleolyn, which the Prior and
    Convent of the Holy Trinity aforesaid have in
    their own use, with its chapels and appurte-
    nances, £39 13s. 4d.,   .   .   .   Tenth 79s. 4d.

    Sum of the totals, £226 5s. 2d.,   .   Tenth £22 12s. 6½d.

---

[1] Tuney.   [2] Bray.

CELLARER'S ACCOUNT.

*Translated from a copy in Christ Church Deeds in Public Record Office,
No. 1115, collated with another copy, Novum Registrum of Christ
Church, No. 218.*

ACCOUNT OF BROTHER WILLIAM TOPP, CELLARER of the Cathedral
Church of the Holy Trinity, Dublin, of money received for buying
wheat and oats in the year of our Lord, 1368 :—

In the first place he received from the treasurer,
 as appears by a tally, ... vi li ix d.
Also in money received from Robert Haket for
 the tithes of Balitybyrt, ... xxiiii s.
Also in money received for the tithes of Kylleny, xvi s.
Also in money received from master Peter, . iii li.
     Sum of all, xi li. x s. ix d.

In the first place he delivered for x crannocs of
 wheat bought ; price of each crannoc, vi s.,   sum iii. li. .
Also delivered for x crannocs of wheat : price of
 each crannoc, vi s. viii d., ... sum iii li. vi s. viii d.
Also delivered for vi crannocs of wheat : price of
 each, vii s., ... sum xlii s.
Also delivered for iii crannocs of wheat bought
 from Geoffrey Hyneley : price of each, v s. iiii d., sum xvi s.
Also delivered for i crannoc of wheat bought, . vi s.
    Sum of the crannocs, . xxx crannocs.
    Sum total of the price, . ix li. x s. viii d.
Also delivered for xii crannocs of oats bought :
 price of each crannoc, iii s. iiii d., . . . sum xl s.
   Sum of the whole payment as appears, xi li. x s. viii d.

COVENANT FOR CELEBRATION OF MASSES FOR
A BENEFACTOR.

*Latin Text of the document of which a shortened translation is given
at pp. 148-51, from the original in Christ Church Deeds, No. 225.*

Universis sancte matris Ecclesie filiis presentem paginam inspec-
turis, Frater Rogerus Goioun Prior Ecclesie Sancte Trinitatis Dublin et
ejusdem loci Conventus salutem in domino sempiternam. Majestatis

divine inscrutabilis altitudo illorum merita condigno premio recompensat qui domus dominice sic amplificant facultates, ut terrena in celestia et transitoria in eterna felici commercio transferant et commutent. Vigor equidem exigit equitatis quod bonorum largicio piis usibus perpetuo titulo amplificata quatenus processerit ex zelo fervide caritatis eatenus firmitatis perpetue robore muniatur ac jugi et continue memorie commendetur. Hinc est quod vestre universitati patefacimus per presentes quod cum noster carissimus Johannes de Grauntsete ad celestia desideria erigens mentem suam, affectansque divini cultus officium ampliare, et ob devotum divini obsequii incrementum, plura ac diversa bona domui nostre ad perpetuam rei memoriam caritative contulisset et impetrasset ac pro juribus dicte ecclesie nostre manutenendis et perpetrandis diversis temporibus multum laborasset grataque obsequia et utilia nobis et ecclesie nostre predicte retroactis temporibus multociens impendisset. Nos prefati Prior et Conventus non astricti nec in aliquo compulsi, set ex mera libera et spontanea voluntate nostra, ac ex pura et sana conciencia excitati ut benefactoribus nostris de beneficiis suis tuciorem reddamus racionem coram eterni judicis tribunali, premissaque in consideracionem deducentes et illa dono spirituali retribuere desiderabiliter affectantes, eidem Johanni in vita et in morte ac Alicie quondam uxori sue et omnibus quibus ipsi tenentur tam vivis quam mortuis, omnium missarum matutinarum precum oracionum jejuniorum elemosinarum suffragiorum vigiliarum diciplinarum ceterorum omniumque bonorum que per dei adjutorium infra dictam Ecclesiam et prioratum nostrum quamdiu mundus duraverit fieri contingent, ita plenissimam participacionem quantam dicte ecclesie nostre fundatori seu alicui alteri summo et specialissimo nostre domus a prima ejusdem fundacione benefactori et amico pure sponte et absolute concedimus per presentes. Volumus eciam et ex unanimi consensu nostro ordinamus et nos ac omnes successores nostros efficaciter obligamus invenire duos Canonicos sacerdotes in Ecclesia nostra predicta sub regulari observancia altissimo famulantes singulis diebus divina officia imperpetuum celebraturos, et celebracionem ipsum die confeccionis presencium solempniter incepturos maxime pro salubri statu ejusdem Johannis dum vixerit et ut cuncta opera sua ad laudem dei inchoata feliciter compleantur, necnon pro animabus predicte Alicie antecessorum heredum benefactorum suorum et omnium illorum quibus iidem Johannes et Alicia quoquomodo tenentur, ac omnium fidelium defunctorum, et cum idem Johannes de hac luce migraverit iidem Canonici celebrabunt cotidie specialiter pro anima ejusdem Johannis et pro animabus predicte Alicie ac omnium predictorum, de quibus duobus canonicis unus celebrabit cotidie missam **beate Marie Virginis** prout moris est, et hoc specialiter pro predicto Johanne et pro anima predicte Alicie ac pro omnibus supradictis, et in qualibet missa pro prefato Johanne et aliis supradictis sic **celebrata vivente eodem** Johanne, **dicet** specialiter illam colectam cotidie pro eodem Johanne, Pretende domine **famulo** tuo dexteram celestis auxilii, ut te toto corde perquirat et **que digne** postulat assequatur, et pro animabus predicte Alicie ac omnium predictorum dicet aliam colectam, Omnipotens sempiterne deus qui **vivorum** dominaris simul et mortuorum **omniumque misereris quos tuos fide et** opere futuros esse prenostis ; te supplices exoramus ut pro quibus effundere preces decrevimus, &c. Et cum dictus Johannes viam universe carnis fuerit ingressus, dictus Canonicus in qualibet missa dicet specialiter pro anima ejusdem Johannis illam colectam, Quesumus domine pro tua pietate miserere anime famuli **tui et** a contagiis mortalitatis exutam in eterne salvacionis **partem restitue** ; **cum alia** colecta, Omnipotens sempiterne deus, antedicta, pro anima ejusdem Alicie ac ceteris supradictis. Alius vero canonicus celebrabit cotidie ad altare coram sancta cruce in dicta ecclesia nostra specialiter pro predicto Johanne et pro anima predicte Alicie ac pro ceteris supradictis et dicet colectas supradictas in forma supradicta. Qui quidem canonici sacris vestibus induti ante introitum cujuslibet misse clam vel palam dicent Pater noster et Ave Maria pro predictis Johanne et Alicia et pro animabus omnium fidelium defunctorum. Et preter hoc anniversaria predictorum Johannis et Alicie in prioratu nostro nos et omnes nostri successores quamdiu mundus duraverit celebrabimus cum tanta solempnitate sicut anniversarium primi et precipui fundatoris nostri et prout solempnius aliquo tempore transacto celebrari consuevit, videlicet anniversarium ejusdem Johannis die Assumpcionis Beate Marie Virginis et anniversarium predicte Alicie sexto die Junii, et omni die qua perfecta fuerit in capitulo nostro vel in choro commemoracio mortuorum, Anime eorundem Johannis et Alicie absolventur inhibi nominatim. Et quoscienscunque aliquis predictorum duorum canonicorum ob infirmitatem vel aliam causam legitimam celebrare fuerit impeditus, tunc alius canonicus de domo nostra suplebit fideliter vicem suam, et omni die sabbati ac aliis diebus cum tabula chori nostri de ebdomodario ac ceteris ecclesie nostre supradicte ministris fuerit ordinata conscripta et lecta, volumus et concedimus unanimiter pro nobis et successoribus nostris ut predicti duo canonici sic celebraturi secundum formam supradictam pro predictis Johanne et Alicia ac ceteris superius nominatis in predicta tabula nostra fideliter ordinentur et conscribantur, ac de eis sicut de ecclesie nostre ministris in lectura tabule nostre supra-

dicte fiat expressio nominalis. Nos eciam frater Rogerus Prior antedictus
et omnes ac singuli Canonici aduniti obligamus nos et successores
nostros et fideliter manucapimus in concienciis nostris quod numerum
predictorum duorum Canonicorum in celebracione hujusmodi minime
minuemus, set ipsam celebracionem fideliter fieri faciemus eamque
manutenebimus et continuabimus quantum in nobis est in forma
predicta debite et decenter, quodque nichil impetrabimus a domino
nostro summo pontifice nec a domino Rege Anglie aut a superioribus
ordinis nostri seu ab aliquo alio cujuscumque fuerit dignitatis preheminencie status ordinis condicionis aut eciam potestatis quominus
celebracio predicta in aliquo subtrahatur. Et similiter quilibet Prior
in nostro Prioratu de novo creatus, in ingressu suo in capitulo nostro
post ipsam creacionem in presencia conventus, ac omnes et singuli
novicii antequam in eodem prioratu nostro ad professionem admittantur
in pleno capitulo nostro juramenti vinculo astringantur, videlicet quod
ordinacionem predictam ac cantariam in singulis suis articulis fideliter
conservabunt et pro posse suo perpetuo manutenebunt, Ceterum ut
presens ordinacio sine diminucione seu aliquali in penis commutacione
perpetuis temporibus perseveret et inviolabiter observetur. Nos
prefati Prior et conventus omnes et singuli subicimus nos et successores
nostros in hac parte jurisdiccioni et cohercioni venerabilis patris
domini Archiepiscopi Dubliniensis ac annuorum visitatorum nostrorum conjunctim et divisim, ut annuatim in visitacionibus suis ceterisque
temporibus necessariis et oportunis possint nos arguere et animaversacione condigna punire et contra nos et nostros in eodem prioratu
successuros canonice procedere juxta regularis exigenciam dicipline si
ordinacionem predictam ex culpa nostra invenerint violatam seu cantariam antedictam in aliquo diminutam vel subtractam. Volumus eciam
et concedimus pro nobis et successoribus nostris quod in omni missale
dicte domus nostre, in margine juxta secretum misse ad perpetuam rei memoriam scribatur, Orate pro Johanne de Grauntsete et Alicia uxore ejus
ac pro omnibus quibus tenentur, et sic sine amocione perpetuis temporibus scriptum remaneat. Et ne oblivio aboleat quod caritativa instituit
gratitudo omni anno bis, scilicet die animarum et dominica in quinquagesima, presens hec ordinacio in nostro capitulo in omnium fratrum
presencia perlegetur ac tota hec convencio et ordinacio de verbo ad
verbum in martilogio nostro ob majorem rei recordacionem inserantur
et transcribantur. Preterea volumus et concedimus pro nobis et successoribus nostris quod ille anulus auri cum lapide precioso et cum
cathena argentea per predictum Johannem de Grauntsete in honorem
sancte Trinitatis in dicta Ecclesia nostra sancte Cruci ibidem oblata,

ab eadam sancta cruce cum dicta cathena firmiter dependeat pro infirmis, ut quos Omnipotens deus virtute preciosi lapidis sanitati restauraverit, pro eisdem Johanne et Alicia apud ipsum omnipotentem oratores habeant, et quod dicte sancte crucis custodes ac eciam anuli predicti hujusmodi infirmis administratores palam injungant et onerent predictos infirmos pro predictis Johanne et Alicia et pro hiis quibus tenentur specialiter orare. Insuper volumus et concedimus pro nobis et successoribus nostris quod ille anulus ibi imperpetuum maneat et a dicta sancta cruce dependeat, et sub pena anathematis per nos super hoc late a nullo hominum umquam ab eadem cruce aliqua de causa aliene-tur. In quorum omnium testimonium atque fidem sigillum nostrum commune unacum sigillo ejusdem Johannis huic scripto indentato alternatim sunt apposita. Datum apud Dublin in domo nostra capitu-lari nono die Julii, Anno domini Millesimo Trecentesimo tricesimo quinto et regni Regis Edwardi tercii a conquestu nono.

INQUISITION AS TO THE CONDUCT OF BROTHER JOHN COMYN.

From the original in Public Record Office, Christ Church Deeds, No. 72. An abstract of this document is given at p. 163.

Inquisicio capta apud Kylkolyn die Veneris in festo sancti Mathie apostoli anno &c. Coram magistro Thoma[1] Kylmore clerico de conve sacione fratris Johannis Comyn et de delapi-dacione bonorum domini Prioris Ecclesie sancte Trinitatis Dublin, apud Kylkolyn, per subscriptos, videlicet dominos Robertum Clenche, dominum Hanr' Mannyng, et dominum Willelmum Le Wite, capellanos, Willelmum Bolloc, Johannem Russel, clericos. Stephanum Ram, Johannem Colbi, Radulfum Mercatorem et Mathm filium Hanr'. Qui jurati dicunt super sacramentum suum quod dictus frater Johannes duxit secum apud Kylkolyn dominum Nicolaum capellanum et Eliam fratres suos et Milsandam consangueneam suam, qui vixerunt ab octo diebus ante natale usque ad festum sancti Walentini, videlicet per octo septimanas ad dampna prioris et conventus x solidorum. Item dicunt quod dictus Nicolaus et Johanna ansilla dicti fratris Johannis scandalisati fuerunt de crimine carnali ad quod scanda-

---

[1] Thome in original.

lum extinguendum dicta Johanna delapidavit de bonis dicti prioris ad valensiam ii solidorum. Item dicunt quod dictus frater Johannes vendidit ii cranocos avenarum pro vi solidis in delapidacione predictorum bonorum, et etiam dicunt quod dictus Johannes amovebat et secum portabat xx runnos fili linei ad valenciam v solidorum et etiam dimidiam petram lani prec' x denariorum, et dictus dominus Nicolaus dedit vi vellera lani pro uno altili ad senam suam. Item dicunt quod per verba dicti fratris Johannis et domini Nicolai fratris sui pomposa et abstraccione sustentacionis garcionum, cultura terre retardatur per viii acras ad dampna iiii solidorum, et unus afris prec' v solidorum moritur. Item tradidit unam carectam exmutuo Hanrico Talloun ad cariendum i molarem, et etiam sibi tradidit unam pessiam ferri prec' ii denariorum ad dampna x d. Item dicunt quod die Purificationis Beate Marie dictus frater Johannes maliciose negavit capellano parochiali ad selebrandum et faciendum officium suum in Ecclesia, propter quod abstracte fuerunt ij libre sere prec' xvi d. Item dicunt quod secum detulit de rebus fratris Nicolai ibidem inventis et aliis diversis rebus ad valenciam xii d.

LEASE OF LANDS OF THE PRIORY.

From the original in Public Record Office, Christ Church Deeds, No. 616.
An abstract of the principal provisions is given at p. 172.

Sexto die mensis novembris Anno domini millesimo ccc° quinquagesimo secundo, apud Dublin, ita convenit inter Religiosos viros Priorem et Conventum Ecclesie Cathedralis sancte Trinitatis de Dublin ex parte una, et Robertum Haketh ex parte altera, videlicet quod predicti Prior et Conventus ex eorum unanimi assensu et voluntate concesserunt dimiserunt et ad firmam tradiderunt predicto Roberto et assignatis suis, totum tenementum suum de Balitypur tam in terra arabili quam in pratis pascuis moris et pasturis et aliis pertinenciis dicto tenemento de Balitypur quoquomodo pertinentibus. Habend' et tenend' totum dictum tenementum cum terris pratis pascuis moris et pasturis et aliis pertinenciis ut predictum est predicto Roberto et assignatis suis usque ad finem sexdecim annorum proximum sequencium, plenarie et totaliter complendorum, termino incipiente die et anno supradictis. Reddendo inde annuatim durante termino supradicto, predicti Robertus et assignati sui predictis Priori et Conventui et eorum successoribus, pro octo annos

proximos sequentes a die confeccionis presencium triginta solidos
argenti annuatim ad duos anni terminos, medietatem videlicet ad
festum Apostolorum Philippi et Jacobi et aliam medietatem ad festum
Omnium Sanctorum proximum sequens. Et pro octo annos alios extunc
subsequentes quadraginta solidos argenti annuatim ad predictos
terminos et sic de anno in annum et termino in terminum durante
termino supradicto. Et predicti Robertus et assignati sui annuatim
durante termino supradicto, terram dictorum Prioris et Conventus cum
caruca sua per unum diem ad semen arabunt yemale et per unum diem
ad semen quadragesimale videlicet super terram dominicorum dictorum
prioris et Conventus apud Clonken. Et metent blada dictorum Prioris
et conventus cum uno homine per unum diem in Autumpno, annuatim
durante termino supradicto. Et cariabunt cum carecta sua blada
dictorum Prioris et conventus ibidem per unum diem, aut cum una
carra per duos dies, aut cum duabus carris per unum diem. Et nichil-
ominus durante termino predicto annuatim dabunt dictis priori et
conventui quociens et quandocunque braciaverint ex certa consuetudine
unum scadabolle servisie continens duas lagenas una cum secta curie
dictorum Prioris et Conventus de Clonken, quociens et quandocunque
fuerint premuniti. Et si predicti Robertus et assignati sui de predicto
redditu in parte vel in toto per unam quindenam post aliquem
terminum predictum aretro fuerint non soluto, extunc cadant a
firma predicta sine ulteriori dilacione, et predictum redditum aretro
existentem integrum solvant. Et predicti Robertus et assignati sui
tenementum predictum nec aliquam partem ejusdem alicui viventi
tradent seu dimittent durante termino predicto nisi uni de consanguineis
suis sine consensu dictorum prioris et conventus. Et si contingat
quod predictus Robertus vel assignati sui infra predictum terminum
obierit vel obierint quod predicti prior et conventus habeant heeriotam
ibidem sine contradiccione aliqua, vel dimidiam marcam argenti ad
eleccionem dictorum prioris et conventus. Preterea predictus
Robertus manucepit quod ipse et assignati sui durante termino predicto, quandocunque et quocienscunque per predictos priorem et
conventum vel eorum successores legitime fuerit vel fuerint premuniti,
ad mandatum eorum cum tanta vi, potestate, secundum posse suum in
consilio servicio et auxilio dictorum prioris et conventus et eorum
successorum veniet vel venient ubicunque infra Comitatum Dublin
sumptibus dictorum prioris et conventus sine contradiccione aliquali.
Et predictus Robertus et assignati sui predictum tenementum cum
omnibus suis edificiis durante termino predicto in bono statu sus-
tentabunt, et in fine termini predicti styf et staunche dimittent, sine

aliqua contradiccione. Et ad hec omnia et singula supradicta facienda fideliter et complenda, predictus Robertus tactis sacrosanctis ewangeliis, corporale prestitit sacramentum. Et predicti prior et conventus tenementum predictum tam in terra arabili quam in pratis pascuis moris pasturis et aliis pertinenciis dicto tenemento de Balitypur quoquomodo pertinentibus predicto Roberto et assignatis predictis durante termino predicto contra omnes gentes warantizabunt. In cujus rei testimonium parti huius scripti indentati penes predictum Robertum residenti nos predicti Prior et conventus sigillum nostrum comune apposuimus. Alteri vero parti penes nos remanenti sigillum predicti Roberti est appensum. Datum apud Dublin die et anno supradictis.

COVENANT WITH VICAR FOR REPAIR OF PARISH CHURCH.

From the Original in the Public Record Office, Christ Church Deeds, No. 635. An abstract is given at p. 181.

Die Dominica in festo Nativitatis Beati Johannis Bapthiste Anno Domini Millesimo ccc^mo quadragesimo septimo, Apud Dublin, ita convenit inter Religiosos viros, Priorem et Conventum Ecclesie Cathedralis sancte Trinitatis Dublin ex parte una, et Dominum Philippum Welsshe capellanum ex parte altera, videlicet quod predicti Prior et Conventus unanimi eorum assensu et voluntate concesserunt et tradiderunt dicto Domino Philippo, Omnes Decimas garbarum et feni pariter et omnes oblaciones et minutas decimas ad Ecclesiam dictorum Prioris et Conventus de Rathothul quoquo modo jure spectantes a die et anno supradictis usque ad finem quinque annorum prox. sequencium plenarie et totaliter complendorum. Tali pacto et condicione quod predictus dominus Philippus solvet predictis Priori et Conventui et eorum successoribus annuatim durante termino predicto, Quatuor marcas argenti ad terminos sancti Petri quod dicitur Ad vincula et Purificacionis Beate Marie Virginis per equales porciones et omnia onera tam infra ordinaria quam extra ordinaria dicte Ecclesie de Rathothul quoquomodo durante termino quinque annorum predicto incumbencia in omnibus subportabit. Et ad inchoacionem unius anni et dimidii, de quinque annis supradictis, bene et congrue gabulum Cancelli dicte

Ecclesie de Rathothul emendabit, et dictum Cancellum bene et sufficienter ita quod sit stuff & staunch duplici bord' ad inicium unius anni et dimidii ut supradictum est faciet cooperire et sic dictum Cancellum stuff et staunch ad finem dictorum quinque annorum dimittet. Et dictum Cancellum inferius pariter et altare pargectabit bene et honeste, et omnes libros infra dictam Ecclesiam existentes infra dictum annum et dimidium ut supradictum est ligabit et sufficienter emendabit et sic eos in fine dicti termini dimittet. Et omnia jura dicte Ecclesie de Rathothull quoquomodo pertinencia durante termino quinque annorum supradicto contra omnes gentes secundum vires suas custodiet proteget salvabit et manutenebit. Et . . . hec que supradicta sunt predictus dominus Philippus vult et concedit per presentes quod si in solucione dictarum quatuor marcarum argenti per quindenam post aliquem predictorum terminorum aut in aliquo de pacto supradicto defecerit quod absit, quod statim sine aliqua contradiccione cadat et a dicta Ecclesia de Rathothul amoveatur, et nihilominus de omni quod tunc de dicta solucione aretro fuerit solvere pariter et de pacti predicti fraccione si in aliquo defecerit complere teneatur. Et ad omnia supradicta bene et fideliter in omnibus ut suprascriptum est facienda pariter et complenda predictus dominus Philippus deosculatis sacrosanctis Evangeliis corporale prestitit sacramentum. Et predicti Prior et Conventus omnes predictas Decimas garbarum et feni, omnes oblaciones pariter et minutas decimas Ecclesie eorum de Rathothul pertinentes dicto domino Philippo durante termino quinque annorum supradicto, ita quod eidem Ecclesie de Rathothul bene et honeste in divinis deserviat seu deserviri faciat, et ea que supradicta sunt bene et fideliter in omnibus compleat, contra omnes gentes warantizabunt et deffendent. In cujus rei testimonium presentibus Indenturis partes alternatim sigilla sua apposuerunt. Datum Dublin die et anno supradictis.

GLOSSARY

OF WORDS OCCURRING IN THE ACCOUNTS.

Acre.—The acre used in the neighbourhood of Dublin down to the 16th century seems to have been measured by a perch of 8 yards. Thus the lands of S. Mary's Abbey were measured in 1539 'per perticam continentem xxiiii pedes juxta consuetudinem patrie ibidem' (*Chartularies*, vol. ii., p. 43). This would make an acre equal to rather more than 2½ statute acres.

Affer.—Better 'afer' or 'aver,' appears to be applied to a poor breed of horses used in farm work, a sense which the word still retains in Northumberland and Scotland (Halliwell's *Dict.*, Jameson, *Scottish Dict.*).

Avener.—An official having charge of the supply of forage. From the Latin *avenarius*.

Bass.—A collar for cart horses, made of flags (Wright, *Provincial Dict.*).

Beamfilling.—Mud or mortar used to finish the top of the side walls of a building, closing the spaces between the rafters.

Bend of iron.—A bundle containing apparently twenty-five of the pieces in which iron was ordinarily sold.

Boly (p. 36).—Irish, buaile. The cattle-yard or cow-house.

Bulchagh.—Said to be the name of a fish, but not identified.

Car.—A vehicle, apparently a sledge without wheels, used in harvest for carrying corn from the fields. Its working value was considered to be only half that of the carecta or wheeled cart. (See pp. 172 and 208.)

Cartebaas (p. 59).—Probably same as bass, above.

Clathes (p. 60).—Irish, cliath. Hurdles of wattle work. The word is usually met in Latin legal documents in the form *claia*. The Mem. Roll of 15 & 16 Edw. II. contains a mandate to the sheriff of Louth, directing him to provide in the neighbouring woods, "120 clais," half to be of the length of 8 feet by 4 feet in breadth, and half 6 feet by 3 feet.

Chippe.—Chep, the part of a plough on which the share is placed (Wright, *Prov. Dict.*).

Cindon for sindon, fine linen.

Cericum for sericum, silk.

Clouts.—Plates of iron for carts.   (See p. 166.)

Crannoc.—The general measure of corn in the English settlements in Ireland to the end of the 14th century.   Its value has been variously stated as from ½ quarter (Sweetman, vol. III., glossary) to 2 quarters (Betham, *Irish Antiquarian Researches*, p. 5).   The exact amount certainly varied, but at the times of these accounts, and long previously, the crannoc of wheat seems to have been nearly equivalent to the English quarter.   By a statute of 53 Hen. III., the earliest recorded Act of an Irish Parliament, the quarter of London was directed to be used throughout Ireland (Betham, *Constitution*, p. 254); and soon after, the crannoc of wheat is found to consist of 8 bushels, that of oats 16 bushels (*Norfolk accounts*).   The latter is repeatedly stated to be equal to 2 quarters (Sweetman, vol. IV., p. 165), so that it may be assumed that the crannoc of wheat was then equivalent to one quarter.   In 1326 the crannoc of wheat still consisted of 8 heaped bushels (*Mem. Rot.*, 19 Edw. II.).   In these accounts it is treated as 7 heaped pecks, that of oats 14 pecks, and of hastiuell 8 pecks—this term being locally used as equivalent to bushel.

At some period an increase of one-third apparently took place in the amount represented by the crannoc.   This is shown by an entry in the Black Book of Christ Church, p. 225: 'Summa de frumento de veteri mensura xlv crannoc et fecit de nova mensura xxxiii crenoc' et vi peck.'' This was written during the latter half of the 14th century, but is obviously copied from some document to whose date there is no clue.

The crannoc dropped out of use soon after the end of the 14th century.

Dealbando (p. 98).—The term seems to refer to a process by which hides were preserved by being dried and bleached.   See ' Fresed Leder,' *Glossary York Fabric Rolls.*

Diversimode.—Properly, ' in different manner,' but frequently used by the writers of these accounts in the sense of ' at different times.'

Draght bord (p. 61).—Apparently boards of extra size (see p. 175).

Euillavit (p. 76)—Evillare seems to be used as an alternative form for devillare, included in Du Cange with the sense of discedere.

Grange.—When, as at p. 36, distinguished from the granarium, Grange denotes the place in which the corn in the sheaf was preserved—the stack yard ; while granarium is the barn in which the threshed grain was kept.

Gropis (pp. 31, 99).—Hooks (*Wardrobe Accounts, Glossary*).

Harness (p. 108).—Baggage and equipment, generally.

Harts (pp. 22, 57).- Hart, a haft or handle.   (Somerset), Halliwell.

Hastiuell.—Probably a variety of barley. Perhaps that known in England as hastybere, said to have been so called from the rapidity with which it came to maturity. That this was also a characteristic of the Dublin hastiuell may be inferred from p. 64, where men seem to have been employed reaping it before the general harvest began.

Heriot.—The best beast which a tenant had at the time of his death, which was by custom due to his lord.

Issue.—The outgoing or produce of the tillage. Used as a title for the grain accounts.

Jantaculum.—Dejeuner, in later use applied to the early dinner in England. Its use in these accounts, however, requires the sense of break-fast. Thus it always precedes *prandium*, which again always precedes *cena*. On p. 5 the three occur on the same day, in the order, *jantaculum*, *prandium*, *cena*. Spelman says, 'quod postea jentaculum dictum est olim prandium appellabatur.' (*Glossary under Nona*).

Lezerlegs (pp. 30–1, 125).—Small iron articles used in the construction or fitting of wheels. In the *Norfolk Accounts* the word occurs in the form 'lerleg.'

Messer (pp. 35, 51–2).—A farm overseer (see p. 167). The messer at Gorman appears to correspond to the serviens or serjeant at Clonken.

Nona.—Properly the ninth hour of the day—the time of the church office of none. The use of the word on p. 14 seems to require the sense of noon, or perhaps of dinner-time, which, according to Wright (*Early English House*) should have been 11 A.M., or earlier. 'Nona. Meridies. Tempus prandii. In antiquis maneriorum membranis Nona crebro usu venit pro meridie, quae inde Anglice appellatur None et Nonetide.'—Spelman, *Gloss. s. v.*

Paindemaine.—Fine cake bread.—See p. 179.

Peck.—The term was locally used in Dublin as equivalent to bushel. In the *Cal. of Records of Dublin*, p. 185, the two words are thus used together. At this time the peck probably represented the English standard bushel (*see* p. 159). At a later time the measure it represented became much larger in quantity. In 1524 a bushel of ale was 16 gallons (*Cal. of Records*, p. 182), and in 1585 a peck of wheat, according to the measure of Dublin, contained 18 gallons, 1 pottle, 1 pint (15*th Report D. K. Records, Ireland*, p. 112).

Penettes (p. 3).—Sugar candy (*Dict. Middle English*, by Mayhew and Skeat). Licorish or pennets . . . other such like pectoral things (Nare's *Glossary*).

Piment.—A compound of wine, honey, and spices.—See p. 183.

Potura (pp. 79, 83).—An allowance of corn for food. 'Potura pro pastura' (Du Cange).

Pykforks.—Pykstelus (p. 41). Pitchforks, and handles for them. From pike, a hayfork; stele, a handle.

Razes (p. 59).—This may also read raȝes. The character ȝ is several times used in names in these accounts where the sound expected is *th*. The word may therefore represent rathes, meaning a frame placed on a cart or waggon for carrying hay (Wright, *Prov. Dict.*).

Sacrista.—See note, p. 147.

Serjeant.—See messer.

Somersadul (p. 99).—A sumpter or pack-horse saddle.

Spennyngs (pp. 34-5, 47, 104, 106).—A local term for first of May.

Speres (p. 39), **spyres** (pp. 40, 61)—Beams of wood. At p. 39 it seems to mean the timber frame for a partition wall, a sense which connects it with the Yorkshire 'spires, timber stands' (*Gloss. E. Yorks. Dialect Soc.*).

Spochour (p. 61).—A vessel used to put water on the mud walls in course of construction.

Stang.—A measure of land, the fourth part of an acre.

Strakes (p. 99), **straknail** (pp. 31, 99).—Iron tires for cart wheels, and the nails which fastened them to the wheels.

Tascha (pp. 28, 66, &c.).—Throughout these accounts *ad tascham* is used of mechanics' wages in the sense of wages in full, without board; in contradistinction to *ad mensam*, wages with board.

Themes (p. 57).—" Themys, cart or plough traces (*Finchal Priory*).

Tublyngs (p. 12).—A kind of fish.

Twistes (p. 120).—Articles bought in connexion with the repair of a lock. The word occurs in the same connexion in Mr. Gilbert's *Hist. of the Viceroys*, p. 544. Perhaps iron springs.

Warrok (p. 120).—A girth (Stratmann).

AUTHORITIES REFERRED TO IN THE NOTES.

Archdall's 'Monasticon Hibernicum,' 1786.

'Babees Book, &c., Manners and Meals in the Olden Time.' Ed. F. J. Furnivall (Early English Text Soc., 1868).

Best's 'Farming Book.' (Surtees Society, vol. 33, 1857).

Betham's 'History of the Constitution, and of the early Parliaments of Ireland' (1834.)

'Black Book of Archbishop Alan': MS. in possession of the Archbishop of Dublin. The references here have been taken from the copy in Marsh's Library, Dublin.

'Black Book of Christ Church': MS. in possession of the Dean of Christ Church, Dublin.

'Book of Howth.' ('Calendar of Carew Manuscripts: The Book of Howth.' Published under direction of the Master of the Rolls in England, 1871.)

Cal. Pat. Rot. 'Rotulorum Patentium et Clausarum Cancellariæ Hiberniæ Calendarium.' (Published by the Irish Record Commissioners, 1828.)

Cal. Pat. Rot. Ang. 'Calendarium Rotulorum Patentium in Turri Londinensi.' (Published by English Record Commissioners, 1802.)

'Calendar of Ancient Records of Dublin,' ed. J. T. Gilbert (1889).

'Catholic Dictionary,' by Addis & Arnold (1884).

'Catholicon Anglicum,' ed. S. J. K. Herrtage (Camden Soc., 1882).

Camden, 'Annals': Annals of Ireland in 'Britain' (edition 1637).

Ch. Ch. Deeds. Original muniments of Christ Church Cathedral now preserved in the Record Office, Dublin. Calendars noticing nearly 1000 of these have been published in the 20th and 23rd Reports of the Deputy Keeper of the Records.

Chartæ Rec. Com. 'Chartae, Privilegia et Immunitates.' (Printed by Irish Record Commissioners.)

'Chartularies of S. Mary's Abbey, Dublin,' ed. J. T. Gilbert (Rolls Series, 1884).

Clyn, 'Annals.' 'Annals of Ireland, by Friar John Clyn,' (Irish Archæological Soc., 1849.)

Cotton: Fasti Ecclesiæ Hibernicæ.

Cowell's 'Law Dictionary' (1727).

' Dictionnaire de l'Académie Française.'

Du Cange, 'Glossarium Mediæ et Infimæ Latinitatis' (Paris, 1840-6).

' Finchal Priory.' 'Charters and Account Rolls of Finchal Priory.' (Surtees Soc., vol. vi., 1837.)

Gardiner's ' Student's History of England' (1890).

Godefroie, ' Dictionnaire de L'Ancienne Langue Francaise' (Paris, 1881-9).

Halliwell, ' Archæic Dictionary.'

' Historic and Municipal Documents of Ireland,' ed. J. T. Gilbert. (Rolls Series, 1870).

' Household and Wardrobe Ordinances of Edward II.,' ed. Furnivall. (Chaucer Soc.)

' Journal of the Royal Archæological Association and Royal Society of Antiquaries of Ireland.'

Lib. Alb. Lond. ' Munimenta Gildhallæ Londoniensis—Liber Albus.' (Rolls Series, 1859-62.)

Lib. Nig. Alani. See ' Black Book.'

Malton's ' Picturesque and Descriptive Views of the City of Dublin,' taken in 1791.

' Manners and Meals in the Olden Times.'—See ' Babees Book.'

' Martyrology.' ' Book of Obits and Martyrology of the Cathedral Church of the Holy Trinity, Dublin.' (Irish Archæological Soc., 1844.)

Mem. Rot. MS. Memorandum Rolls of the Court of Exchequer in Ireland. The notices in this volume are from transcripts made by the Irish Record Commissioners, which, as well as the originals, are preserved in the Record Office, Dublin.

' Mortilogium et Martyrologium Ecclesie Cathedralis,' &c. See ' Martyrology.'

' Norfolk Accounts.' MS. Accounts of the Estates of the Earl of Norfolk. Ministers' Accounts, Exchequer, Record Office, London.

Pipe Roll. Court of Exchequer in Ireland. MS. preserved in Record Office, Dublin.

Plea Rolls of the King's Courts in Ireland. MS. preserved in Record Office, Dublin.

Prompt. Parv. ' Promptorium Parvulorum,' ed. A. Waye. (Camden Soc., 1843, 1853, 1865).

' Red Book of Ossory,' ed. J. T. Gilbert. (Historical MSS. Commissioners, Report 10. Appendix.)

' Regesta Pontificum.' (Bliss's Transcripts from the Vatican MS. Record Office, London).

' Roman Transcripts.' (Bliss's Transcripts from the Vatican, General Series. MS. Record Office, London.)

Spelman : 'Glossarium Archaiologicum,' authore Henrico Spelman. (London, 1687.)

Stratmann : 'Middle English Dictionary,' ed. Bradley. (Clarendon Press, 1891.)

Sweetman : 'Calendar of Documents relating to Ireland. Published under the direction of the Master of the Rolls in England.'

Tusser, ' Five Hundred Points of Good Husbandrie,' ed. Payne & Herrtage. (English Dialect Soc., 1878.)

Walter of Henley's ' Husbandry,' &c. Ed. Elizabeth Lamond. (1890.)

' Wardrobe Accounts.' (' Liber Quotidianus Contrarotulatoris Garderobæ, 28' Edw. I., ed. Nichols, 1787.)

Ware, 'Antiquities.' 'The History and Antiquities of Ireland,' revised by W. Harris, 1764.

Ware, ' Bishops.' 'History of the Bishops of Ireland,' being vol. i. of the Works of Sir James Ware, as revised by Harris, 1745.

' White Book of Christ Church.' MS. in possession of the Dean of Christ Church, Dublin.

Wright's ' Vocabularies.' (' Anglo-Saxon and Old English Vocabularies,' by Thos. Wright, ed. by Wülcker, 1884).

' York Fabric Rolls.' ' Fabric Rolls of York Minster.' (Surtees Soc., vol. xxxv., 1858).

INDEX.

THE END.

Printed by PONSONBY & WELDRICK, *Dublin.*